*This Tight Embrace:*

*Luisa de Carvajal y Mendoza*
*(1566-1614)*

Edited, Translated, and Introduced
by
Elizabeth Rhodes

MARQUETTE
UNIVERSITY

PRESS

Milwaukee, 2000

REFORMATION TEXTS WITH TRANSLATION (1350-1650)
Kenneth Hagen, General Editor

**Women of the Reformation, Volume 2**
Merry Wiesner-Hanks, Series Editor

Cover art: Sean Donnelly,
from an early portrait of Luisa, artist unknown

## Library of Congress Cataloging-in-Publication Data

Carvajal y Mendoza, Luisa de, 1566-1614.
   [Selections. English & Spanish]
   This tight embrace / Luisa de Carvajal y Mendoza ; edited,
translated, and with an introduction by Elizabeth Rhodes.
      p. cm. — (Reformation texts with translation (1350-1650).
Women of the Reformation ; v. 2)
   Includes bibliographical references and index.
   ISBN 0-87462-704-4 (pbk. : alk. paper)
   1. Carvajal y Mendoza, Luisa de, 1566-1614. 2. Spiritual life—
Catholic Church—Early works to 1800. 3. Christian poetry,
Spanish—Translations into English. 4. Carvajal y Mendoza, Luisa
de—Correspondence. I. Rhodes, Elizabeth, 1955- . II. Title.
III. Series.
BX4705.C334A25 2000
282'.092—dc21

                                                        00-008585



Member, THE ASSOCIATION OF AMERICAN UNIVERSITY PRESSES

**MARQUETTE UNIVERSITY PRESS**
MILWAUKEE

The Association of Jesuit University Presses

2000

*Surgam, et circuibo civitatem;*

*per vicos et plateas*

*Quaeram quem diligit anima mea . . .*

Canticum Canticorum 3: 2


I will rise now, and go about the city

in the streets, and in the broad ways

I will seek him whom my soul loveth . . .

Song of Songs 3: 2

# Table of Contents

## Prologue

> "... they should not be read under any circumstance,
> since they treat matters of conscience"

With these words, written in English, the Spanish missionary Luisa de Carvajal y Mendoza sealed the envelope containing important documents she had composed during her life. Knowing that she was dying, she left them wrapped in the following instructions: "I request and order my female companions that, should I die, they keep these papers under lock and key without anyone breaking their seal, and if my confessor is in England, they be given to him, and if not, that every one be burned before their very eyes."[1]

Inside this important packet, Carvajal stashed several manuscripts: her spiritual life story, written for her confessor as part of her petition to go to England as a missionary, her "cuentas de consciencia," or individual records of significant spiritual events in her life, perhaps her poems, copies of the 178 letters she wrote that are now extant, her vows, and her will. All of these documents now rest, with Carvajal's remains, in the Reformed Augustinian Convento de la Encarnación in Madrid, where the nuns of the community welcome those who care to examine them. Like her unburied body, which sits awkwardly in a corner of the convent's reliquary room, her writings rest uncomfortably in history, unsettled and unsettling.

There is an abundance of material about Carvajal other than what she wrote herself. Because it was so unusual, her life produced a large amount of records, many of which still need to be located and examined. For example, documents related to the diplomatic crisis provoked by her second arrest in London are still coming to light (Loomie 1996). Her story is one of the few about which several layers of written sources remain. At the core are her own manuscripts, but no less telling and important are the books and records written about her by men: the early biography composed by Walpole; a second biography, largely based on the first, written by the renowned Jesuit biographer Luis Muñoz (published in 1631), and the 1966

[1] From the manuscript biography of Carvajal written at an unknown date after her death by her confessor in England, Michael Walpole, SJ (129ᵛ).

rendition of her life by Camilo Abad, SJ.[2] Also interesting are the documents prepared between 1625 and 1627 for the Cause of her beatification, testimonies which are also in the Encarnación.

The hagiographic haze around Carvajal, which she herself built into her self-representations, thickens with each remove from her own pen. Thus, anyone seeking historical information about her should read with caution her own writings and all accounts of her life, for they were written to satisfy confessional exigencies more than those of a positivist type. As the epigram cited above indicates, her personal papers were never intended to be read by the general public, and they provide an intentionally limited and extremely slanted account of her life.

Overall, there is a certain amount of violation and voyeurism built into any investigation such as this one into the nooks and crannies of an early modern woman's private relationship with God, which is what Carvajal's confessional documents were meant to reveal. Likewise, reading Carvajal's letters violates the seal that still clings to some of them, and draws us close to other illegitimate readings, such as those of the individuals who intercepted them on their way to their destinations (see Letter 78 ¶2). The invasive nature of inquiries such as the one offered here can be counterbalanced by reading from among all the many types of texts she wrote, not just those composed for her male superiors.

The style and tone of Carvajal's confessional writings are faithful to the expectations of their original readers and portray a submissive, obedient woman who rejoices in the sacrifice of her entire self to the service of God and the men who interpret what that entails. Fortunately, Carvajal left a large quantity of documents which also reveal a much less humble and cowering woman than do those she wrote for her confessors: her will and her letters are examples. Indeed, her fiery temperament and passionate nature, reminiscent of Princess Juana of Austria's imperious character, radiate from those writings: she bosses Philip III's Prime Minister around with amazing verve in her correspondence from London, and composed an Order for her religious companions that could vie with that of Ignatius himself in its severity, conservatism, and purposeful ambiguity. In most of her letters, she seems little bound by the exaggerated humility she claims to have so fervently embraced in Spain. She writes from London on 17 Dec. 1607 to Inés de la Asunción: "Do me the favor of sending me the

---

[2] Complete references are in the list of Works Cited. The Muñoz biography was published again in Madrid, 1897.

verses that are in the book I left behind by Father Fray Juan de la Cruz . . . And be careful not to forget to do that. . . . I need the scissors and skeins of golden thread. . . And watch out, because if Father Richard Walpole leaves the College, they have to store all my things in your convent, since I myself have so written to you, and I believe to the mother prioress. And send me as well the recipe for sugar and starch frosting . . ." (*Epist.* 235).

Documents by Carvajal can be divided into two sets: those she composed to justify her English mission, ridden with self-abnegation and humility (1598-1604) and those she wrote while on it, of a much more assertive nature (1604-1614). Gifted with a sharp intelligence and superb education, Carvajal ably performed the male construct of her gender in her writings for men. She nimbly played the role dictated by dominant expectations for women, until she had attained what she perhaps had sought all along: freedom of thought and movement, which came to her in London once her English was proficient. The fact that she was enacting rather than spontaneously producing this performance is evident in her writings for women, in which she performed quite different, more subtle roles, such as that of the spiritual mother, needy sister, lonely companion.

Once in England, Carvajal had little immediate access to her spiritual superiors, and instead had to rely on the slow and capricious rhythm of the mail packets dispatched from England via the Spanish Embassy and secret delivery systems. She thus enjoyed a liberty that was unheard of for a woman of her day, and suspended her performance of the submissive, self-effacing holy woman to greatly expand her repertoire of personae. Priests in London made themselves known at great peril during the years Carvajal lived there, a situation which bereaved her of the physical proximity of her spiritual advisors, but simultaneously freed her not only to experience God as she wished but to teach Catholic doctrine and preach in modest dimensions with little if any supervision. There is no evidence that the content of Carvajal's theology was the least bit subversive. On the contrary, it represents the militantly conservative wing of Spanish Catholicism to perfection, and for this reason fell in so well with the Jesuits. The performance of her theology, however, which staged a woman vowing martyrdom in the high drama of international intrigue and politics, could not have been more subversive.

Not coincidentally, all of Carvajal's documents recording intense and painful mystical experiences date from her years in Madrid, the period when she was searching for a means to carry out her mission, enduring an extremely ascetic lifestyle and practicing severely penitential piety whose execution almost killed her. That severe lifestyle was a requisite for her to attain direct contact with God, which in turn was indispensable for her to legitimize her unusual apostolic plans. It is perhaps no surprise that she evidently found little need for penitential excesses once her own ambitions were being realized (ambitions she describes as God's). It is indeed tempting to theorize that the intense mystical experiences recorded for, by, and about hundreds of Spanish women during Carvajal's day are as much the result of what options women had to exercise as anything else. Without exterior and public means of expressing their ambitions, women turned inward and looked upward. Given a public space in which to vent her considerable energies, Luisa de Carvajal abandoned the self-destructive penitential piety described in much seventeenth-century women's religious writings.

The fact that Carvajal did not write anything describing her intimacies with God once her confessors stopped requiring her to do so also says something very important about women's spiritual life stories of early modern Spain, of which there are over fifty samples extant: their authors wrote them because they were required to, and, as Teresa of Ávila observed in hers, it was a very embarrassing charge to carry out (*Book* 27:13).[3] While there is little question that many of the religious women of this period wanted to write, evidence indicates that, given the choice, they would not have composed first-person accounts of their intimacies with God rather other, more authoritative narratives. Thus, the extent to which confessional documents are revealing of early modern Spanish women's lives on earth deserves ongoing consideration, for they capture a moment of obligation and constitute a highly ritualized rite of passage more than spontaneous self-expression. The ritualized aspect of women's confessional documents is manifest, for example, in the substantial borrowings from saints' lives they display, a requisite for religious women's "self"-representation during the period. Such melding of the saints' lives into their own facilitated their acceptance into the Catholic writing community during a period when any sort of novelty was viewed with great suspicion by superiors. In Carvajal's spiritual life story, it is hard to know where the subject is Raymond of Capua's St. Catherine of Siena, or Martín de Lilio's St. Elizabeth of Hungary, and where it is Luisa de Carvajal. It is clear that, during Carvajal's lifetime, the distinction was less important that the similarity.

---

[3] Poutrin includes a catalogue of many known samples of spiritual life stories.

Much work remains to be done on Luisa de Carvajal, and there is an abundance of archival and documentary research awaiting attention. There is no complete study of Carvajal's life in English, and those available in Spanish serve the confessional interests of their authors. Many women readers will cringe in bitter understanding over passages in her writings that have gone virtually unperceived by her male editors and biographers, such as the image of a lonely six-year-old girl seeking a solitary place to cry over her parents' sudden death, and the quiet but constant mention of her uncle next to every penitential act she describes.

Abad's apology for the Marqués de Almazán's impertinent scrutiny of young Luisa's penitential practices is paradigmatic of the approach to her works that still enshrouds their interpretation: "It was quite natural that the Marqués should take care to demand an accounting from Luisa of what she had done during the day" (Intro. *Epist.* 24). This observation, telling for its very presence (if it was so natural, then why mention it?), elides the detail that her uncle did not inquire about her needlework, letters, or how far she had walked at midday, rather about how she felt as she was flagellating herself.

Contact with Luisa de Carvajal is inspiring and horrifying, for her relationship to the repressive ideologies that almost killed her several times is difficult to ascertain. Seeking to understand what Carvajal called the *amor terrible* between herself and God, and the distressing paradoxes in her life and works, I offer what follows to readers in the hope of sparking interest in this singular woman.

## METHODOLOGY

I have modernized Carvajal's spelling and normalized punctuation according to modern usage throughout. Archaic words themselves, however, remain (*aqueste, veríades*, etc.). The translation is more literal than adaptive, respecting Carvajal's elaborate and uneasy syntax. Like most prose religious discourse of her day, Carvajal's is based on sermon rhetoric, embellished with anaphora of the conjunction "and," with which almost every clause begins. This style is typical of the times and does not signal any traits of gender or linguistic register.

Throughout the translations, I revert to early modern meanings of words and expressions, which appear to draw the English away from a literal rendition. For example, "extraño" today means "strange or odd" but in Carvajal's day signified something singular or unique, with positive connotations.

Biblical translations are from the King James Bible, with the exception of the Books of Wisdom not in that translation, whose Latin quotations I have translated. I maintain Spanish titles of address (Marqués, Marquesa, don, doña) but translate all others (Saint, Master, Father).

All translations are mine unless otherwise indicated. References to Teresa of Ávila's writings include the title of the work and the paragraph; the cited translation is that of Kavanaugh/Rodríguez.

Reflecting early modern usage, references to the divinity are translated as masculine, and pronouns referent thereto are capitalized.

English names are used in the Index, and Carvajal's spelling of them often differs.  Index references are to the translation only.

## Abbreviations (complete references in Works Cited)

| | |
|---|---|
| DNB | *Dictionary of National Biography* |
| EA | Luisa de Carvajal, *Escritos autobiográficos*, ed. Abad |
| *Epist.* | Luisa de Carvajal, *Epistolario*, ed. Abad |
| LS | Luisa de Carvajal, "Spiritual Life Story" |
| Let. | Luisa de Carvajal, Letters |
| *Mis.* | Abad, *Misionera española* |
| *Tesoro* | Covarrubias, *Tesoro de la lengua castellana* |
| Test. | Testimonios del Proceso |

Thanks to the following people who provided invaluable assistance in the compilation of this volume: the community at the Encarnación, Leticia Sánchez, James Amelang, Henry Kamen, Merry Wiesner-Hanks, Joan Skocir, María Luisa Guardiola, Lisa Loberg, and Enric Bou.

❧

# *About Luisa de Carvajal y Mendoza*
## 1566-1614

"Her entire life has been a strange thing . . . "
(Letter from Ambassador Sarmiento to Philip III, 25 Feb. 1614)

Luisa de Carvajal y Mendoza was born in 1566 to wealthy and noble parents in the small town of Jaraicejo, in the western province of Extremadura, Spain. She was their sixth child and represents herself as their first, long-awaited daughter (LS ¶1). When Luisa was five or six, her father, Francisco de Carvajal y Vargas, was made the ruling official of the city of León, in Castile, and the family moved to his new and prestigious post. Her mother, María de Mendoza y Pacheco, whom she describes as very pious and to whom she was extremely devoted, died shortly after their arrival, from a fever brought on by her tending Luisa's own illness or by a contagious disease she caught while overseeing the burial of a poor man.[1] Her father died almost immediately after her mother.

Her father's will stipulated that the young Luisa be raised by a maternal aunt, Petronila Pacheco, the Marquesa de Ladrada, until the age of ten, at which time she was to be placed in a convent until she was old enough to choose her vocation. However, for reasons unknown, Luisa was separated from her brothers and was sent to live with her maternal grandmother's sister, doña María Chacón, who was the governess of the crown prince and princesses and who lived at the court in Madrid. Carvajal spent the next four years, from age six to ten, in her aunt's care, living in the quarters of Philip II's sister, Princess Juana de Austria, at the royal convent of Las Descalzas Reales. Princess Juana herself, ill with the cancer of which she died in 1573, was then in residence at the Escorial with King Philip, and it is unlikely that Carvajal had much direct contact with her. However, Juana's secret Jesuit vows meant that members of the Society met the religious needs of most of the household, and the young girl had her first Jesuit confessor there (LS ¶31). This marked the beginning of

---

[1] The latter suggestion, made by Carvajal herself (LS ¶18), has a hagiographic ring to it and would assuage her guilt over being the one to pass on to her mother the illness that killed her.

1

Carvajal's lifelong intimacy with the Jesuits, whose founder was said by some to be her uncle.[2]

Since her birth, Carvajal's governess had been the severe Isabel de Ayllón, the only person with whom she had uninterrupted contact until age thirteen. Although Carvajal represents herself as caring for Ayllón, she does not hesitate to describe her governess's extreme disciplinary measures (LS ¶37). These measures inspire nothing but praise from Carvajal's male biographers, although Carvajal herself repeatedly suggests that they reached beyond normative discipline and provoked heroic endurance on her part.

When her aunt suddenly died in 1576, the young Luisa faced yet another severe loss and was assigned to the guardianship of her maternal uncle, Francisco Hurtado de Mendoza, who had previously attempted, without success, to claim her as his ward. This uncle, the Marqués de Almazán, was a prominent figure in Spanish politics; when Carvajal joined his household, he was serving as Philip II's ambassador in Germany, a position he held from Jan. 1570 to Sept. 1576. While the Marqués and his wife were abroad, their two younger daughters were in residence at the family estate in Monteagudo, in the central province of Soria, and Carvajal was taken there immediately after her aunt's death. Three months later, the girls were moved to the family estate in Almazán, also in Soria, where they would live for the next two and a half years. Some seven months after Carvajal's arrival at Almazán, her aunt and uncle returned from Germany, her aunt moving directly into the house at Almazán with the rest of the family, her uncle stopping only briefly there on his way to the court in Madrid. On 6 Feb. 1579, Philip II officially named don Francisco the Viceroy of the province of Navarra, and he left to discharge his duties in the city of Pamplona after sporadic contact with his niece.

Carvajal was a budding adolescent of ten when committed to her uncle's care. She spent the next sixteen years of her life under his control. Thanks to the initial vigilance of his wife, she was given an outstanding education in domestic and intellectual matters, as well as guidance in the practice of charity, one of a noblewoman's most important occupations. Although Carvajal scoffs at her early Latin lessons, it was clearly this early education provided by the Marquesa

---

[2] Rodríguez Moñino cites seventeenth-century documents describing Luisa de Carvajal as Ignatius of Loyola's niece, and a familial relationship would explain the intensity of Carvajal's alliance with the Society. Her uncle had done the Spiritual Exercises with the future saint Francisco de Borja in 1553 (Iparraguirre 271); the early date and the prestigious spiritual director suggest special status.

that fostered what eventually became Carvajal's great familiarity with classical and early Christian writings (LS ¶50).[3]

When Carvajal was thirteen, her uncle ordered her to join him in Pamplona, with his daughter Isabel and her husband, and his other daughter Francisca. It is not known why he did not send for his daughter of Luisa's age, María, to join them at that time; she arrived with the Marquesa at an unspecified later date. The death of Ayllón's mother, just before Carvajal's move to Pamplona, required Ayllón to remain in Almazán to claim her estate, forcing a separation from her governess upon the young girl. Thus, Carvajal moved into the Marqués's palace in Pamplona without her aunt or her governess to supervise her relationship with her uncle. Although the Marquesa eventually joined them, Carvajal's subservient relationship to her uncle had been established during her absence, never to be broken until his death. Any mitigating influence that the Marquesa might have exercised was probably tempered by her frequent absence from the estate (LS ¶74). It is interesting that Carvajal's clean copy of her life story ends precisely when she reaches the date that her uncle came into her life (LS ¶38).

In Pamplona, under the "spiritual counsel" of the Marqués, Carvajal was obliged to participate in a series of violent and remarkable penitential activities, which she describes in the manuscript of her spiritual life story (LS ¶¶67-78; 100-03; 124-26). As The Catholic Truth Society's rendition of Carvajal's life bluntly but accurately states, "She was to be the slave of servants" (*Spanish* 6). These are the activities of which even a restrained biographer like Abad says, "The horrible penitence to which she submitted herself during this period, obeying her uncle . . . remains an enigma to us" (*Mis.* 24). Carvajal does not specifically mention that her uncle witnessed these highly theatrical spectacles, but it seems likely that he watched their enactment from some unseen locale. By age fifteen, Carvajal had been "instructed" by her uncle in the "pious" practices that stand out starkly in her life story.

Today those practices appear to constitute a form of voyeuristic child abuse. Carvajal's closest friend, Inés de la Asunción, testified that they "exceed all the limits of reason" (Test. 267[r]). Her description of other episodes in Carvajal's relationship with her uncle, such as his falling asleep with his head in her lap, or his habit of depriving

---

[3] In a 1608 letter to Joseph Creswell, she asks forgiveness for any errors in her numerous [flawless] Latin quotations, insisting, "I cannot check them because of my haste, nor am I as expert in it as some here believe" (*Epist.* 242).

her of permission to "attend to human necessities" (presumably to urinate and defecate), suggest perversion to modern eyes (Test. 270ʳ; 272ᵛ). Without underestimating the dangerous nature of the penitential practices in which the Marqués engaged his niece, it is important to recall the penitential mode of piety that dominated sixteenth-century Spain and Italy at this time, which found ample expression in the works of extremely popular writers such as Luis de Granada. When she wrote of these experiences, Carvajal was a well-educated noblewoman who described them for a confessor. The scarcity of documents by women in similar conditions to hers makes it difficult to know how to interpret the "exercises" she describes, although her age when they were carried out suggests serious impropriety. Carvajal's aversion to being touched at all by anyone, a repulsion which she carried into death by insisting that her body not be exhumed or defiled in any way, is sadly understandable in light of her childhood history.

It is no surprise that, in one of her spiritual declarations, Carvajal claims to have had "great desires to be a martyr" since the age of seventeen (EA 189); death had been thrust upon her literally and symbolically since the age of six. Modern psychology suggests a relationship between her expressions of vehement desires to die, desires much darker than Teresa of Ávila's similar longings, and the death of her mother, since Carvajal describes her feelings as aspirations "to die for the sweet Lord who died for me" (EA 189). Furthermore, if "the desire for martyrdom is the desire to be completely purged of sin and reformed by grace as well as an expression of love for God and for neighbor" (Daniels 82), then Carvajal's craving to die for God served a double function: cleansing of her problematic experiences with her uncle, and apostolic fervor related to her Catholic mission.

Lust for martyrdom increased as Christian missionary activity around the world intensified with improvements in navigation techniques and cartography, on the one hand, and with the rise of the cult of the primitive church, on the other. Tales which likely inflamed Carvajal's own desires told of men such as Paul Miki, John Soan de Goto and James Kisai, Jesuits crucified in Japan in 1596, who reportedly rushed to embrace the cross upon which they would die. Martyrdom, "religious conviction and controversy concretely embodied and dramatically displayed" (Gregory 5), was then one of the few fields upon which women could manifest courage of conviction and earn praise for it. Daniels has aptly summarized its meaning, somewhat alien to most readers today, saying, "Ardent love of the passion meant single-minded desire to conform oneself to Christ's death. . . .

For perfection comes only when [the viator] finds his heart not merely willing, but intensely longing, to die for his neighbor's salvation" (75; 80).

On 4 Dec. 1581, the Spanish ambassador to England, Bernardino de Mendoza, wrote a letter describing the execution of Edmund Campion, SJ, by the Anglican state. The account circulated in Madrid, telling about the brilliant priest who had entered England disguised as a jewelry merchant in 1580 and a year later, on 1 Dec. 1581, was arrested, tortured, hanged, and his body drawn and quartered. Abad and Ortega are sure that this text was the motivating force behind Carvajal's English mission (*Mis.* 24; "Spanish" 106); Peralta insists that it inspired "holy envy" in doña Luisa (2ᵛ). Regardless, her uncle's very close relationship with the Jesuits assured her awareness of important events such as these, which served to justify her later intentions.

In an undated spiritual recollection, Carvajal recalls that before leaving Almazán, in 1583 (at age seventeen), she wrote to the famed Dominican preacher and writer Luis de Granada, and his later-defamed confessant Sor María de la Visitación, for advice about her designs on an English mission (EA 190).[4] Sor María's failure to respond does not seem to have deterred Carvajal, nor does the ambitious nun's compromised reputation seem to have intimidated Carvajal in the least. Sor María's defamation, however, surely taught Carvajal the importance of manifest obedience of powerful men and strict observance of Catholic protocol, both inclinations she represents herself as having from childhood.

As the severity of her religious practices augmented, Carvajal plunged herself ever deeper into the female sacrificial model of holiness, in part due to the lack of options available to her as a headstrong, highly educated, ambitious woman, and in part due to the series of losses she suffered throughout her youth which probably made Christ an especially attractive father and husband figure: He

---

[4] Sor María de la Visitación (María de Meneses), "The Nun of Lisbon," as she came to be known, was a young and successful Dominican prioress and ecstatic who allegedly received the stigmata on 7 Nov. 1584. Her wounds were authenticated by the Spanish Inquisition and celebrated by Pope Gregory XIII. When she was suspected of speaking out against the Spanish occupation of the Portuguese throne (1588), her hands were submerged in soap and water (a test to which they had never been subjected before), and the "stigmata" dissolved. Luis de Granada, one of her many ardent supporters, was discredited (see Luis de Granada, *Obras* v. 17 and Huerga, *Fray Luis* 291-310). Her experience held a menacing specter over many ambitious religious women for years.

would never, as did so many earthly figures, abandon or disappoint her. Until she left Spain, Carvajal channeled her considerable energies in the most acceptable direction for an ambitious woman at that time: self-mortification, which to the secular reader today suggests powerless sacrifice.

In Oct. of 1586, when Carvajal was twenty, the Marqués de Almazán left Pamplona for Madrid to take up his new assignment as a member of the King's War Council and the President of the Council of Orders, leaving his son-in-law to carry out the duties of Viceroy of Navarra. Carvajal returned to Almazán with her aunt and cousins, but at an unknown date, before 1591, she moved into the house where her uncle lived at court, on the prestigious Calle Mayor. Within a few years, she was clearly anxious to get out from under her uncle's control. In 1591, when she was twenty-five and legally able to make her own choices about her life but socially still bound to her uncle's will, he refused her petition to move out of his house, but allowed her to live in semi retirement from the world with a few companions on the top story of his Madrid palace. This move to the upper rooms of her uncle's house was a clear imitation of Catherine of Siena, whose pious practices Carvajal describes as her own on many occasions, although without openly drawing the parallel herself.[5]  During this phase of her life, she began living with Inés de la Asunción, who stayed with her until Carvajal left for England (1591-1604).

The Marqués died the following year (1592), and six months later, so did his wife. Curiously, the Marqués's brother, who wanted Carvajal to live with him, also died immediately (*Mis.* 68-69). Carvajal writes that upon their deaths, "I raised my eyes to God and gave Him immense thanks, because I saw myself then free to follow, without hindrance, in the scorn and abandonment of Christ which my soul so desired" (EA 211).[6] She began to plan for her life of holy virtue, rejecting not only marriage and the convent, but Spain as well: she had long been hatching a scheme to go to England, where the execution of Catholic men, particularly Jesuit priests, distressed her greatly. After her uncle's death, her relationships with the Jesuit community intensified, and she leased the house on the Calle de Toledo in Madrid

---

[5] Fullerton cites several of Carvajal's contemporaries whose retirement from the world outside the convent could have inspired Carvajal (78). Catherine of Siena was likely the model for them all.

[6] Catherine Mooney has studied such "un-womanly" sentiments of holy women, expressions of liberation usually glossed over in male biographies of them ("Dutiful").

belonging to the Order, the same house in which the Imperial College was later built.

To express her newfound freedom, the first thing Carvajal set about doing was dispossessing herself of her substantial estate, which she eventually willed to the Jesuits after a twelve-year lawsuit against her guardians and other members of her family (who were likely disturbed to see the family fortune go to the Society). That law suit began in 1592 and dragged on until just before she left for London, and the fact that she was willing to bear the ongoing weight of such an enterprise, rather than simply renounce it to seek true poverty, indicates the degree of control she still wanted to maintain over her own money. Although later, she writes in an undated document, she was indeed ready to give up on the suit, the Jesuits — obviously anxious to get the money — would not let her ("no me era permitido" EA 225). Such obedience to the Society surely won her some leverage in her struggle to obtain support from her superiors to go to England.

Carvajal's biographers describe her life in Madrid as one of abject poverty, and they mention that she put herself under the obedience of women who had formerly been servants in her own household. Inés de la Asunción testified that Carvajal told the women living with her "that, until then, the world had been calling her our lady, and that then she was but our sister and servant" (*Mis.* 72). On the one hand, such behavior was a re-enactment of social reversals common in hagiographic accounts of late medieval noblewomen, and Carvajal herself tells of having to learn how to cook and clean, and describes how her family ostracized her because of her unseemly behavior, particularly her monastic dress. On the other hand, accounts of Carvajal's obedience of her social inferiors are of relative historical value, for in her testimony for Carvajal's beatification, Inés de la Asunción also recalls of their life in Madrid "that there was in the house a glass or plate from Talavera [famous for high-quality ceramics] which some person had religiously given to them, and the lady [Carvajal] had ordered immediately that it be given to the poor. There was carelessness in obeying her. The good lady took it and threw it out the window" (Test. 260$^r$). Carvajal, it seems, was ultimately the person in charge of the household, and such behavior evidences the pro forma disdain of material goods that only the wealthy can afford.

Carvajal's loud declarations of poverty and humility must be nuanced within a seventeenth-century context, in the same way as words like "naked" (which meant anything from stark naked to being partially clothed) and "fasting" (which could mean eating nothing, eating a restricted diet in comparison to one's usual intake, or anything between). Her own words qualify her supposed humility: in September 1598 she wrote from Madrid, describing the women living with her named Isabel and María, "these two women serve at the house, because I'm no good for serving anything" (*Epist.* 99). Similarly, the license granted to Carvajal in 1597 to hold mass in the oratory of her Madrid house indicates not only status, but space. That document refers to her as having visitors as well as servants (*Mis.* 375), indicating official understanding that she was still living within the social paradigm of her class, if conspicuously avoiding some of the material benefits to which that class entitled her.

Carvajal's vows are testimony to her slow but sure release of powerless sacrifice and her steps toward empowering herself, specifically moving into a geographical space of high risk and independence. The first steps in this metamorphosis were necessarily accomplished by a *via negativa*; before moving into a role of her own design, she had to appear to disengage herself from her wealth and social status, no easy task for a woman of her rank. The years between the death of her uncle and her departure from Spain, 1591-1604, witness her transformation.

In 1593, at the age of twenty-seven, Carvajal began making a series of promises to herself, her superiors, and God. First was a vow of poverty, whose explicit judicial language betrays a keen financial mind and a poverty best described as relative (see Vows). Two years later, she vowed obedience to her spiritual superior or confessor, a document which reflects the same educated finesse. The same year she took a vow of greater perfection, related to her vow of obedience.

Carvajal's confessor from 1591 to 1596 was the Rector of the church at the Jesuit College, Juan de Sigüenza. She was probably engaged in a controlled but intense battle with him over her access to the Host, which he resolutely limited to twice a week. She expressed joy upon finding a confessor more to her liking (*Epist.* 99; EA 215), Father Gaspar Pedrosa (of whom little is known); and shortly thereafter, in the spring of 1597, she was given permission to commune daily, a privilege reserved for the highest spiritual elite. Not surprisingly, her ecstatic experiences intensified. It is likely that most if not all of her poetry dates from this period, and even through the illnesses which plagued her, she maintained the sense of freedom and autonomy that she represents herself as first feeling when her uncle and aunt died: in one of her poems, a daughter rejoices to her mother saying, "and now I belong to no one / except to Love" (Poem 31, ll. 15-16).

Carvajal's impassioned desire for the Host, evident in her spiritual writings and her poetry, displays early modern women's problematic relationship with power in vivid colors. The motivation behind Eucharistic fervor such as Carvajal's continues the trends of female piety identified by Caroline Bynum for the later Middle Ages: women compensated for their increasing exclusion from rituals of power by intensifying their identification with Christ's humanity, his female component. By the early modern period, however, the Host had accrued a political meaning it had lacked during the Middle Ages, specifically in relationship to the doctrine of transubstantiation.[7] Carvajal used the Eucharist not only as a personal symbol of her union with the suffering Christ, but also as a signal of her passionate alliance with the Spanish Counter Reformation Church; she thirsted for the universal political dominion of Catholicism indistinguishably from Jesus.

Carvajal established a type of *beaterio* in her residence in Madrid, meaning a community of single women who devoted themselves to the ideals of the primitive Christian church while living in the world (versus the cloister). They did not take the solemn vows of religious orders, rather those which could be rescinded upon need, in circumstances such as those Carvajal describes in the introductory paragraph to her own vows. Two of her companions in Madrid became important correspondents later: Inés de la Asunción, mentioned above, and Isabel de la Cruz, Inés's cousin. In her testimony for Carvajal's beatification, Inés described life in Carvajal's house in Madrid, where they followed a pious schedule similar to the one Carvajal later established for her Society of the Sovereign Virgin, in London (see Society). These statements indicate that Carvajal was regularly called to visit noble and royal ladies, to provide consolation and consultation, a standard duty of prominent holy women. Importantly, this testimony identifies the women with whom Carvajal had this contact as "ladies of the Society," meaning other female patrons of the Jesuits.

---

[7] "By the early seventeenth century, the intellectual leaders of the Counter Reformation, notably the Jesuits, were absolutely and resolutely convinced that the Eucharistic doctrine of transubstantiation was the bedrock of Catholicism" (Carroll 162). On the changing meaning of Eucharistic piety from the late medieval to early modern period, see Rhodes ("God on Earth").

While in Madrid, Carvajal fit the profile of the noble female saint: frenzied reliance on the Eucharist to sustain herself, dangerous abstinence from normal amounts of sleep and food, and charitable activities centered on the poor and prostitutes. This behavior was the required prerequisite for the authorization of her character and faith which followed, and can be summed up in Father Hernando de Espinosa's evaluation of Carvajal's life in Madrid, included in his testimony for her beatification: "Among many and very fervent souls he knew and dealt with, not one did he find more fervent or that made less noise and demonstration of being so, than the servant of God's [Carvajal's], because without seeming like doing anything, she acted; with speaking, she prayed; without moving, she moved hearts and brought them to love of Our Lord and pangs of conscience, if they were impure" (in *Mis.* 115). Such paradoxes aptly capture the ideal female model whose standards any woman had to meet, or appear to meet, before engaging the larger world with her own ideas.

While in Madrid, Carvajal did public battle with what she called her honor, meaning her preoccupation with what others thought about her. In her desire to eradicate all worldliness from her soul, she engaged in humiliating activities such as sweeping the steps of the Jesuit residence in broad daylight and emptying the garbage basket of her community in plain view of passers-by, both scandalous acts for a woman of her birth. In an exhibition that suggests playing at poverty to modern eyes, she requested and gained permission to beg with the truly needy. Her sublimation of the event is clear in Inés's recollection of how, rather than eat the porridge she was given on her first begging excursion, Carvajal took it into the church and prayed over it for hours (Test. 279ᵛ). The emotional turmoil engendered by such radical displays, combined with her sparse eating, sleeping, and dressing habits, produced an illness in her with which she struggled for the rest of her life. Inés describes her as having shaking fits similar to epilepsy and great pains in her heart. Both maladies are typical of early modern holy women, and indeed physical infirmity was required for such individuals to be accepted as orthodox during this period (Rhodes "Name").

Carvajal's own writings, and writings about her, illustrate an important development in attitudes toward poverty which were evolving during this period. In descriptions of her supposed rejection of material goods, Carvajal and her biographers alike emphasize not the actual poor relief such rejection provided (which in any case was nil), rather the social spectacle of public female degradation, which was celebrated as exemplary. Carvajal's public deeply esteemed the symbolic impact delivered by her renunciation of material and social security, and her willingness to debase herself and her family in the eyes of the community. Although such actions were originally intended to confirm the presence of Christ in the poor, by the late sixteenth century this notion was outmoded and had been replaced by an understanding of the poor as a problem to be solved, a class of little if any redeeming features. The increased esteem for earning one's keep that came about during the Reformation, described by Jütte, greatly complicated the lives of ambitious women like Carvajal, who found themselves caught in a time during which a model like Catherine of Siena's embrace of the poor was no longer functional as a paradigm for Christian merit. According to the new paradigm, the poor needed material uplifting, not imitation. For this reason, perhaps, Carvajal abandoned her experiments with poverty, to create a paradigm that harmonized better with both her personal loyalties and her age's attitudes about who the acceptably disadvantaged were (in her case, the Catholics in England).

Carvajal's later missionary activities were rehearsed in her early attempts to integrate with the destitute of the urban center. Although her Spanish rehearsal of these activities was a failure, for she ultimately abandoned self-degradation as an objective in itself, her London work with the outcast was a huge success. In England, she could exercise her apostolic vocation with a freedom she was denied in Spain where, as a member of the dominant class, her radical outreaches to the marginalized were seen as merely scandalous and superfluous. In England, however, she herself was marginalized by virtue of her nationality, her gender, and her religion, a status that provided her with a bridge across which to reach those she found in need. Visiting prisons, the poor, and execution sites was, in a way, visiting herself in London, comforting herself. In Spain, the same actions meant merely demeaning herself.

In 1598, at the age of thirty-two, Luisa de Carvajal took the extraordinary vow to seek out all legitimate ways to become a martyr (see Vows). Although she never completely abandoned the role of the death-seeking zealot that seems to have come naturally to her, it was not a totally repressive role, and Carvajal probably worked on the assumption that her own degradation was necessary for the later privileges she enjoyed. It was precisely her death-seeking posture which afforded her the multitude of opportunities to grow and thrive, in her own way, that she found in England. Her life thus evidences a major paradox of women's lives: without promising to die, Luisa de Carvajal could never have lived as she did. Her vow of martyrdom, startling as it is, was not the suicidal declaration it may seem, but rather a confirmation of her alliance with Jesuit ideals of apostolic endeavor and Spanish Catholic imperialism.

Carvajal's promise to die for God, while probably a sincere expression of her religious ambitions, was also an able strategy on her part to get to England, for it manifested the same fearlessness toward danger that was expected of all men sent to the Jesuit missions. She was intimate with the individuals writing and reading reports of such dangers. A few years earlier, Carvajal's friend Joseph Creswell, an English Jesuit, had published his *Historia de la vida y martirio que padeció este año 1595 el P. Henrico Walpolo*, [*History of the Life and Martyrdom that Father Henry Walpole suffered in this year 1595*]. Henry Walpole had studied in Spain, and it is likely that by the time of his execution Carvajal was in touch with his brother, Michael, who was to be her confessor until her death. Inés de la Asunción declared that Carvajal always carried Creswell's book with her and slept with it under her pillow (Test. 238ʳ). In 1599, the *Historia particular de la persecución en Inglaterra* was published [*Detailed History of the Persecution in England*], an account written largely by Creswell but published in Diego de Yepez's name. This book was extremely popular at the Spanish court, and it contained two long accounts by Elizabeth Sanders of the harried adventures of some English nuns, formerly at Syon Abbey, before they settled in Portugal. These texts surely inspired Carvajal, who later opened her house in Valladolid to recusant women seeking shelter on their way to convents of their choice.

In January of 1601, the Spanish court moved to Valladolid and Carvajal, needing the court to pursue her lawsuit, moved there as well. Valladolid at this time was a hotbed of active religious women. Mariana de San José and Inés de la Encarnación were in residence there, as was most notably Marina de Escobar, whom Carvajal also met. Escobar, eventually the foundress of the Brigittine Order in Spain, was the paraplegic, ecstatic confessant of the important Jesuit Luis de la Puente, also in residence in the city.[8] Escobar's courageous style of

---

[8] Mariana de San José was later the foundress of the Recollect Augustinians in Spain and became Carvajal's close friend. Inés de la Encarnación, another of Luis de la Puente's spiritual daughters, wanted to join Carvajal in England, but de la Puente denied her permission. Poutrin says of her "This modest woman without intellectual culture had the gift of inspiring numerous religious vocations in people around her and then recruiting benefactors with the necessary dowries for the young women" (311). See Fernández del Hoyo on Valladolid. Luis de la Puente's biography of Escobar, allegedly based on Escobar's own writings, is an astounding and frightening document which exalts female debility and objectification to alarming degrees.

operation, which grew bolder as she aged, is evident in documents such as the letter she wrote to the Provincial of the Dominican Order and the Conde de Benavante defending the Immaculate Conception. In that epistle, Escobar refers to her own position as "our holy opinion," and states from the outset, "The thing is, My Lord, that it is an infallible truth that the Most Holy Virgin Our Lady was conceived without original sin. And I know this from God Himself, who is infallible truth which cannot be deceived nor deceive us, and since this is the heart of the matter, let it suffice" (Escobar, 114ʳ). Daring women such as Escobar surely inspired Carvajal to seek out her own niche in the aggressive Catholic assault against Protestantism, as well as the equally aggressive female assault upon what women perceived to be men's weak efforts at defending the faith.

While in Valladolid, Carvajal intensified her already close relationship with the Jesuits. The house she rented there shared a wall with the Jesuit College of St. Alban's, where students for the English mission were trained. Joseph Creswell, with whom Carvajal later corresponded from London, was then the Vice-prefect of the College, and it is likely that Carvajal continued to deal regularly with both Richard and Michael Walpole while there. These individuals were important figures in the diplomatic circles moving between Spain and England, and Carvajal became intimately aware of their problems while in Valladolid. She was on the verge of helping found a convent specifically designed for English women ("English women of importance," she called them in a letter), a foundation that the wealthy widow Mariana de Cortés wanted to endow. The Jesuits themselves manifested no enthusiasm for the enterprise, which ultimately failed due to complications in the income from doña Mariana's estate. There was no lack of will, however, on the part of the would-be foundress or Carvajal, who added a postscript to a letter to a friend in Brussels about the foundation saying, "I don't think those Fathers [Jesuits] will get in the way of this good work. The important thing is to win over Father Persons; Your Grace should write to him" (*Epist.* 124). Frank moving and shaking for selected projects did not seem to fall beyond the purview of Carvajal's "humility" or "retirement from the world."

The longer she stayed at court, the firmer became Carvajal's connections with noblewomen who would support her English mission financially, women she mentions in her letters or writes to directly. Among them are most notably the Condesa de Castellar, but also the Duquesa de Medina de Ríoseco, the Condesa de Miranda, and the Condesa de Puebla, and others. These relationships provide evidence of women's substantial financial activities in not only the foundation of religious institutions but also their support of other women's work. As Carvajal's network of wealthy noblewomen grew, so did her conviction about her own role. She wrote to her friend Magdalena de San Jerónimo from Valladolid in August of 1602 saying, "Among these ladies of the court there are very Christian people, and the Condesa de Miranda, as Your Grace says, is so in great measure. But the continual occupations and the multitude of things which occupy the hearts of the ladies of the earth, under the guise of very important and necessary business, tend to leave the smallest amount of time for works of great importance in the service of Our Lord, because, since these women must give themselves wholeheartedly to who they are, upon arriving at God they find their hearts so busied and their energies so spent in the business of their estates and so absorbed by all that comes with it, that they have to be ever forging ahead to find a resting place" (*Epist.* 120). This is laudable rhetoric. However, in practice, Carvajal merely exchanged secular occupations for religious concerns of a very similar nature, and continued to fret over questions related to inheritances, budgets, schedules, and administration, interests whose distance from the world now seem to be of a questionable degree.

Elizabeth I of England died in 1603, and in 1604 the Treaty of London was ratified, arranging peace between Spain and England under James I. At the end of 1604, James sent all Catholic priests jailed in England to the continent, theoretically ridding his country of them. This void (in law if not in fact) probably inspired Carvajal's superiors to support her trip to London to work for the Catholic cause: the men simply could not do it, as Edwards observes, saying, "It became high treason for a Jesuit or priest trained in one of the new seminaries abroad to be in England" (24). Thus the doors opened for Carvajal to realize her mission, and things began to fall quickly into place, in a way that moved Muñoz to comment, "Who can work against the will of God or doubt that His Divine Majesty is powerful enough to work great wonders through very weak instruments?" (*Vida* 262). Although Muñoz categorized Carvajal as falling into the tradition of weak instruments of which the divinity avails itself to confound men, she would continue to prove herself to be anything but weak.

Carvajal had made a commitment to depart for England by February 1604, thereby obeying God's will, as she repeatedly insisted. One of her superiors advised her to do the Spiritual Exercises related to election at that time, and she modestly recalls that in January or

February of that year, she did "that part of the Exercises most appropriate to this end," meaning to the fulfillment of God's will. Women were not usually led through the last week of the Exercises, when life-changing decisions were made, and the special privilege is overt acknowledgment of her extenuating circumstances.[9] During that self-examination, she overcame any doubts she had and later wrote of completing the Exercises, "I came out of that resolved" (EA 225). What her specific mission was in London she either did not know or hid. Although she had been convinced — so she says — since age seventeen or eighteen that God wanted her in England, she was less sure of exactly what she was supposed to do there, and expressed this doubt overtly as late as 1607, at the end of her second year in London: "I can't figure out what His Majesty might want from me in England, although it seems he wants me to persevere here, at least so far" (Letter 78 ¶4).

Although the decision to go to England was Carvajal's, she wisely consulted all the men she could find who would approve her plans before leaving, and for her efforts managed to received enigmatic blessings from them. Such was the mixed blessing of Luis de la Puente, who described his response to her apostolic intentions saying, "that he would not dare advise her to undertake the journey, and much less would he advise that she not do so." After citing this reticent consent, Muñoz adds, "The case, finally, was reduced to terms such that not to support the journey was to go against the will of God" (*Vida* 262). In this light, Carvajal's long history of submission and representing herself as soldered to divine will, to the effect of annihilating her own, clearly reaped the desired fruit.

The resolution of Carvajal's law suit in her favor on 2 Aug. 1604 enabled her to write her will, which she did on 22 Dec. 1604, naming the Virgin Mary as her universal heiress, with Robert Persons, SJ, representing the Virgin's interests.[10]   By early 1605, Carvajal was preparing her departure in earnest, without telling anyone what she

---

[9] Iparraguirre notes that religious women were guided through "open Exercises," thus called because they lacked precisely those related to Election (271, n. 173).

[10] Persons used the funds to found the English novitiate in Louvain, which opened in Feb. 1607. Earlier, however, on 25 June 1605, the General of the Society, Claudio Aquaviva, accepted the foundation and granted a certificate of "brotherhood" with the Jesuits to its foundress. Carvajal's novitiate quickly acquired a notoriety similar to that of its foundress, and according to Senning, "With the conversion of England as its ultimate objective, small wonder it was that her foundation quickly became the object of particular concern to James's ministers in London and Brussels" (45).

was planning to do because of the need to conceal the entire trip. Michael Walpole, her Jesuit confessor in Valladolid, was probably secreted into England with her and accompanied her disguised as her servant.[11] Realizing the risk she was about to undertake, she took her leave in writing of those dearest to her. Most moving is the letter she wrote to her companion Inés, who had planned to accompany Carvajal to England up until the moment when their common confessor, Lorenzo Da Ponte, detected personal as well as professional motivations behind Inés's desires to go, and prohibited her from leaving Spain at the last minute.

Carvajal's nerves finally gave out on her just before her departure, which was delayed because of her serious illness. She wrote to Inés three days before leaving, "I am torn up, sister. But for the fact that this is all for God's majesty, I don't think I could have gotten this far." A bit below, clearly weakened at the prospect of her imminent break with her homeland and friends, she wrote, "I hope in God that He will bring news of your soul that my soul desires, for I carry it [your soul] in mine with true love. And we do not need softness in this, but strength, leaving the softness for when his divine love asks for it, so He can please you with it" (*Epist.* 146).

Interestingly, Carvajal's trip to England has been attributed to the need to cement the Catholicism of Anne of Denmark (1574-1619), James I's wife. Of the Queen, it is said, "With these [Catholic] endeavors may perhaps be connected the journey from Spain to England, contrived by the Jesuit Walpole in 1605, of a lady, who is manifestly to be identified with Donna Luisa de Carvajal, 'with purpose to convert the queen our mistress to the Roman religion.' Great hopes were entertained of this visitor, but already in the same years her endeavors are said to have met with little success" (DNB I: 438).[12] Carvajal's friend Magdalena de San Jerónimo appears to have been informed of a similar plot, since in a letter to Magdalena from London, dated 2 Feb. 1606, Carvajal corrects her friend's information saying, "His Majesty [God] knows how far my designs have been from wanting to see the Queen, and neither has that [rumor that she was meant to convert her] spread about here; it has only been said

---

[11] Her letter to Christopher Walpole, dated 16 Feb. 1606 from the road to Bordeaux, refers to the identity of "el padre" ('the father') being in jeopardy, and instructs him to tell anyone who asks that she is going to Rome (*Epist.* 148-49). Her declaration of vocation, dated 22 June 1606, declares outright that he was with her in Brussels in 1605 as she prepared to enter England (EA 226).

[12] The DNB is notoriously slanted toward Protestant interests. Other sources plainly state that the Queen was a practicing, if not baptized, Catholic.

among the principal ministers and gentlemen that I came to see if the Catholics were in such a dire straits as I had heard, and with desire to suffer trials together with them. And they say that with great gentleness and benevolence, without displaying any unpleasantness toward me, and I believe they hold it to be true. That other business that Your Grace says must have been said by some odd people off the top of their heads. . . . My job here has been to keep quiet, since I have always been where no one understands my language [in England], turned into a child by it" (*Epist.* 155-56). Whether the rumor was true or not, it is interesting that an attempt to justify Anne's Catholic tendencies would use Carvajal as means to do so, and attests to the notoriety she attained while in London.

On 24 Jan. 1605, in the dead of an ugly and wet winter, Carvajal's small party left Valladolid: three men on horseback, a serving woman, and two youths who accompanied them on foot, guiding Carvajal's mule. In a document dated 22 June 1606, she recalls some points of her itinerary: from Valladolid she went north to Burgos, and on to San Sebastián (with a devout/tourist visit to the house of Ignatius of Loyola), then to Paris where she was warmly welcomed by the Discalced Carmelites, and Rouen. She specifically avoided Brussels, so as not to meet up with Governess Isabel Clara Eugenia, her childhood companion. It is likely that the Princess would have tried to stop her from continuing to England, since Isabel Clara was among those who later protested Carvajal's presence there. She stopped in St. Omer for a month at the house of Robert Person's sister-in-law, while Walpole sought final confirmation of their plans from Jesuit authorities, which arrived in good time (EA 227). The final moment of her journey upon her, Carvajal put aside her fear of water, paid for all the passages on the boat that took her across the Channel (so as to avoid being identified by anyone) and arrived at Dover—so she says—on 1 May 1605, after a trip of five months (EA 232).[13] Her penitential instruments were confiscated by English customs officers as she entered the country, and she was forced to find other ways than whipping herself to vent her considerable energies. She laments their loss

---

[13] The symbolic date is suspect, and Senning says she arrived in April (43). Father Oswald Tesimond described his own journey from Valladolid to London, undertaken in the late 1590s, as taking four months. It took so long because of men's need to change their disguises at least four times along the way to avoid being discovered, and other subversive strategies (see Loomie, "Creswell"). Carvajal's trip was long for different reasons: her gender and social status required her to seek out befitting locales to spend the night, and the fact that Walpole was with her probably necessitated extreme caution.

in letters through 1606, by which time she had other matters to worry about.

The Superior of the Jesuit English Mission, Henry Garnett (1555-1606), made arrangements to have Carvajal housed at White Webbs, his residence ten miles north-east of London, where she surely met some interesting women such as Anne Vaux (see Letter 47 ¶4).[14] Three months after she arrived there, her companions found out that White Webbs, a Catholic hideaway, was about to be raided, and its residents dispersed in all directions. Carvajal describes an unsettling period moving to different locales in the London Catholic underground, probably guided by Garnett, since the women who had rushed her to London from White Webbs fled immediately back into the countryside (EA 228).

On 5 Nov. 1605, the plans of several English noblemen to blow up Parliament were discovered, the famous Gunpowder Plot.[15] Official response was to tighten measures against Catholics and assure the populace's conformity with royal authority. Persecution intensified, and Carvajal was in a dangerous position. In a letter of 1606, she recalls the frightening experience of being in a house that was searched [for Catholics], during which the agents left her alone after pulling off her bonnet (her hair was cropped), probably inquiring about her odd coiffure, and realizing she spoke no English (*Epist.* 154). To protect her from any further incidents, Garnett prudently contacted the Spanish Ambassador in London, Pedro de Zúñiga, asking that he take her in, despite Carvajal's protests that she had not come to England to live with Spaniards.

The Ambassador's confessor kindly let Carvajal have his suite at the embassy, and she lived there with two English companions until renting her first house, right next to the Spanish embassy, which she had done by Jan. 1607. Carvajal's initial enclosure in the Spanish Embassy for months, combined with the awareness she acquired while there of the intense dislike of the English Anglicans for Spaniards specifically and Catholics in general, produced a frustration in her that surfaced immediately in the boiling rhetoric of her letters. Al-

---

[14] Fullerton, citing unidentified sources, says that during her first few months in England Carvajal lived at the house of Magdalen, Viscountess Montague, a residence then known as "little Rome" (176). She may have spent time at both.

[15] Two of the conspirators had earlier been involved in attempts to win Spanish support for military resistance of James's accession to the throne, attempts carried out at the Spanish court in 1602-03. Joseph Creswell and other Jesuits in Spain were involved in these petitions, called "the Spanish treason," and Carvajal may have known of them as well (see Loomie "Guy").

ready in 1606 she was referring to England as "this mangy desert of wild beasts" (*Epist.* 170) and even her references to pious matters betray a violent streak: about her cousin's desire to abandon the world, she wrote in May, "great glory to God follows from giving the world that great smack in its vain and haughty face" (*Epist.* 169).[16]

Carvajal's realization of the greater power that political interests exercised over those of the faith infuriated and energized her from the outset. In March of 1606, she wrote to Magdalena de San Jerónimo: "And I don't get involved in temporal things, for I abhor a lot of war and the spilling of blood, but as far as the lifting of spirits and helping the missions to grow, and working so that these souls be converted and many saved every new day, I run out of patience with the lethargy I see in the hearts of some Catholics who are jealous of the Church's good. And what I fear is that those things related to the glory of God will be overrun by reasons of state, gilded and showy as they are, which, by law of reason, requires that they [reasons of state] be attended to. And they tend to be evil beasts, because they displease God and He usually lets fly a heavy hand against that very state which pretended to conserve or improve itself by following that route" (*Epist.* 164).

The year of 1606 was probably the hardest of Carvajal's entire mission. Once word of where she was reached Spain, a hue and cry arose to have her returned home, initiating an international debate that was to plague her for the rest of her life. Her close friend of twenty years, the Bernardine nun Magdalena de San Jerónimo, stopped writing to her in 1607 after an intense correspondence that ended in jealousy and disagreement, because, as Carvajal complained to Mariana de San José, "Magdalena de San Jerónimo has tried with great persistence to remove me from this land by means of strong letters and the Princess [Isabel Clara Eugenia in Brussels]. . . . They fear that the peace will be broken because of me, and they can all be assured that it will not, at least not because I have meddled in anything beyond my profession, with Our Lord's help" (*Epist.* 171). Pressure was also exerted by many others to get Carvajal back to Spain, and opinions on the matter were registered by high- and low-ranking Jesuits (mixed opinions); the Ambassador's priest (who said she should return - did he want his rooms back?); Pope Paul V (she should stay); Marina de Escobar (she should return); and the future saint, Juan de

---

[16] The insult was more a function of religion than nationality. Elizabeth Smith, a recusant, wrote to Carvajal from Lisbon about saving her sister and mother from "our miserable country" (unpublished document, Carvajal papers, Encarnación).

Ribera (she should stay, and he wanted to be her confessor!) and others. The early phase of this dissension provoked a crisis in her vocation during her first year in England, when she considered leaving to found an Augustinian convent in Flanders, but after praying over it she realized that God wanted her where she was, and thereafter she resolutely turned her back on anyone who tried to tell her otherwise.

While living at the Spanish embassy, Carvajal enjoyed not only immunity from persecution but access to the sacraments as well, something of vital importance to her. Before the year was over, she had detected a market in London for needlework in threads of precious metals, something at which Spanish women were expert, and she started pumping her correspondents for supplies from Spain to do the work (she continued to request such supplies; see Letter 94 ¶21). In spite of her attempts to maintain herself and her companions by selling needlework, her extensive missionary activities and her lack of affiliation with a religious order left her in a tenuous financial situation, and Walpole attests to how she was perpetually in debt, although as time went by she accumulated more and more patrons ("Vida" 89ᵛ). She repeatedly relied on the generosity of the Spanish ambassadors for financial aid. The pension of 300 *reales* a month that King Philip III arranged for her, in recognition of her service to the state and church, was generous but, in true bureaucratic fashion, it did not actually begin to reach her until just three months before her death.

Whereas she had been willing to acknowledge divine assistance in her acquisition of Latin skills, Carvajal insists repeatedly that she learned English on her own and with much effort. The effort seems to have paid off, for in secular and religious court testimonies alike, it is the content of Carvajal's speeches that people recalled, not her accent or intonation. No sooner did she attain a modicum of proficiency in English than she was on the streets of London. Her first undertaking was the visitation of jailed priests, to console them and encourage them to face the worst rather than recant their Catholic faith (Letter 40 ¶7). It did not take her long to establish a network of (bribed) sources to tell her in which jails there were Catholic prisoners, and prison visitation was one of her primary occupations.

Carvajal's activities during her eight years in London eventually acquired a colorful variety. Her administration to jailed Catholics went beyond religious and moral encouragement, and she obtained money to give to the poor in jail, particularly the less fortunate whose few belongings had been confiscated by the English state. She distributed Catholic literature, mostly books, to needy readers in England and abroad, and likewise helped secret the latest Anglican and Protestant texts into Spain (she read widely in "heretic" writings).[17] Her work as a patron included collecting funds from her noble connections abroad to pay for women's dowries to enter convents in Catholic lands and to finance young men's passage to the continent and procure funds for their placement in noble households or Catholic colleges. For example, Joyce Smith, a Catholic Englishwoman whose transfer to Portugal in 1611 Carvajal patronized, wrote thankfully to Carvajal from Lisbon in February of 1612, adding: "Maddam, I am bolde to presume to crave one favour at your handes, that is that it would please you to send us some English bookes of the mother Teresa of Jesus and some other of Frere Lewis de la Puente of Meditationes or other spirituall bookes, as you shall thinke best, but especially those of the mother Teresa, for here we can get none of them in English; they are very much esteemed of here."[18]

Carvajal's houses, the one in London as well as the one she rented later in the outskirts of the city, probably served as a hideout for Catholic priests. Walpole was arrested at her London residence in 1610 and was also at the house in Spitalfields when Carvajal herself was arrested in 1613, which suggests he spent a good deal of time there. She invited women to visit her at home for discussion of religious matters, and received men and women sent to her for catechism, either study for conversion or a refresher course in Catholicism (presumably for those to whom the differences between the various faiths then available were unclear). Carvajal herself was also asked to call on both Catholic and Anglican noblewomen, and she was always on the lookout for potential converts among the upper-classes, whose mentality she understood perfectly and whose example she believed was important for all. She had the reputation of being a kind and humble yet genteel person, with extraordinary abilities in spiritual consolation, and was probably something of a celebrity whose visits brought social points to the nobility, or at least satisfied their curiosity. After a few years in London, she was a source of current information about the whereabouts of all prominent individuals, of any nationality, as befitted a woman of her station. Thus, for example, in

---

[17] For example, Peralta: "She knew Latin well . . . and had read with particular care some of the books related to controversies against the heretics of that kingdom . . . She understood Catholic dogma well and could cite at length the Scriptures, information related to saints, and [decrees of] Councils" (4ᵛ).

[18] Unpublished letter, Carvajal papers, Encarnación.

Sept. of 1611 she writes to Creswell of Arabella Stewart's imprisonment in the Tower (*Epist.* 331).

Carvajal's residences functioned as a clearing-house for the body parts of executed Catholics, which she treated as relics and had forwarded in lead coffins to the continent, probably thanks to her close relationship with the London embassies of Catholic countries. The bodies of individuals executed for treason were drawn and quartered and then sometimes scattered throughout various graveyards, to keep Catholics like Carvajal from recovering them. Whether scattered or not, they were dumped into common graves with the remains of other criminals. This posed a practical problem for Carvajal and her grave diggers, who nonetheless made every attempt to recover all the parts of each body before receiving them with due ceremony at her house, bathing them, and sending them off to a Catholic state. In 1611, she devoutly received the body parts of the Benedictine John Roberts, who himself had sent the bodies of others to her for safe-keeping.[19] Conducted at night to lessen the likelihood of discovery, the ceremony of admission into Carvajal's home involved a processional candlelight welcome through the front door, followed by the bathing and vigil of the body parts by the women in Carvajal's Society.

Carvajal's profuse adoration of dead and mutilated bodies, repellent as it is to modern tastes, reflects Baroque Catholicism's exalted cult of the saints, with its consequential adoration of saintly bodies and what Holquist has called "the ontological primacy of physical experience" (2). From Carvajal's point of view, the men whose arms, legs, and headless torsos she processed through domestic rituals of devotion were martyrs of her faith, mirror images of Christ, and therefore worthy of adoration. Passages in her works describing these activities, including her sending "relics" to her patrons on the continent, are stunningly grotesque. In a letter of 1611 to her cousin's husband, the Marqués de Caracena, in which she enclosed some piece of John Roberts's body, she wrote (describing the bodies of Roberts and Thomas Summer): "Their heads were put on the bridge, with those of other martyrs, but their bodies [were] buried beneath those of ten and six thieves [respectively]. The two Fathers died together, and on one side of them, eight thieves [were executed], and on the

---

[19] In his memory, an anonymous Benedictine nun authored the play *Donna Luisa of Carvajal*, published in 1922. The title page of this work contains a copy of the stained glass window at Tyburn Convent depicting Carvajal washing Roberts's feet in prison before his execution. Roberts's remains, of which Carvajal had custody, now rest at the Monastery of St. Gregory in Douai.

other, another eight. They were removed from there [Tyburn], and one night a Benedictine Father came to ask my permission to have them brought to my house. I provided an English coach, and therein they brought Father Roberts, less one leg which fell out on them, since the guards were pursuing those who had removed the bodies, and half the body of the other saint [Summers]. I believed myself to be most fortunate to have such guests and to be able to serve them in such great need, for not a single safe spot, not even one halfway safe, could be found in which to put them. To arrange them, they put an arm with its half chest and back on the ground, and the other with the other half. Strange spectacle and motivation for prayer it was, to see that fragile armor with which they fought without fragility, valiantly. They flew up to heaven, increasing the number of intercessors there, and brought fortune upon my house with such rich booty. Some priests, who found out that I had done that, tried to make me afraid of what the Council would do, but not me, and I almost got mad at them about the entire business. I would not refuse to receive them for all the world together, nor ten lives of mine: I never dreamed I would be so fortunate in my life. I made the Father to whom they belonged give me some pieces [of Roberts's body], but I could not obtain the relics I wanted from him. One of these days they will take him [Roberts's body], it behooves me not to say to where, and therefore I have erased [the information from] the letter to my lady cousin. And let this be for Your Excellency and my cousin only and your daughters, so that no Englishman nor Flemish person get wind of it, for these people make themselves out to be all goodness there and, once they are here, they are great scrooges and heretics" (*Epist.* 324-25).

There is no doubt but that Carvajal was sensitive to the political importance of Catholics' bodily presence in England, and the English state was likewise fully cognizant of the perils involved in the execution of individuals whose lives would then be exalted to counterproductive heights. Catholic presence in England signified the equation of Rome and holiness, an equation that the Anglican church-state challenged. Discussing the nature of executions in England after the Gunpowder Plot, Bossy remarks, "This and later examples of the execution of justice in England, attended as they were by a ritual cuisine requiring dissection of the victim, boiling of entrails and placing of heads in public situations, might well be considered sacrificial rites in the temple of monarchy, a deity fancying the boiled where older gods preferred the roast" (158).

Carvajal made no secret about her position in the political debate that was churning around her. The aggressive political rhetoric that had surfaced in her letters as early as 1606 gradually intensified into florid violence, as she readily joined the resistance against absorption of the holy by the ideology of political sovereignty, resistance evident in the writings of Spanish political theorists such as Juan de Mariana, SJ (1536-1624) and Francisco Suárez, SJ (1548-1617). Carvajal's own religious interests cannot be distinguished from her political designs on the world at large, and she repeatedly shows herself to be a member of the noble Spanish class that yearned after Spanish imperial dominion in alliance with an infallible Pope.

Toward the end of her life, Carvajal no longer distinguished His Majesty the Lord from His Majesty the Spanish King. Daringly, she wrote to Rodrigo de Calderón in 1613 that Philip II had been cowardly in his defense of the faith for letting things in England get as out of hand as they were, and four months later complained bitterly to him of Philip III's peace with the Dutch: "Where I want His Majesty [Philip III] to show his hand is in Holland, in the greatest way. Oh, Lord, if only that peace and truce could be broken! And while Spain's friendship with France is fervent, the best opportunity is being lost. Those of us who desire his royal honor and service will not rest until we see the Dutch humiliated beneath his feet, little vermin with respect to His Majesty" (*Epist.* 396; 400).[20] These political ambitions had probably throbbed beneath Carvajal's religious intentions all along.

Although Carvajal wrote almost exclusively of prominent individuals in her letters, Walpole's manuscript biography describes her work with the less fortunate, mentioning the standard activities of Catholic holy women such as tending to the ill, recruiting prostitutes to a better life, helping women give birth, making sure babies were baptized. The political edge on her management of infant baptism, however, singles her out from the masses: whenever she found out a child had fallen ill, she hastened to have her or him baptized by a Catholic priest (probably not an easy job), especially if the family were Anglican, and so assure that child's place in heaven ("Vida" 81-82).

---

[20] Carvajal began to correspond with Calderón in 1609, when it was said that all of Spain's affairs were carried out by him and the Duke of Lerma, Philip III's favorite. A man of dissolute habits, Calderón had married Carvajal's cousin Inés in 1601. Upon his exemplary death (he was executed in 1617), it was said, "He lived very badly and died very well" (Abad, "Don Rodrigo").

Carvajal began her life in England with two anonymous companions, probably women assigned to her by Garnett before his death. By 1608 she had three Catholic women living with her, of her choice, and there were four by the end of the year. By 1609 Carvajal had five women living with her whom she had selected, and her Society of the Sovereign Virgin Mary Our Lady was functioning (see Society). She evidently had difficulties finding women like herself to join her mission, women able to sustain the difficult balance between prayerful withdrawal from the world and active, dangerous engagement in it. Writing to Lorenzo Da Ponte in June of 1608, she describes the troubles she was having in finding suitable companions, as well as her great ambitions for her Society, saying, "I have been very distrustful of the possibility of finding a[nother] suitable companion, because if a woman has any devotional abilities, she directs it all toward becoming a nun in the Low Countries. I have been left with three ladies as good as gold, and not counterfeit, who certainly show true virtue well beyond the ordinary. And if many could be introduced to the life of spiritual perfection, it would be a great thing. Your Grace should beseech this of God" (*Epist.* 256).

The women in Carvajal's Society were of a mixed class. One, who lived the longest with Carvajal, was Anne, one of Henry Garnett's cousins. In the testimonies for Carvajal's beatification, there is evidence that another was Mary Ward's aunt.[21] Identifying them is difficult because in her letters Carvajal refers to these women by first name only, to protect their identities. Carvajal's instructions for her companions are official documents describing a rigorous, enclosed life of prayer which prudently passes over all of the street-wise activities in which they were really engaged (see "Society"). These ladies, who dressed up as washer women from the Spanish Embassy to gain access to Carvajal while she was in prison, were evidently as astute as their mistress in moving around London. About this education, in the praxis of religious espionage and politics, Carvajal wisely wrote nothing.

---

[21] Abad mentions the testimony (*Mis.* 315) and also believes that Carvajal's second house, in Spitalfields, was formerly Garnett's residence and was perhaps the place where Ward set up the first house for her English Ladies in England (they were moved to St. Omer in 1609, where they were protected by Princess Isabel Clara Eugenia, Carvajal's childhood companion). Carvajal and Ward do not seem to have met, although Ward knew about Carvajal's Society. Ignatius of Loyola's prohibition of a women's branch of the Jesuits before his death tormented both of these determined Catholic apostles.

The notion that Carvajal's womanhood protected her from the swift and deadly punishment that would have been meted out to a man engaged in exactly the same activities is borne out by the fate of John Ogilvie, SJ. Ogilvie had entered Scotland in disguise in 1615 because of the persecution of Catholics there and carried out his priestly work secretly in Edinburgh. He was caught entering a prison to console those incarcerated because of their Catholicism, for which he was arrested, tortured, and hung that same year. Carvajal was sensitive to the advantages of her sex, as were her superiors, and Londoners' unwillingness to believe that a woman would have the nerve to speak as publicly as Carvajal did about the dangerous subjects she chose is evident in their calling her a priest disguised as a woman (Letter 94 ¶4). It is likely that Carvajal's foreign status also protected her from arrest. The English noblewoman Anna Vaux, Henry Garnett's accomplice, was arrested in March of 1606 while visiting Newgate prison, the same one Carvajal frequented (*Epist.* 165).

Carvajal's less prudent proselytizing activities eventually got her into the kind of trouble she longed for. Aside from ripping up antipapal propaganda on the street and kneeling to adore the cross at Cheapside in plain view of all, she took to speaking about religion with anyone who would listen. One day in early June 1608, she was arrested for having gone on at length about the virtues of Catholicism while shopping in Cheapside. She spent four days in jail (something of a misnomer, since she paid to be kept in a room of the jailer's own house; see Letter 94). While she was under arrest, the Spanish ambassador Pedro de Zúñiga not only refused to have her freed but also insisted that she move out of London upon her release (which eventually came about simply because Robert Cecil owed Zúñiga a favor; Walpole 75ᵛ). In spite of the ambassador's reprimands, this arrest only excited Carvajal's apostolic zeal and served to highlight her profile.

Her life, however, soon took a turn for the worse. Zúñiga left England in 1610, and Carvajal lost her most important patron. His successor Alonso de Velasco, like Zúñiga before him, spoke no English, but Velcaso's lack of Zúñiga's aggressive diplomatic talents probably made some of Carvajal's movements and financial exchanges more difficult. Michael Walpole was arrested while attending Carvajal in 1610, and after six months in jail was exiled from England; Robert Persons also died that year. These losses surely discouraged Carvajal, and her illnesses began to disable her more frequently thereafter.

George Abbott became Archbishop of Canterbury on 9 April 1610 and Carvajal's problems began in earnest. Abbott had held a personal vendetta that predated his investiture against this woman who was rumored "to be more effective with her words and her works than several priests together" (Abad, ed. *Epist.* 55). He was also unrestrained by his predecessor's reluctance to arrest a foreign noblewoman. Abbott ordered that Carvajal be allowed into any prison she visited and then not be allowed out, an order that she heard of in time to avoid capture. Such a serious cramp on her activities, however, surely depressed her and put her into a difficult moral position regarding her vow of martyrdom: she could not shirk any occasion to die for the Catholic cause, but neither could she seek out death overtly, which would qualify as suicide. The line between the two was extremely thin and Carvajal was walking it unaided by her long-time friend and supporter, Michael Walpole. Her health began to deteriorate and she fell gravely ill in June 1612. Her doctors advised her to get away from the foul air of London, so she rented a house next to the Venetian embassy, where she could have access to the Host, in Spitalfields. The enclosed life she led after this point only further aggravated Abbott for its semblance of monastic retirement, and in September he gave orders that Carvajal be arrested wherever she was found (outside an embassy).

Fortunately for Carvajal, the diplomatic expert Diego de Sarmiento, Conde de Gondomar (1567-1626), arrived in London during August of 1613, to take the place of Velasco. Unlike his predecessors, Gondomar spoke eloquent English, had a flair for effective theatrical postures, and had an acute sense of honor. His solution to the all-points bulletin issued by the Archbishop was to escort Carvajal wherever she wanted to go in his carriage. His wife, Constanza de Acuña, became Carvajal's close friend and joined in the campaign to frustrate Abbott. The tension in Carvajal's life during this year was extremely difficult for her to bear, as documents written by the women living with her explain (see Rhodes, "Luisa").

Senning summarizes Carvajal's mission saying, "An able propagandist, well versed in sacred learning, she gained many by persuasion. Others she won by distributing alms among the poor and by other acts of service to the needy. All in all, her efforts were said to be remarkably successful" (46). He also cites evidence that her Spitalfields house was being used as a refuge by Jesuits and seminary priests, and indicates that Michael Walpole had established a secret headquarters there (50).[22] There was obviously a litany of reasons why the Arch-

---

[22] Walpole was back in England, probably hiding in Carvajal's house, by August 1611, when Carvajal added a codicil to her will specifying that he be given all her papers (*EA* 252).

bishop wanted Carvajal removed from England. The ones given by the Council of State to Sarmiento after her second arrest were the least of them, as Carvajal indicates herself (Letter 178).

On the evening of 28 Oct. 1613, the Sheriff of London broke into Carvajal's house with some of his men and arrested her, warrant in hand. Walpole was there, and his life was saved by the rapid appearance of the Flemish Ambassador who, upon seeing Walpole on site, treated him as one of his household servants and ordered him home (see Letter 176). While the officers searched the poorly furnished house, Carvajal had time to burn some compromising documents before being taken to prison. There was no amiable sheriff's house awaiting her as there had been the first time, and she was deposited in the jail for common criminals. Importantly, she was not given the chance to answer to the accusations made against her this time, nor was she allowed any contact with visitors while in prison. Three of her companions were arrested with her, but were put in the cell with other recusants. One ill companion was left at the house and died the next day, and the fifth, upon returning to the house and finding it swarming with the sheriff's men, fled the scene.

Carvajal's second arrest produced a diplomatic crisis which is described in Sarmiento's reports to Philip III (see Senning). The chivalric Ambassador's strongest efforts did not suffice to have her released to his custody, and she spent three days (28-30 Oct.) in jail. During all daylight hours, several ambassadors' wives posted themselves at the prison, refusing to leave until she was set free. Abbott and King James, however, were in no mood for negotiation. Francisco Súarez, SJ, had just published his *Defensio fidei* against the Anglicans, leaving James greatly angered, and James refused to let Sarmiento have Carvajal without deporting her. Sarmiento, on his part, refused to debase Carvajal by allowing her to be deported. After some face-to-face confrontation, Sarmiento received custody of Carvajal with the provision that he have her escorted out of England immediately.

Installed once more in the Spanish embassy, Carvajal had recovered sufficient composure and health within a month to write letters about her second imprisonment, the first extant one being to her Carmelite friends in Brussels (Letter 176). She lost no time in lobbying against the Council of Castile's orders that she return home, which she knew were on the way from Spain, and took up her pen to beg the King's favorite, the Duke of Lerma, to leave her alone (Letter 178). However, the English ambassador in Madrid had specifically requested her extirpation from his homeland, and at that point (if not before) Carvajal became more of a diplomatic liability than a benefit to the faith. Walpole describes her status at that moment, saying, "If we consider the time that Our Lord removed her from this world, it was when almost all those who knew her in it, friends and enemies alike, although for different reasons, wanted to get her out of England against her will" ("Vida" 122ʳ). Bitter awareness over her status as *persona non grata* surely affected Carvajal's health, and once the exaltation from yet another brush with martyrdom had subsided, she became seriously ill with what Walpole calls colic, defined at that time as "an illness of the intestine, which is altered and twisted either with gas or some choleric humor" (*Tesoro* 333).

Shortly after her release from this second prison term, Luisa de Carvajal died quietly at the Spanish embassy in London. It was her forty-eighth birthday, 2 Jan. 1614. Her biographers attribute her final illness directly to her prison term, thereby justifying her qualification as a martyr. However, her physical state had been deteriorating since long before her second arrest, and one of her companions had died after her second arrest, of what could have been a contagious illness. Whatever the cause, by the time the Council of Castile had recalled Carvajal to Spain, she had already found her way home.

Able negotiating on the part of Sarmiento allowed her companions to be temporarily released from prison to be with her when she died, and they were the only ones to tend her dead body, as Carvajal had meticulously specified. Sarmiento kept her corpse, soldered into a lead box, at the embassy in London, hoping to bring it to Spain with him at the end of his ambassadorial tenure.

In exchange for turning her inheritance over to the Jesuits, Luisa de Carvajal had asked in her 1604 will that they find a place in one of their churches for her body to be buried, "for the deep affection which I have always had for their sacred religion"; lacking space in one of their churches, she asked to be buried in one of their colleges (EA 246). Although Carvajal delivered on her promise, the Jesuits did not honor her will. Her body went instead to a women's convent, with no known efforts on the part of the Society to claim it. After a saga involving Rodrigo Calderón's maneuvers to secret her corpse into a church of his own, her remains were gratefully recovered by her friend Sor Mariana de San José, foundress of the Reformed Augustinian Convent where they now rest.

Carvajal's London legacy appears to have lived on in her companions. In response to Philip III's orders of 5 March 1614 that the Spanish Ambassador to England send her body to Spain and tend to the members of her Society, Diego de Sarmiento responded: "Her companions have all been freed and are exercising freedom of conscience, without having been asked to take the Oath nor having any restrictions put on them in matters of religion, which has been a point that cost me a lot of work and obliged me to speak with the King about it many times, in which Count Somerset exercised his office very well. And that was necessary because of the emphasis that the Archbishop of Canterbury put on saying that they were founding monasteries here, and that they were nuns, and that they were converting people. And about that last item, he is right, and so they are doing even now, and this is the reason why they do not wish to leave this kingdom. I have told them about the situation that the Marqués de Sieteiglesias [Rodrigo Calderón] has offered them [to give them dowries to enter convents in Spain]. They respond that they may perhaps accept that offer in the future, and with this in mind they are trying to learn Spanish, which right now not one of them understands" (*Mis.* 413; appendix 17).

Doña Luisa de Carvajal y Mendoza, herself so adept at slipping between rules while appearing to be in conformity with their makers, would have beamed at this legacy of female competence and independence.

## Introduction: Spiritual Life Story

*T*he first-person document that follows is not an autobiography. Although over fifty Spanish women wrote this type of narration during the sixteenth and seventeenth centuries, at that time no specific name existed to denominate them. I refer to them as spiritual life stories, to call attention to the features that distinguish them from autobiographies, such as the age at which their authors wrote them (around 40, not the end of their lives) and their heavy borrowings from saints' lives. Spiritual life stories were confessional documents that served religious purposes and, in their first manuscript versions, were not expected to circulate beyond the coterie of men who were their intended readers. Teresa of Ávila referred to her text of this kind as her "Book"; it is known today as her *Life*.[1]

Like Teresa's "Book," Carvajal's text was written for the purpose of providing her confessor with evidence that she was a trustworthy, orthodox member of the Catholic community. Abad maintains that Michael Walpole insisted she write it (EA 132, n. 4). Like Teresa, Carvajal was required to compose the document at a mature but not advanced age, when she was an expert not only in prayer, but also in the Catholic textual tradition, an expertise that her spiritual life story was expected to display. Confessors required ambitious religious women to write texts describing their childhood and their intimate relationships with God before confirming their authors as potential religious activists whose future conduct the religious establishment would consider condoning. Women who failed the test of orthodoxy were labeled heretics or false saints, silenced immediately, and their texts destroyed.[2] Since the spiritual life story ends exactly where the woman's career really begins, it made possible but does not contain her most energetic pursuit of the holy. Teresa of Ávila stopped writ-

---

[1] On the politics of such categorization, see Rhodes, "Name."

[2] For example, the Dominican holy woman Sor María de la Visitación, to whom Carvajal wrote of her early ambitions to go to England, wrote a spiritual life story upon orders of her Provincial, which Luis de Granada had in his hands as he wrote his biography of her (Luisa de Granada, *Obras* XVII: 13). When Sor María was denounced as a fraud in 1588, she was exiled to a convent outside Lisbon, and her text disappeared.

ing her "Book" when she caught up with herself holding her pen, just as she was beginning to found convents; Luisa de Carvajal's wrote hers before beginning her English mission.

Spiritual life stories by important women such as Teresa of Ávila, Luisa de Carvajal, Marina de Escobar, and Mary Ward frustrate modern readers because they are incomplete. While the sense of incompletion is accurate, it is not due to the author's gender, women's supposed inevitable relationship with an other, or any similar modern preoccupation, but rather to the simple fact that the text's purpose was to produce an image of an obedient woman whose greatest aspiration was to manifest the will of God through her body. They are passports to a life beyond the normal, written by an individual whose relationship with the divine would prove beneficial for the Catholic community at large. If authors of this type of text had produced complete and rich self-images that faithfully captured their frustrations and ambitions, their readers would have censored them and we would not have the texts today.

Life stories such as Carvajal's adhere to narratives that are larger than an individual life, and their authors' task was much more complex than reconstructing their own memories. The Catholic Church at this time was little interested in the representation of ambitious women, but the same institution was quite determined to eradicate any whisper of heresy from its spokespeople. Since authors of spiritual life stories were inevitably women who either already had or were planning to trespass the boundaries of normative piety and launch into apostolic missions of one variety or another, of great dimensions or small, they were subjected to careful scrutiny before given permission to continue in their intense relationship with God. Not surprisingly, men were not required to produce this type of document, since their powers of discernment were believed to supersede those of women, whose "natural debilities" left them dependent on greater wisdom than their own to determine whether it was God or the devil inspiring them to great things. Religious women's very aspirations and achievements tagged them as suspicious, and their gender by default suggested diabolical origins for those aspirations and achievements. Hence spiritual life stories devote considerable space to describing God's presence in the woman's life, a presence detectable from the moment of her birth if not before.

It is not known exactly when Carvajal wrote her spiritual life story, since none of its three sets of folios are dated. It recounts events of her life through the time she lived with her uncle and aunt in Pamplona. The final folios of all three sets end describing the abusive penitential practices in which she was then engaged by her uncle, events she seems to have stumbled over so much that she never finished her life's account. Subsequent, separate confessional documents written to describe her spiritual state for her confessor provide fragmented descriptions of some events in her life through 1606, just before her departure for England. It seems likely that Carvajal, like many other ambitious women in her position, was asked to write her life story by her confessor as part of the Jesuit's evaluation of her worthiness to undertake her English mission, an ambition so unheard of as to be scandalous. They were obviously quite interested in assuring themselves of the orthodoxy of this wild woman, whose rhetorical performances were all milk and honey, but whose actions packed a serious weapon that the Catholic Church could put to good use, and did.

Further evidence of a close relationship between Carvajal's life story manuscript and her seeking permission to go to England is provided by the carefully chosen points she emphasizes in her religious self-fashioning. For example, describing her behavior before the age of six, she specifies that she kept a coffer of coins, which she regularly distributed to the poor: "I was very careful about putting the key away and dividing it all up among the poor, especially those in jail" (LS ¶15). This detail, down to the coffer itself and her prudence in locking it up, was surely included to convince her readers that she had long practiced precisely the activities she would need to carry out in London, such as alms-giving and the consolation of the imprisoned. Indeed, if read as a factual recollection it is compromising, for sixteenth-century Spanish jails were filled with criminals, not recusants and Jesuit priests, and it would have been unseemly for a noblewoman, and especially a noble child, really to have had contact with imprisoned individuals. Similarly, Carvajal paints a portrait of her mother's virtues, describing her pleasure in a well-arranged oratory and her extraordinary respect for priests (LS ¶¶17-20). This description actually mirrors Carvajal's own virtues, whose exercise she reveals in the events of own her early life. The fact that she twice refers to customs practiced "in Spain" (LS ¶¶67; 97) might indicate that she was out of the country when writing some or all of the text.

Carvajal, perfectly aware of the need to represent herself as meek and mild, obligingly represents herself via episodes firmly entrenched in the Catholic hagiographic tradition, borrowing from female saints' lives so as to make her own life reflective of a narrative larger than her individual existence. One of her most important textual models was the *vita* of Catherine of Siena by her confessor Raymond of Capua, which had been translated into Spanish under the patronage of Archbishop Jiménez Cisneros in 1511 specifically for placement in convents for the edification of nuns. The other important influence is the *vita* of Elizabeth of Hungary (1207-1231), a princess famous for her charity who was reportedly rejected by her family because she embraced poverty, as was Carvajal.

The manuscripts of Carvajal's life story indicate that she was preparing a final draft of the document, all of which remains, when she abandoned the refining project. This suggests that she was engaged in composing the final version at the point when she left for England or when she left the Continent in 1606. Both of these departures were abrupt and related to the need to secret her confessor Michael Walpole into England (perhaps in relationship to the Gunpowder Plot of 1606). Whether she wrote the first sections of her life story in 1606, or earlier, perhaps while living in Madrid when she was refining her plans to go to London, the existence of the document itself points to serious scrutiny of her piety. Such scrutiny could have been provoked by any of the unusual facets of her life at that time: her disowning her substantial social status, her handing over her entire estate to the Jesuits, her exaggerated and public self-abnegation, or her mystical experiences themselves, whose descriptions are laced with a lust for suffering which any levelheaded confessor would have felt obliged to investigate. And indeed, the document Carvajal produced would not have disappointed anyone seeking to know the origins of her peculiar sacrificial ethics: a long history of severe personal loss and displacement (not necessarily unusual for noble children during this period, but not inconsequential either), and a lengthy cohabitation with a guardian whose behavior with his ward can generously be labeled perverse.

The sections describing Carvajal's "discipline," as systematic religious flagellation was then called, vary in sordidness from the general nature of her final draft to more explicit descriptions of the whipping incidents in which her uncle ordered her to participate, descriptions included in versions she edited out of her final draft, probably for the sake of prudence. Importantly, the draft versions remained among her papers. Equally important is that fact that Carvajal's renditions are the only witness's accounts extant. Other evidence indicates that abuses in the practice of religious flagellation were rampant during Carvajal's lifetime. Sebastián Covarrubias, writing in 1611, defined "to discipline" saying "It is particularly practiced among religious people and those who mortify the flesh, in remembrance of the lashes that Christ our Lord endured for our sake, and if this is done under the appropriate circumstances, God unites said penitent's blood with His and gives him courage and merit. But those who whip themselves out of vanity are abominable, foolish priests of Baal. And prelates, as secular governors, should throw out of processions anyone who disciplines his body profanely and should severely chastise them, for since the excesses which occur are as notorious as they are, I do not elaborate on them here, and because it shames me to repeat them. In Germany there was a sect of heretics called the Flagellants; they were great fools and drunkards, and they were indeed condemned as such" (*Tesoro* 426).

It is extremely difficult to know what to make of these episodes, of which Carvajal left three different renditions, until the social history of flagellation is better understood than it is now. As Christian reminds us, "If we impose modern categories and issues, we learn — perhaps — more about ourselves, but miss much about them" (3).[3] According to Carvajal, when so ordered by her uncle she obediently took up the practice of whipping herself, probably engaging in what was officially called *sursum disciplina*, meaning that which involved the upper body only. Like many young enthusiasts of the Catholic life, she became quite adept at self-flagellation. Although its spiritual intent and potency are authentic, her description of her torn skin resulting from the wounds on her back (LS ¶103) recalls sixteenth-century Passion narratives, such as Luis de Granada's *Libro de la oración y meditación* (1558), so closely as to call its historical veracity into question. On the other hand, the "head-to-toe" whippings that Carvajal describes, carried out on orders of her uncle by servants who stripped her and tied her to a column constructed for that purpose, are unusual in their details and describe incidents which lurk in the darkest corners of Catholic penitential practice.

There is little doubt that Carvajal believed that her submission to these acts made her a more perfect Christian. Neither is there any doubt that their value was believed to reside in the direct experience of innocent suffering and ritualized physical pain, similar to the sacrificial rites endured by Christ. Such considerations, however, must be tempered with queries into why the Marqués singled out his young niece to be the object of hired servants' ritualistic humiliation and whipping, rather than have his own daughter, the same age as Carvajal, participate in them. Why he was unsatisfied with Carvajal's long-

---

[3] Christian cites the increasing popularity of flagellation brotherhoods in sixteenth-century Spain, and cites references to women's membership in them, usually with their husbands (186). These floggings were public and self-inflicted, in contradistinction to Carvajal's interactions with her uncle's servants.

standing practices of self-flagellation, a more seemly and more normal practice at the time, must also be considered. Although there are hagiographic precedents for incidents such as these, none pass the frontiers of discretion to the extent that Carvajal's do, for her uncle lacked not only moderation but ecclesiastical jurisdiction over his niece. Lilio's 1558 *vita* of St. Elizabeth of Hungary, for example, describes Elizabeth's failure to attend a sermon that her confessor gave, for which "he ordered her stripped to her undergarment with some of her ladies who were guilty with her and had her harshly whipped" (459ᵛ). While not overtly pornographic in themselves, these texts are underpinnings of a pornographic society, and Lilio's differs from the activities described in Carvajal's only in degree.[4]

Carvajal's own accounts of these incidents discreetly indicate that her uncle had attempted to force her to elaborate to him on how her penitential exercises made her feel, and also tried to force her to beg him to beat her (LS ¶72). Carvajal, who was consistently described by individuals who knew her as extremely reserved in matters of conscience, resolutely and wisely considered him unworthy of such intimacies and refused to talk or comply with his unseemly inclinations. In response to her resolute silence, the Marqués humiliated her in acts which he could observe directly, should he so choose, thereby forcing her to reveal what she would not on her own. The resulting episodes tell us more about him than about her, and provide evidence of physical and psychological abuse of an adolescent girl justified as the imitation of Christ. Carvajal's uncle and her biographers alike exalt her silent obedience to these acts and point to her "perfect submission" as one of her major virtues. Such "perfect submission" is the founding principle of modern domestic abuse, whose basic tenet is that women have natures which demand violent control by men and benefit from the violence used against them. While it would be presentist to interpret Carvajal's unusual experiences of youth solely in light of twenty-first-century standards, it would be just as intellectually dishonest to ignore the evidence of alarming practices they reveal, practices of a marked influence on twenty-first-century life.

The following selections are transcribed from the manuscripts, correcting lapses and errors in Abad's edition (EA 131-88). Material I do not translate is cited from EA. The polished version of Carvajal's story is contained in LS ¶¶1-37, all of which follow. LS ¶¶39-103 make up one draft section, nine and a half unnumbered folios of

---

[4] On the relationship between women's spiritual life stories and the pornographic society, see Rhodes, "Women on their Knees."

unclean copy. LS ¶¶104-132 are found on five folios of clean transcription with many marginal notes by the author. Although I have numbered the paragraphs consecutively, their chronological content overlaps. I italicize all of Carvajal's marginal notes; those whose position in the main text she marked with a cross are inserted into the text where she so indicated; those whose position she left unspecified are in notes.

Ihs.

1. Sirvióse la dulcísima virginidad de Dios de echarme en este mundo tras muchos ruegos y oraciones de mi madre, que con instancia le pedía una hija. Lo mismo deseaba mi padre, tras cinco hijos varones que les había dado, aunque sólo el uno vivía. Y así, nací con una grande y común alegría de la casa.

2. Catorce infelicísimos días estuve sin bautizar; causaríalo el mucho frío de aquel tiempo. Por especial devoción de mi padre me llamaron Antonia; Luisa, por gusto de mi madre. Dábame Dios salud y con entrambos tanta gracia, que cada día crecía su amor para conmigo. Y notábase mucho en mí extraordinaria mesura, y dicen que tenía la más proporcionada disposición de cuerpo y linda cara que se podía en una niña desear. Siendo de edad de cuatro años, pisándome la basquiña una muchacha, caí sobre una piedra muy aguda que me rompió la frente y, bañada la cara en sangre, llegué donde estaba mi madre con muestras de no pequeño corazón. Ella quedó como fuera de sí de dolor, y yo muy cercana a la muerte con aquella peligrosa caída y, despachando a toda diligencia por un gran cirujano que estaba [a] catorce leguas de allí, por su medio me sacó Dios de aquel peligro, quedándome una señal blanca en la frente, de modo que no causa nota.

3. Yéndose mi padre a otra provincia por causa de negocios, el temple diferente y contrario a mi complexión me quitó la salud, y caí en muy recias cuartanas, siendo de edad de cinco años.

# [*Spiritual Life Story*]
## [I. Childhood and adolescence, 1566-1572][1]


Ihs.


1. The most sweet virginity of God was served to cast me into this world following many entreaties and prayers of my mother, who beseeched of Him a daughter. So also wished my father, after five sons that He had given them, although only one was still alive. And thus I was born to the great and communal rejoicing of the family.[2]

2. I spent fourteen most unhappy days without being baptized, probably because of the extremely cold weather at the time. My father named me Antonia out of special devotion; Luisa was my mother's choice. God gave me health and with both of my parents such grace that their love for me grew every day. And much restraint was noted in me, and they say that I had the most well-proportioned body and lovely face that could be desired in a little girl. When I was fourteen, a girl stepped on my skirt and I fell on a sharp stone, opening my forehead and, my face bathed in blood, I reached my mother showing not little bravery. She was beside herself with grief, and I close to death from that dangerous fall, and dispatching with all haste for a famous surgeon, who was fourteen leagues away, God removed me from that danger by means of him, leaving me with a white scar on my forehead that is not noticeable.

3. When my father moved to another province for business reasons, the different climate, which was contrary to my constitution, made me unhealthy and I had a series of fevers, being five years old.


---

[1] In the first section of the manuscript, Carvajal describes her early tendencies to devotion and her exaggerated adherence to pious Catholic protocol. The qualities she attributes to her childhood self (imitation of a saintly mother, inclination toward physical suffering, devotion to a religious order, tendency to charity) are all features of noble women saints.

[2] In investigations for beatification, one of the questions put to witnesses was whether they would affirm that the individual in question was "a child of prayers," meaning that someone had literally prayed that person into life, a signal of divine favor. This paragraph was designed to provide an answer to that question.

Pasábalas vestida por la mayor parte, sobre una camilla en el aposento de mi madre.

4. (Necesario será, hasta los doce años, tratar de niñerías, pues tan de veras manda vuestra merced que no deje nada de cuanto se me acuerda.)

5. Habíaseme ya pegado de mi madre gran codicia de dar limosna, o por imitarla, o por darle gusto (que en todo, dicen, procuraba dársele, como si tuviera más edad). Y cogiendo cuanto podía, quejábanse los de casa a mi madre, y ella se reía y gustaba que lo hiciese así. Cuando me ponían en la cama blanda y caliente, muchas veces lamentaba la miseria de los pobrecitos, que yo decía que se hallaban entonces sin cama y sin casa, temblando de frío.

6. Mostraba tanta estima de los Padres descalzos franciscanos, a quienes mi madre estimaba y quería muchísimo, que cuando venían a casa, me ponía a sus pies y se los besaba. Y decíame un Padre agustino, deudo nuestro, por qué no se los besaba también a él; y respondíale yo, que los pies de los descalzos eran de oro, y los suyos no. Y algunas veces gustaba yo de descalzarme, sin que nadie lo viese, y pasearme a solas en algún aposento, y en tiempo muy frío, con grande contentamiento de ver mis pies por el suelo desnudos. Y si alguien acertaba a pasar, abajábame de manera que cubriese mi vestido los pies; y, en yéndose, tornaba a pasearme. Y aun siendo más niña, de tres ó cuatro años, me dicen fingía tener chinillas dentro de los zapatos, para que me los quitasen. Y después, no quería consentir

I got through them fully clothed for the most part, on a cot in my mother's room.[3]

4. (I must, until reaching my twelfth year, relate childish things, since Your Grace so truly asks me not to leave out anything I can remember.)

5. From my mother I picked up a burning desire to give alms, either to imitate her, or to please her (for in everything, so they say, I tried to do so, as if I were older than I was) and, gathering up what I could, the members of my mother's household complained, and she used to laugh and was pleased that I would do such a thing.[4] When they put me in my soft, warm bed, I used to lament the misery of poor children, who, I said, were at that time without bed and home, trembling from the cold.

6. I showed such affection for the Discalced Franciscan Fathers, whom my mother held in great esteem and loved very much, that when they came to the house I would sit at, and kiss, their feet.[5] And an Augustinian friar, a relative of ours, used to ask me why I didn't kiss his as well, and I would answer that the feet of the Discalced Fathers were golden, and his were not. And sometimes I enjoyed going barefoot, without anyone seeing me, walking around some room alone, and in very cold weather, delighted to see my bare feet on the floor. And if anyone happened to pass by, I would stoop down so that my dress covered my feet, and once that person left, I would start walking about again. And even when I was younger, three or four, they tell me that I used to pretend to have pebbles in my shoes so someone would take them off. And afterwards I didn't want them

[3] They moved to the city of León, where Carvajal's father had been made *corregidor*, or magistrate. Only in grave illnesses did women fail to dress in the morning, even though sickness may have kept them in bed. The presumed pleasure derived from undressing for bed made it a target for penitential exercise: Pérez de Valdivia's guide for *beatas* recommends that on Thursdays and Fridays they "go to bed at night completely clothed, being content with merely loosening their belts and relieving their feet [by removing their shoes]." Similarly, penance for immodest acts was "to go to bed clothed one night" (241; 616).

[4] The *puer senex* topos, meaning the child who is old beyond her or his years, was standard in classical biographies of exemplary individuals and was passed down to the Christian tradition as a requisite for the heroic figure. Carvajal insists regularly on her preternatural maturity.

[5] "Rural Iberian monasticism in the early modern period was predominantly Franciscan. . . . The Franciscan influence, still growing in 1575, partly explains the intense devotion of the period to the crucifix and the Passion" (Christian 15-16).

que me los pusiesen, sino andar algún rato descalza, pero en esto no sé lo que me movía, porque no me acuerdo.

7. Imitaba mucho a mi madre en aborrecer liviandades y poco recato de puertas y ventanas. Y no podía sufrir, aun en tan tierna edad, cosa alguna de aquellas que yo le oía desaprobar y tener por malas, y de cualquiera semejante que viese, la avisaba. Y diciéndole una criada, privada suya, que no me diese crédito porque siendo tan niña, era fácil mentir, respondía mi madre, "¡Oh, no; la niña nunca miente!" Y así me dicen que mentía poquísimo, o casi no acertaba a mentir, y que fácilmente me dejaba cargar de culpas que no tenía. Y de esto se aprovechaban las de casa, cuando perdían o quebraban algo del gusto de mi madre. Y si le parecía cosa imposible, preguntábame si era así, y con gran simplicidad le respondía, "Mi madre, yo no me puedo acordar de haberlo hecho así."

8. Con ser mi madre mujer de rarísimo ejemplo en modestia y honestidad, decía yo de ella a las de casa, "¡Qué llana es mi madre, pues deja que tantos la visiten! Cuando yo sea grande, no tengo de dejar que me visiten tantos." Juzgábalo con llaneza y no por falta de recato, y con todo, no lo aprobaba. De esta suerte, dicen, discurría en otras muchas cosas, con que daba mucho gusto a los que me oían.

9. Hallábame muy embarazada con galas, y no las podía sufrir, y era menester engañarme con algo que me daban para que me dejase componer, de lo cual gustaba mi madre. Y así, me hacían muchas galas, aunque de ordinario me traía con un hábito de San Francisco muy lleno de pasamanos de seda parda, de arriba abajo. Y esa devoción

put back on but wanted to go barefoot for awhile, but I don't know what moved me to this, since I don't remember it.[6]

7. I used to imitate my mother's abhorrence of lascivious things and her modesty around doors and windows.[7] And I could not bear, even at such a tender age, anything I heard her disapprove of or say was evil, and whenever I saw such a thing, I told her. And when one of her personal servants told her not to pay any attention to me because, since I was so young, it was easy for me to lie, my mother responded: "Oh no, the child never lies!" And so they tell me that I lied very little, or never managed to lie at all, and that I would easily accept blame for things I did not do. And those of the household used to take advantage of this when they would lose or break something of which my mother was fond, and if it seemed impossible to her [that it had been I who had lost or broken it], she would ask me if it was true, and with great candor I would reply to her, "Mother mine, I can't recollect having done such a thing."

8. Even though my mother was so very exemplary in modesty and virtue, I used to say to those of the household, "How informal my mother is, for she lets so many people visit her! When I grow up, I will not let so many call on me." I judged her behavior straightforwardly and not as lack of modesty and even so, I didn't approve of it. Thus, so they say, I went on about many things, which greatly pleased those who heard me.[8]

9. I was very annoyed by frills and could not stand them, and they had to fool me by giving me something so I would let them dress me up, which pleased my mother. And so they dressed me with extreme elegance, although I usually wore a Franciscan habit decorated with brown silk braiding top to bottom.[9] And this devotion

---

[6] The qualifier is important, since the motivation behind saintly behavior was considered as important as the behavior itself; had she been motivated by vainglory, her desire to get others to take her shoes off and see her go barefoot would have been sinful. In Spain, going barefoot was considered extremely unhealthy.

[7] Virtuous Mediterranean women were expected to stay away from doors and windows to avoid being seen from the street. Capua's *Vita* of Catherine of Siena says, "she never peeked out of windows or the door of her house to see those who passed by" (5ᵛ). The topos traveled to the New World: Pedro de Loayza's 1619 *Vida* of Santa Rosa de Lima insists, "She never stood at a door or window, nor attended festivities" (73).

[8] This repeated insistence on how pleasing she was to others is a crucial component of exemplary female behavior. The primary objective of exemplary little boys, in contrast, was not to please others, rather to excel in an activity.

[9] Cf. Lilio's 1558 life of St. Elizabeth of Hungary: "Raised in royal pleasures, she disdained all things of youth . . . and she despised immodest dress and loved only virtuous clothing" (459ʳ).

del hábito era por miedo que no me muriese, y con él pensaba preservarme. Y decía que, cuando yo fuese de edad de diez años, si vivía, me había de poner totalmente como monjita y enderezar mi ánimo a que quisiese ser monja descalza; que, a su parecer, era la mejor suerte que me podía caber; y ella sin duda la escogiera para sí, si no la hubieran casado tan niña como la casaron.

10. Retirábase mi madre con aquella doncella que ella quería bien, a solas en su aposento, para tratar de las cosas de su casa y lo demás que le parecía. Y como para mí no había puerta cerrada, ni quien me pudiese apartar de mi madre casi en todo el día, aunque ella me rogaba muchas veces que me fuese a jugar con los otros niños, entraba luego allá y metíame en sus mismas pláticas, como si fuera de mucha edad. Y solía decir mi madre, "Ya viene Luisina a darnos también su parecer y poner su cucharadita."

11. A esta criada que, por su virtud y grande entendimiento que tenía, igualmente mis padres amaban mucho. Por este respeto [le] mostraba yo el mayor amor que me era posible, sin embargo de que conmigo era recia, y la que solamente osaba reñirme, y no veía cosa de regalo que no lo quisiese para ella. Y en esto, y en cuanto echaba de ver que les daba gusto, les pagaba el gran amor que me tenían, en que dicen mostraba extraordinarísima capacidad de niña. Y decía mi madre que deseaba considerasen estas cosas en mí, los que decían que ella dejaba de amarme y me adoraba, y verían cuánto le merecía todo lo que me amaba.

12. No sé a cuánto llegaba mi malicia en aquellos casos de aborrecer falta de recato, y notarlo, y decirlo a mi madre. Aprehendíalo por malo por decirlo ella así. Y mi inocencia llegaba a tanto en esta edad, que me enviaba mi madre en brazos de uno de sus criados a la celda del guardián de San Francisco, a cuya iglesia ella iba a misa, por estar junto a su casa entonces, y mandábame confesar con él de todos mis pecados, apuntándome algunas cosas que yo hacía o decía mal, por gracia y donaire, y yo la obedecía puntualmente. Y él, colgándome del brazo una cestica de rosquillas, o cosa tal, decía que aquella era la penitencia que me daba por mis pecados.

13. Ni parece que era amiga de hacer ningún daño, porque fuera de lo ya dicho, callaba en otras cosas.

for the habit was out of fear that I would die, and with it she hoped to keep me alive. And she used to say that when I turned ten, if I lived, she would dress me all up like a little nun and lead my soul to the desire to be a Discalced nun, which, in her opinion, was the best lot that could befall me, and she doubtless would have chosen it for herself had they not married her as young as they did.

10. My mother used to retire alone to her quarters, with that maiden she was fond of, to attend to the business of the house and other things she deemed appropriate. And since no door was closed to me, nor could anyone separate me from my mother in almost the whole day, even though she entreated me many times to go play with the other children, I used to go in there and join in their conversations as if I were quite old. And my mother used to say, "Here comes little Luisa to tell us what she thinks and throw in her two cents' worth."

11. My parents both cared a great deal for this servant because of her virtue and great understanding. Out of respect for this regard, I demonstrated the greatest love [to her] that I could, even though she was harsh with me and was the only one who dared scold me, and I never saw any object of comfort that I didn't want for her. And in this, and in anything through which I saw it was clear that I was pleasing them, I repaid them the great love they had for me, in which they tell me I showed a most extraordinary capacity as a child. And my mother used to say that she wished that those who said she [the servant] didn't love me, when she really adored me, would consider these things and they would see how much all the love she had for me was repaid.

12. I don't know how far my bad behavior went in those cases of abhorring immodesty and noticing it, and telling my mother about it. Since she said it was evil, I held it to be so as well. And my innocence was such at this age that my mother used to send me in the arms of one of her servants to the cell of the prelate at the Franciscan convent, at whose church she attended mass, since it was close to the house then. And she sent me to confess all my sins to him, writing down some wrong things that I did or said out of playfulness or wit, and I would obey her to the letter. And he, hanging a little basket of fritters or some such thing from my arm, would say that was the penance he gave me for my sins.

13. It doesn't seem either that I was much given to wrongdoing, since aside from what I've already said,[10] I was silent about other things.

---

[10] Her tendency to be a tattletale about immodest behavior.

14. Una noche, estando acostada una criada que dormía conmigo por respeto de mi cuartana y friísimo invierno que hacía, quiso calentar para sí la cama y pegóme el calentador a una piernecilla, de modo que abrasó grande parte de ella. Pusiéronme remedios que templasen el dolor, y la mujer temía no lo supiese mi madre, porque era cosa muy probable el echarla luego de su casa. Y yo callé tanto que no lo pudo entender mi madre en ninguna manera. Y con no sé qué ocasión haciendo que me descalzasen en su presencia, muchos días después, vio la señal del fuego, y admirada de ello, hacía gran pesquisa para saber la causa; pero yo callaba, y así, no pudo entender quién lo había hecho.

15. Habíame dado mi madre una arquilla con un candado de plata, que fácilmente se abría, en la cual guardaba yo cuanto dinero me daba ella y mi padre para los pobres. Y hartas veces estaba casi llena de cuartos y reales, aunque no era pequeña. Tenía yo mucho cuidado de guardar la llave y repartirlo todo en los pobres, especialmente de la cárcel. Y los criados de casa, por gustar de la gracia e inocencia que ellos hallaban en mí en estas cosas, abrían el candado y sacaban la mayor parte del dinero, y tornábanle a cerrar. Y dicen estaba donosa cuando venía a la arquilla y dudosísima en si había dejado tan poco dinero.

16. Todo mi contento era que me trujesen muchos pobrecillos desarrapados de los de las calles, de mi misma edad, y sentarme en medio de ellos, y repartirles algunas cosillas dulces y otras de comer que yo allegaba para aquello. Y cuando me dejaban sola con esta buena gente, abría un escritorio grande de terciopelo verde que yo tenía lleno de brincos lindísimos y muñecas de Ciudad Rodrigo, y dábaselo. Y ellos procuraban escaparse con ello, sin que los de casa los viesen, porque se lo quitaban. Y era mi gran pasatiempo que me sentasen sobre una mesa alta, y viniesen los pajes de casa y todos los otros que yo podía traer allí y que me llamasen su reina, e hiciesen grandes humillaciones y reverencias, y yo derramaba sobre ellos una cesta o grande toalla de manzanas y peras, nueces y castañas y cosas así.

14. One night when I was in bed, a servant, who slept with me because of my quartan[11] and the extremely cold weather at the time, wanted to heat the bed up for herself, and she pushed the heater against my poor little leg, burning a great part of it. They treated it to quell the pain, and the woman feared that my mother would find out about it, since it was likely that she would throw her out of her house. And I kept so silent that my mother never managed to find out about it. And on some occasion or another, ordering that my shoes be removed in her presence, she saw the scar from the burn and, astounded, investigated endlessly to find out how it had happened, but I kept quiet and so she never knew who had done it.

15. My mother had given me a little chest with a silver lock that was easily opened, in which I kept the money she and my father gave me for the poor. And many times it was almost full of coins although it was not a small chest. I was very careful about putting the key away and dividing it all up among the poor, especially those in jail. And to make fun of these things that I did, which they thought were cute and innocent, the household servants used to open the lock, take out most of the money, and then lock it again. And they say I was adorable when I opened the chest and was amazed that I had left so little money in it.

16. My greatest delight was when many poor little urchins of my own age were brought to me from the streets, and I sat amidst them and gave them sweets and other things to eat that I had collected for the occasion. And when I was left alone with these good folk, I would open a big green velvet lap desk that I had, full of lovely trinkets and dolls from Ciudad Rodrigo, and I would give them out to them, and they managed to get out of the house with them without anyone seeing them and taking them away. And it was my great entertainment to be sat on a tall table with all the pages of the house and all the others [servants] I could assemble and have them call me their queen and humble themselves before me and bow, and I would empty among them a basket or big towel full of apples, pears, walnuts and chestnuts and such things.[12]

---

[11] A quartan is a fever that recurs every fourth day.

[12] Emphasis in this section, which relates the years during which Carvajal's mother was alive, is on food and charity toward others. After describing her mother's death, the narration never recovers this thematic abundance or nurturing, either physical or emotional. Her later sustenance of the poor under her aunt's tutelage entails painful self-denial (¶79). The figure of the charitable woman, however, reaches much further back than Carvajal's mother: cf. Lilio's 1558 rendition of the life of St. Elizabeth of Hungary: "And so sweetly and humbly did she give herself to the children of the poor that they all called her mother. And whenever she entered the house, all of them came up to her like a mother and stood before her. And when

17. Aquel último invierno de la vida de mi madre, me acuerdo que salía cada día, después de levantada de la mesa, a los corredores de su casa, con su mantellina de terciopelo negro y traje tan modesto y reportado como su condición, y dos de sus criadas, con una gran canasta de pan, partido en pedazos, y olla de carne y berzas. Y allí, asentados por orden muchos pobres, les iba por su mano repartiendo sus porciones muy suficientes. Y dándome a mí algunas de las escudillas o platos, me hacía hacer lo mismo. Su piedad y devoción llegaba a lo que sus fuerzas con quien quiera que la había menester, y cuando aun los más bajos mozos de su casa o pobres vecinos del barrio do[nde] moraba estaban malos, salía al anochecer disimuladamente a visitarlos, y acompañada de un criado y una o dos criadas, les llevaba bizcochos y almendradas y otros regalos o cosas de que ella veía tendrían necesidad.

18. Al cabo, apretándome muchísimo mi cuartana, ella se quedaba vestida junto a mi cama muchas noches y me lloraba por muerta. Pero ella murió el primer día de enero de aquel primero año, de un tabardillo muy fuerte, pegado, según oí, de un pobre a quien ella fue a hacer enterrar personalmente, como lo acostumbraba, y de tener los enfermos en su mismo estrado y en sus almohadas de terciopelo y lados de su chimenea. Murió de 27 o 28 años de edad.

19. Era en extremo hermosa, y decían que sus cabellos parecían finísimas hebras de oro, y así era cierto, que yo los vi, muchos años después. Fue siempre grande su virtud y rara su modestia desde que era niña, y ni en aquella edad no podía sufrir cosa contraria a ella, ni le podían hacer que se pusiese corpiño, o saya con cuerpo bajo, como se usaba entonces. Tuvo extraordinario respeto a los sacerdotes, y mostrábasele en cualquier ocasión y modo de cortesías, y en topando algunos en la calle o en otra alguna parte, les hacía una reverencia bajísima, aunque ellos no lo mirasen, ni le hiciesen a ella cortesía. Frecuentaba mucho su oratorio, que siempre procuraba tenerle muy bueno. Y decíame una hermana suya que cuando tenía nuevas de gusto, luego se iba a dar gracias al Santísimo Sacramento de la iglesia

17. That last winter of my mother's life, I remember her going out every day, after getting up from the table, to the exterior walkways of her house, with her black velvet mantle and a dress as modest and restrained as her nature, and two of her servants with a large hamper of pieces of bread and a pot of meat and cabbage. And there, to many poor folk seated in an orderly fashion, she would distribute ample portions. And giving some of the bowls or plates to me, she had me do likewise. Her piety and devotion were equal to her abilities, for whomever had need of her, and when even the lowliest youths of her household or poor folk of her neighborhood were sick, she discreetly went out at nightfall to attend them and, accompanied by a manservant or one or two serving women, she would bring them cakes and almonds and other gifts or things she saw they might need.

18. Finally, when my quartan became intense, she remained by my bed fully clothed for many nights and cried for me as if I were dead. But she died the first day of January of that first year, of a bad case of typhoid fever, caught, so I heard, from a poor man whom she went to bury personally as she used to do, and from having the sick in her own receiving room and on her velvet pillows and beside her hearth.[13]  She was 27 or 28 when she died.

19. She was extremely beautiful, and they said that her hair was like the finest strands of gold, and so it was, for I saw them, many years later.[14]  Her virtue was ever great and her modesty remarkable since childhood, and not even at that age could she bear anything that violated that modesty, neither could they make her wear a sleeveless bodice or a garment with a low neckline, as was the fashion then. She was extraordinarily respectful to priests and demonstrated it on any occasion by means of all courtesies, and whenever she ran into some on the street or anywhere else, she would bow deeply to them, although they didn't notice or show her any courtesy.[15]  She frequented her oratory often, and was always careful to have a good one. And one of her sisters told me that when she received good news, she would go immediately to the Holy Sacrament at the church

she carried some little glass toys that she had ordered bought for the children in her cloak, they fell out onto some stones without breaking" (460[r]).

[13] Following Moorish custom, Spanish women received visitors in a room with a large raised wooden platform covered with wicker mats, under which heaters were placed in cold weather. The women sat on pillows on the platform.

[14] Perhaps in a portrait or a saved lock of hair. Idealized women always had golden hair during this period; Carvajal herself was brunette.

[15] Spanish honor made much of who bowed to whom, and people were assassinated on the spot for violating standards of courtesy and social hierarchy.

cercana a su casa. Amábala más que a todas su hermano mayor, que era el tío que me crió en su casa. Y porque era tal que se puede estimar en mucho su calificación, dicen que muchas veces me solía llamar "hija de la mejor mujer del mundo." Y cuando yo, siendo moza, mostraba, aun en muy delgadas y menudas cosas, grande modestia y recato, me decían que era en ello un vivo retrato de mi buena madre.

20. Confesó y comulgó, y a lo último, tuvo turbado el juicio, aunque volvía presto en sí.

21. Como mi padre la entraba a ver y se sentaba cerca de la cama, pegósele el tabardillo y, doce días después, cayó enfermo, estando resuelto de hacerse sacerdote y de vivir muy virtuosamente de allí en adelante. Era muy erudito y señalado en la lengua latina y griega. Conoció con tiempo su peligro y, enviando por el P[adre] Rector del Colegio de la Compañía de Jesús, se confesó con él generalmente y recibió el Santísimo Sacramento con gran devoción y lágrimas, asistiéndole el mismo Padre. Ordenó su testamento y todo cuanto le tocaba. Así acabó harto mozo y bien, al parecer de todos, gracias inmensas sean dadas a Dios. Sin duda le ayudó mucho el gran entendimiento que Nuestro Señor le había dado, y él no empleádole en la devoción ni virtud que mi madre. Fue de modestísimo exterior y notablemente ahidalgado de talle. Dejóme en su testamento una buena cantidad de dinero.

22. Trujéronme a Madrid, do[nde] estaba el curador que nos había dejado, con otros cuatro hermanos míos, el mayor de todos como de diez años u once. En llegando yo a otros tantos, había ordenado mi padre me pusieran en un monasterio, hasta que tuviese edad de elegir estado, y en el ínterin, en casa de la Marquesa de Ladrada, deuda nuestra. Pero una hermana de

close to her house to give thanks. Her older brother loved her more than any other woman, and he was the one who raised me in his house. And since his reputation was such that his opinion can be held in esteem, [I repeat the fact that] they say that many times he used to call me "the daughter of the best woman in the world." And when I, being a young woman, showed signs of modesty and reserve in even the smallest and most minor things, they would tell me that I was the very image of my good mother.

20. She confessed and took communion, and in the end, her mind was disturbed, although she would quickly come back to her senses.

21. Since my father went in to see her and sat close to the bed, he caught the typhoid fever and, twelve days later, fell ill, having resolved to become a priest and to live very virtuously from then on. He was very erudite and distinguished in Latin and Greek. He recognized the danger he was in [of dying] in time and, sending for the Father Rector of the College of the Society of Jesus, he made a general confession with him and received the Holy Sacrament with great devotion and tears, with the same Father attending him. He made his will and set all his affairs in order. Thus he died quite young, and well, as all agreed, immense thanks be given to God. Doubtless the great understanding which Our Lord had given him helped him greatly, and he did not put it to use in the devotion or virtue that my mother did. He kept up a modest appearance and cut quite a gentlemanly figure. In his will he left me a good sum of money.

## [With her aunt, María Chacón, at the Royal Palace in Madrid, 1572- 1576]

22. They brought me to Madrid, where the guardian was whom he had left us, with four other brothers of mine, the oldest of whom was then about ten or eleven.[16] When I reached that age, my father had ordered that they put me in a convent until I should be old enough to choose my profession, and in the meantime, [I was to stay] with the Marquesa of Ladrada, a relative. But a sister of my

---

[16] Carvajal corresponded with her eldest brother, Alonso, while in London. She mentions the death of her brother Juan in letter of 1600 (*Epist.* 104) and in her will refers to her youngest brother, Francisco, as having died at age four (EA 249). Abad says that her father's will refers to a son, Gutierre, as then studying law in Salamanca, probably a half brother, to whom she refers in ¶53. Her rocky relationship with her siblings is visible in some of her letters; see, for example *Epist.* 98-99.

mi abuela la Condesa Doña Luisa, aya de los hijos del Rey, me tomó luego consigo, sin consentir fuese llevada a otra parte.

23. Posaban entonces en casa de la Princesa de Portugal, doña Juana, su tía, pegada a las Descalzas Franciscanas que ella fundó, con puerta abierta al monasterio en la cámara de las Infantas, por cuyos claustros jugábamos, haciendo harto ruido a las religiosas, entre las cuales yo tenía tías y otras deudas.

24. Al cabo de algunos meses, caí en grandes calenturas, remate de mis cuartanas. Y diciendo que tenía peligro, decíale a Isabel de Ayllón (que era aquella criada que amaban mucho mis padres, y él la señaló para que me criase y tuviese a su cargo) que me pesaba mucho de morir tan chiquita que no pudiese ser válido mi testamento en lo que deseaba dejarla, pero que ella no se descuidase de encomendarme a Dios después de mi muerte, porque había sido muy gran pecadora, con lo que la hacía enternecer muchísimo. Sané de esta enfermedad y ya empezaba a sentir la soledad y falta de mis padres. Y retirada algunas veces do[nde] nadie me oyese, a solas lamentaba y lloraba su temprana muerte.

25. He oído que, aun siendo tan niña, escuchaba con extraordinaria atención a las personas de alguna importancia que hablaban delante de mí en cualquier grave materia, o cosas de ingenio, cualquier largo tiempo, sin mostrar cansancio. De donde procedía que, quedándome muchas de ellas en la memoria, después me aprovechaba en las ocasiones. Me tenían por niña de buen entendimiento y debíale a Nuestro Señor un corazón tan piadoso, que no podía tolerar aflicciones de otros, ni aun un tanto como ver castigar [a] las muchachas de casa. Y si veía pasar los azotados por justicia, cuando no estaba en palacio, luego alzaba los ojos y manos al cielo con muchas lágrimas y preguntaba cómo los podía yo ayudar.

grandmother the Condesa Doña Luisa, governess of the King's children, took me right away with her, not allowing that I be taken anywhere else.[17]

23. They [the King's children] were then residing in the household of the Princess of Portugal, doña Juana, their aunt, which adjoined the Discalced Franciscan convent that she founded, throughout whose cloisters we played, making plenty of noise for the nuns, among whom there were aunts and relatives of mine.[18]

24. After some months had passed, I had a high fever, a recurrence of my quartans. And [since they were] saying that I was in danger, I said to Isabel de Ayllón (who was that servant whom my parents loved much and he [my father] singled her out to raise me and take charge of me) that it grieved me greatly to die so young, since my will could not be valid with regard to what I wished to leave her, but [I enjoined her] that she not forget to commend me to God after I died because I had been a very great sinner, which touched her very much. I recovered from this illness and then began to feel lonely and miss my parents. And removing myself sometimes to places where no one would hear me, I would lament and weep alone over their early deaths.

25. I have heard that, even being as young as I was, I listened with extraordinary attention to people of any importance who spoke before me about any serious matter or witty things, for no matter how long, without showing fatigue. From which it came about that, since many of them stayed in my memory, I made good use of them when the moment was right. I was understood to be a child of keen understanding, and to Our Lord I owed such a pitying heart that I could not tolerate others' afflictions, not even such a thing as seeing the serving girls of the household disciplined. And if I should see those who were being whipped for criminal offenses pass by, when I was outside the palace, I would straight-away raise my eyes and hands to heaven with many tears, and asked how I could help them.

---

[17] This great aunt was María Chacón, mother of Bernardo Sandoval y Rojas, then Archbishop of Toledo. One wonders whether Doña María was trying to keep young Luisa out of the hands of her uncle, who nonetheless attempted to extract Luisa from her care (see ¶32 below).

[18] Princess Juana de Austria, Philip II's younger sister, was the mother of Sebastián, Prince of Portugal. She was one of the wealthiest and most powerful women of Europe when she died on 7 Sept. 1573 at age 38. The convent she founded, Descalzas Reales, admitted women of only the highest rank and its foundress was a closet Jesuit. See Bataillon, Retama, and Rahner 52-67. The fact that Carvajal had relatives in the convent shows her social status.

Pues cuando sabía que azotaban [a] un esclavo negro de casa de mi tía, ya viejo, porque era fugitivo, la eficacia con que procuraba fuese perdonado era grandísima, y si no lo alcanzaba, luego lamentaba el trabajo y miseria de Pedro como si lo hubiera de pasar yo misma, con que no poco se entretenían las criadas. Dicen que decía con grande aflicción, "¡Pobre de ti, Perico!, ¿qué será de ti? ¿Quién te ayudará en tanto trabajo?" Ver correr toros y los hombres cerca de sus cuernos, me ponía como difunta y fue para mí siempre intolerable fiesta.

26. Para con los pobres no tenía ordinariamente la ocasión que con mi madre, pero durábame el blando corazón, deseoso de ayudarlos. Y cuando los Hermanos del hospital de Antón Martín pedían limosna en palacio, tomaba algunas veces su esportilla, con grande gusto, y subía a pedir para ellos al estrado de las damas y a el de las doncellas de cámara.

27. Amaba muchísimo a Ayllón, mi aya, sin embargo de la aspereza de condición que mostraba en gobernarme, y no podía sufrir estar ni un día sin ella. Parece que conocía lo que me importaba cuanto ella hacía por enderezarme a virtud y destruir lo que puede impedirla. Si se murmuraba de su rigor, me entristecía, y la defendía siempre. Y cuando más me apretaba, lo más que yo hacía era congojarme un poco y decir que creía que Ayllón me quería comer viva. Sentía bravamente que me azotase, por lo que tocaba a la honra, y como no se entendiese, cualquiera dolor sufriera de buena gana.

28. Llevábame mi tía consigo al monasterio de Santo Domingo el Real, que tenía breve para entrar, y una hija allí monja, llamada doña Magdalena de Rojas. Y ella contaba, siendo yo ya mujer, que le solía decir a su madre, "¿Veis, señora, [a] esta niña? Pues ella vendrá a ser una persona que cause gran contentamiento a sus parientes."

29. Fui muy seca y huraña con mi contrario sexo, propiedad con que parecía haber nacido.

30. De esta edad me acuerdo que ya rezaba con mucho afecto y devoción las que Ayllón me enseñaba, y hartas veces de la manera

Indeed, when I knew that they were beating a black slave in my aunt's household, an old man, because he was a fugitive, the efficacy with which I tried to get him pardoned was most great, and if I did not manage it, I lamented the trails and tribulations of Pedro as if I would have to endure them myself, which gave the servants not a little entertainment. They tell me that I would say with great affliction, "Poor thing, Perico! What will become of you? Who will help you in such great trials?" To watch bullfights, with men close to the bulls' horns, distressed me to death and it was always an intolerable event for me.

26. I didn't ordinarily have the opportunities to be with the poor that I did with my mother, but my soft heart endured, desirous of helping them. And when the Brothers of the Hospital of Antón Martín begged for charity in the palace, I would sometimes take their alms basket, with great pleasure, and go up to beg for them in the ladies' drawing room and in the chamber of the ladies-in-waiting.[19]

27. I loved Ayllón, my governess, very much, in spite of the harshness she displayed in governing me, and I couldn't stand to be a day without her. It seems that I knew how important everything was that she was doing to direct me on the path of virtue and destroy whatever might hinder it. If anyone gossiped about her strictness, it afflicted me, and I always defended her. And when she was the most strict with me, the most I did was get a little upset and say that I thought Ayllón wanted to eat me alive. I resented it fiercely when she whipped me, for what it did to my pride, and I willingly suffered any pain so that no one would find out about it.

28. My aunt took me with her to the Royal Monastery of Saint Dominic, since she had a papal brief to get in and a daughter who was a nun there, named doña Magdalena de Rojas. And she told me, when I was a woman, that she used to say to her mother, "Do you see this little girl, madame? Well, she will turn into a person who will bring great happiness to her relatives."

29. I was very curt and withdrawn with the sex opposite to mine, a quality with which I seem to have been born.[20]

30. Of this age I recall that I prayed the prayers that Ayllón taught me with much zeal and devotion, and many times as if I had before

[19] Spanish palace quarters were rigidly segregated by gender; see Wilkinson Zerner.

[20] I translate literally because the turn of phrase is unusual. Innate aversion to men is a standard feature of female *vitae*: Cape's *vita* of Catherine of Siena remarks, "nothing pained her more than to see men and be seen by them" (4ʳ). Cruz attributes this aversion to Carvajal's psychological history, also important ("Luisa").

que si tuviera visiblemente delante [a] aquel gran Señor a quien enderezaba mi oración. ¡Él sea para siempre bendito!

31. Era aficionadísima a confesarme muchas veces, y en viniendo confesores al oratorio de Sus Altezas, que era lo más vecino en las ordinarias ocasiones que allí había, corría luego por mi manto. Y como no me le daba Ayllón, diciendo que no había para qué irme a confesar sin propósito, tomaba por remedio callar y cubrirme la cabeza con la falda de mi ropa y así me confesaba, que entonces acudía más allí un Padre de la Compañía de Jesús.

32. Desde que el [Mar]qués, que estaba fuera de España con su mujer e hijos mayores, entendió la muerte de su hermana y cuñado, hizo mucha fuerza por cartas para que me llevasen con dos hijas que había dejado en ella. Pero, en oyéndolo yo, me entristecía y hacía pucheros, temiendo no me apartasen de mi tía doña María. Ella me amaba mucho y me decía, "No temáis, hija mía, que nadie os quitará de conmigo, porque no lo consentiré yo."

33. Deprendía a leer y hacía alguna labor, pero muy poca, porque la mayor parte del día pasaba jugando con las Infantas a las muñecas o a las señoras. Y si mi aya me detenía, ellas venían por mí, sin embargo de aquella grandeza y autoridad con que las criaban. Queríame tanto el Príncipe niño, hermano suyo, que lloraba en estando sin mí, y ellas también me querían tener consigo, por lo que había ordinario pleito. Y porque no le hiciese daño al niño llorar, mi tía en persona me iba a buscar muchas veces, porque con menos diligencia, no había sacarme de sus manos; y algunas me escondían de manera que mi tía no me podía hallar.

34. Los pecados de estos años no fueron muchos en número, a lo que me puedo acordar, pero de harto grave calidad, de que se duele mi alma. Llegué un domingo casi al cabo del primer evangelio de la última misa, por haberme embebido en jugar con una señorita de las de palacio, de mi edad. Y por ello fui reprendida y castigada ásperamente de mi aya. Y un viernes, levantando los

me that great Lord to whom I directed my prayer. May He be forever blessed!

31. I was most fond of confessing often and when confessors came to the oratory of Their Majesties, which was ordinarily the closest place there was, I would run right away for my cloak, and when Ayllón wouldn't give it to me, saying there was no need for me to confess without a reason to, I solved the problem by keeping silent and covering my head with my skirt and thus I would confess, for it was a Father of the Society of Jesus who attended us there the most.

32. From the time that the Marqués [de Almazán], who was out of Spain with his wife and eldest children, heard about the death of his sister and brother-in-law, he made many attempts in letters to have me taken where his two daughters were, whom he had left in Spain. But, upon hearing that, I was saddened and threatened to cry, fearing that they would take me away from my aunt doña María. She loved me greatly and would say to me, "Don't fear, my child, for no one will take you from me, because I won't allow it."

33. I learned to read and did some handwork, but very little, because the greatest part of the day I would spend playing dolls or dress-up with the Princesses.[21] And if my governess detained me, they would come for me, in spite of that greatness and authority with which they were raised. The young Prince, their brother, loved me so much he would cry when he was apart from me, and they also wanted to have me with them, which usually caused a ruckus.[22] And so the little boy wouldn't be hurt by crying, my aunt came in person to get me many times because with less diligence there was no way to get me out of their [the Princesses'] hands. And sometimes they would hide me so my aunt couldn't find me.

34. My sins during these years were not many in number, as far as I can recall, but of a sufficiently serious nature that my soul aches over them. I arrived one Sunday almost at the end of the first Gospel reading of the last mass because I got distracted while playing with a little girl of my age from the palace. And for that I was harshly reprimanded and punished by my governess. And one Friday, removing

---

[21] The daughters of Philip II and Isabel de Valois: Isabel Clara Eugenia (1566-1633), was later regent of the Netherlands, and Catalina Micaela (1567-1597), who bore ten children in eleven years, dying in her last childbirth. Catalina kept the affectionate letters written by her father to herself and her sister, documents whose discovery in 1884 revolutionized historian's understanding of Philip II.

[22] Fernando was born on 4 Dec. 1571 to Ana de Austria and Philip II, but died young.

platos de carne de la mesa de sus Altezas, comí un poco de uno de ellos; parece me iba olvidada totalmente de que era día prohibido. Y una vez tomé unas es[tampas] iluminadas de unas *Horas*, y viéndolas Ayllón en las mías, por afrentarme,[1] teniéndolas todas juntas en la mano, me dijo, "Mire aquí lo que ha hurtado. Pues yo las voy a dar luego a su dueño," con lo cual quedaba muy conocido el ladrón. Y otras tres o cuatro veces creo que fueron las que tomé escondidamente los lienzos a Sus Altezas, cayéndoseles en el suelo, en tiempo que yo había perdido los míos, por consejo de una de las otras niñas, para satisfacer a mi aya, que, aun por cosas tan menudas, me reñía demasiadamente. Llegarían estas y otras semejantes faltas como a doce, y no sé que fuesen más, ni con qué malicia pecaba. Paréceme, cuando hago más reflexión, que no había llegado a alcanzar qué cosa fuese pecado mortal, y que Dios no se ofendía de estas tales cosas más de lo que mi aya o tía, cuando se enojaban poco, porque cuando su enojo era más, teníale por demasía, y no la imaginaba en Dios.

35. Deseaba quedar de asiento en palacio, creo que por desearlo Ayllón. Pero Nuestro Señor había resuelto lo contrario misericordiosísimamente, y eso se ejecutó por medio de la muerte de mi tía doña María, que era gran sierva de Dios, y muy probable que Su Divina Majestad se la llevó al cielo. Habíase ido al Escorial la Reina y llevado allá a las Infantas, y ordenado el Rey que el Príncipe entrase en Toledo en público; creo que era la primera vez. Llevábale mi tía sobre sus faldas, sentado en un litera, en día muy caluroso, y dióle a ella una gran calentura que la acabó. Y pareciéndole a mi curador buena ocasión para que se cumpliese el gusto del Marqués, mi tío, sin esperar que volviesen los ausentes, con sólo la licencia de don Bernardo de Rojas, que ahora es Cardenal de Toledo, hijo de la tía difunta, y tenía a su cargo las cosas que tocaban a su madre, me llevaron a Almazán, y entregaron

---

[1] [tachado] las fue luego a dar a su dueño, con lo cual el ladrón quedaba conocido

the meat dishes from Their Highness' table, I ate a bit from one of them; it seems that I had totally forgotten that it was forbidden that day.[23]   And once I stole some illuminations from a book of hours, and when Ayllón saw them, holding them all in her hand, she said to me, "Look here what you have stolen. Well I'm going to return them straight-away to their owner," whereby the thief was made well known.[24] And I believe it was three or four other times that I secretly took Their Majesties' handkerchiefs, when they fell on the ground, at times when I had lost my own, on the advice of one of the other girls, to get back at my governess who, even for such small things, punished me too much. These and other such faults probably add up to twelve, and I'm not aware that there were more, nor do I know out of what malice I was sinning. It seems to me, when I reflect more on it, that I hadn't attained an understanding of what a mortal sin was, and that God wasn't offended by such things any more than my governess or my aunt when they got a little angry, because, when they really got mad, I thought they were exaggerating, and I didn't imagine that anger in God.

## [Ward of her aunt and uncle, in Soria, 1576-1579]

35. I wanted to remain permanently in the palace, I think because Ayllón desired to. But Our Lord had most mercifully resolved the situation otherwise, and that was carried out by means of the death of my aunt doña María, who was a great servant of God, and [it is] very probable that His Divine Majesty took her up into heaven. The Queen had gone to the Escorial and had taken the Princesses with her, and the King had ordered that the Prince was to appear in public in Toledo, I believe for the first time. My aunt carried him on her lap, seated in a litter, on a very hot day, and from it she got such a great fever that it finished her. And since it seemed to my guardian to be a good occasion for the will of the Marqués my uncle to be carried out, without waiting for the return of those who were away, with only the permission of don Bernardo de Rojas, who is now Cardinal of Toledo (the son of my dead aunt, and [who] had charge of his mother's affairs), they took me to Almazán, and they handed

---

[23] Members of the nobility served the royal table. Luisa was not permitted to eat meat on Fridays, whereas Their Majesties evidently were.

[24]  The original ending to this sentence, which Carvajal blacked out, is still legible: "in mine [book of hours], so as to cause me embarrassment, she went straight-away to give them to their owner, so that the thief was revealed."  The drama increased in the rewriting.

a don Pedro González de Mendoza, hermano de mi abuelo, a cuyo cargo estaban las hijas del Marqués y el gobierno de su estado. Y él mismo me llevó luego a la fortaleza de Monteagudo, do[nde] estaban las primas, doña Isabel y doña María, niña de mi edad.

36. Llegando ya a los diez años, empezaba ya a hablar cuerdamente entre las mujeres de edad, con avisadas advertencias y discursos en muchas cosas; mas, por otra parte, amaba los juegos y entretenimientos de niña, muy como tal. En tres meses, poco más o menos, que estuvimos allí, pasé el tiempo en leer y deprender a escribir mejor, y jugar con la primita. Acudía a confesarme cuidadosamente, cuando nos traían confesor religioso de Almazán, porque allí no había más que clérigos seculares, en que me iba aprovechando no poco no por [ilegible] en la que ellos no hacían más que oír la confesión y absolver. Hallábame (muchas veces) con gran devoción por medio de un libro antiguo de la Pasión, afectuosísimo, en que yo leía muy de ordinario.

37. Trajéronnos a Almazán y, antes de pasar adelante, diré cuánta fue la merced que Nuestro Señor me hizo en darme por aya a Isabel de Ayllón, a la cual mi padre muy de veras me encargó a la hora de su muerte. Decía ella que no quería tener de qué dar cuenta a Dios en materia de mi dirección. Enseñábame esta virtuosa doncella un modo de proceder modestísimo y de muy extremado recato y honestidad, aun en cualquier menuda acción, siendo en esto tan exacta que aun en el desnudarme y componerme en la cama, no se descuidaba. No me permitía echar sobre el lado izquierdo, porque no corriese fácilmente algún humor dañoso al corazón, y hacíame cruzar los brazos sobre el pecho en forma de cruz. Y luego, tirando la camisilla hasta los pies, hacía que un doblez de ella dividiese las rodillas, y en el verano hilvanaba la ropa de la cama por los dos lados, por la salud y por la modestia, de que tanto ella cuidaba. Exhortábame a huir de flojedad y muchas veces repetía, "La flojedad nunca hizo cosa buena. Y es bien cierto que tan muelle fundamento no podrá sufrir en sí

[me] over to don Pedro González de Mendoza, my grandfather's brother, in whose care the Marqués's daughters and estate were. And he himself took me right away to the fort of Monteadugo, where my cousins were, doña Isabel and doña María, a girl of my age.[25]

36. When I turned ten I began to talk intelligently among older women, with experienced bits of advice and speeches on many things; but, on the other hand, I loved games and girls' play, just like one. During the three months, more or less, that we were there I passed the time reading and learning to write better and playing with my little cousin. I went to confession carefully, when a religious confessor was brought for us to Almazán, because there were only secular clerics there, of which I took not little advantage, not for [word illegible] in which they didn't do more than hear confession and absolve. I found myself (many times) moved to great devotion by an old book about the Passion, extremely poignant, from which I read quite regularly.[26]

37. We were brought to Almazán, and, before proceeding, I shall say how great the mercy was which Our Lord gave me in giving me Isabel de Ayllón for a governess, to whom my father quite sincerely charged my care at the hour of his death. She used to say that she didn't want to have to account to God for matters related to my guidance. This virtuous maid taught me an extremely modest way of behaving for every minute deed, being in this so exacting that, even in undressing and tucking me into bed, she neglected nothing. She didn't permit me to lie on my left side, so that no harmful humor would run easily to my heart, and she made me cross my arms over my chest in the form of a cross, and then, pulling my nightdress to my feet, set a fold of it between my knees, and in summer she basted shut the sheets on both sides, for my health and my modesty, to which she paid so much attention. She exhorted me to flee from weakness and many times repeated, "Weakness never did a good thing. And it is quite certain that such a soft foundation can't bear up under

---

[25] Carvajal's guardian had removed her to the Marqués's estate without waiting for the Princesses, her close companions, to return to the palace, something she observes specifically in a draft version of the text (EA 178). Carvajal makes it clear that the decision about her fate and her departure from the palace were contrary to her own wishes.

[26] Abad suggests that she refers to the *Passio duorum* (EA 143 n.15). Its Spanish title was *Tractado de deuotissimas y muy lastimosas contemplaciones de la passion* (*Treatise of Most Devout and Very Moving Meditations on the Passion*). Published in 1538, it was an extremely sentimental rendition of Christ's Passion by an anonymous Franciscan.

ninguna que lo sea." No me consentía traerle nuevas ni parlarías, por menudas que fuesen, y decía que me había de avezar a que supiese callar tan bien y ser tan cuerda, que toda la casa le dijese, primero que yo, las nuevas y cosas que yo oía. No me consentía jurar ningún género de juramento, ni tomar un libro en la mano que no fuese espiritual, como lo eran todos los que ella tenía, ni estar donde se leían de caballerías y amores y ficciones vanas. Y si sospechaba que había algo allá (que era cierto muy acaso, porque jamás me incliné a tal lectura), dejaba su labor e iba a buscarme y traíame consigo, y hacíame leer un rato de espiritual lección, que ella oía, o que hiciese labor. Reñíame, si me arrimaba a alguna parte, diciendo que "qué más haría si tuviera ochenta años." Conservábame en tanta limpieza de manos, cara, y vestidos (que siempre eran buenos), y tan discreta y pulidamente adornada, que todos tenían qué mirar. Enseñábame toda suerte de cortesías, trato apacible y muy cuerdo, y a que fuese muy sufrida y no me descompusiese ni con ninguna otra niña, aunque me diese ocasión. Y si me veía hablar alto o más de lo que quería, que era poco, me corría, diciéndomelo delante de otros. Deseaba ella que yo aborreciese las livianas costumbres y pláticas y desordenadas acciones de algunas mozas, nuestras conocidas, y cuidaba mucho de preguntarme a solas qué me parecía de aquellas cosas, para conocer mejor mi ánimo e inclinación. Y responiéndole yo que malísimamente, que era lo que deseaba saber, me daba de nuevo doctrina, abominándolo. Hacíame estar en misa y en lugares con respeto y quietud, no olvidando (*borrón*) cuando se ofrecía ocasión. No sé que hubiese ningún género de buen pensamiento que ella no procurase estampar en mi tierno corazón, gastando la mayor parte de su tiempo. Y parece que todo su cuidado era eso. Si me hallaba en cosa contraria a su deseo, lo pagaban mis brazos, de manera que los traía llenos de cardenales y señales grandísimas (que después que pasé de muy pequeñita, no me azotaba) y así me decía, "Yo no la tengo de gobernar por vía de azotes, que es cosa de las niñas, y es menester que tome pensamientos de mujer y sea muy cuerda y grave desde ahora." Procuraba yo no supiesen el rigor que usaba conmigo nadie de casa, ni las otras niñas que en ella había, porque aun sólo

even anything weak." She would not allow me to bring her news of gossip, no matter how trifling, and she used to say that she had to get me used to keeping quiet so well, and being so prudent, that the entire household would tell her the news and things that I heard before I did. She would not allow me to swear in any form, nor to pick up any book that wasn't spiritual, as were all those which she had, nor to be where stories of chivalry and love and books of idle fiction were being read. And if she suspected that there was any of that going on (which was definitely quite rarely, because I was never inclined to such reading), she abandoned her handwork and went to find me and brought me back with her and made me read a bit from spiritual reading, to which she listened, or made me do handwork. She scolded me if I clung to any place, asking, "What more would you do if you were eighty years old?"[27]   She kept my hands, face, and clothes (which were always of high quality) so clean and so discreetly and neatly adorned that everyone had something to behold. She taught me all kinds of social graces, even-tempered and very sound behavior, and to endure much and not to lose my temper even with another little girl, although the occasion might present itself. And if she saw me speaking loudly or more than she wanted, which was little, she embarrassed me, telling me about it in front of others. She wanted me to abhor frivolous habits and chatter and the uncontrolled actions of some girls, our acquaintances; and she was very careful to ask me alone what I thought of those things, so as to better know my disposition and inclination, and upon my responding [that they seemed] most bad, which was what she wished to hear, she preached at me again, abominating it. She made me sit in mass and in [other] places with respect and quiet, not forgetting [hole in ms.] when the occasion arose. I'm not aware that there was any type of good thought that she didn't manage to stamp into my tender heart, devoting the greater part of her time [to that]. And it seems that all of her concern was to do so. If she found me involved in anything contrary to her desire, my arms paid the price, such that I had them full of bruises and very large marks (since after I was no longer a baby, she didn't whip me), and thus she would say: "I don't have to govern you by means of lashes, which is a childish thing, and you must take up womanish thoughts and be very prudent and serious from now on." I managed not to let anyone at the house know about the rigor with which she treated me, nor the other girls who were there, because the

---

[27] Perhaps referring to the tendency of the elderly to attach themselves to places.

lo que se veía, que era lo menos, tomaba muy mal la Marquesa. Y la gente moza decía era cautiverio, y para qué sufría aquellos rigores y penalidades de mi criada ni la obedecía, siendo su señora. Y las oía, y reparaba en ello. Y al fin me resolvía en amarla y estimar lo que hacía, cada día más, hallando facilidad en perdonar demasías que me llegaban a la virtud y apartaban de vicio tan conocidamente.

38. En este tiempo, que fueron siete meses u ocho después de estar en Almazán, vino el Marqués. . . //

39. Vinieron mi tío y tía (que también era mi deuda, y casádose con dispensación), de fuera de España, ocho o nueve meses después de nuestra llegada a Almazán, y fue tanta mi alegría con ellos, que lloré de contento. Mi tío me mostró, desde el primero día, muy grande amor, y notaba en mí muchas cosas que le daban gran gusto, y, con él, las contaba a los otros. Detúvose allí muy poco, y pasó a la corte, y yo quedé con su mujer e hijas allí en Almazán por dos años.[2]

40. Deprendíamos la prima niña y yo a escribir bien y leer cualquier género de letra, y a contar, y hacíamos alguna labor. Y de estos ejercicios ahorrábamos todo el tiempo que podíamos, para tenerle mayor para jugar y salir al campo y riberas de[l] Duero, que son amenísimas, y de lindos montes, de caza tan abundante, que delante de nuestros ojos atravesaban los ganillos y los ciervos, desde la parte do[nde] iban, y los conejos pasaban de una a otra, y las liebres saltaban cuando menos pensábamos, cosa allí muy ordinaria.

41. Gustaba mucho doña María de jugar a las muñecas, pero yo no tenía flema para ello, ni gracia mayor del mundo para

---

[2] *Lo que perseguíamos a Aguilera, por sólo jugar y entretenernos.*

Marquesa took very badly even just what could be observed, which was the least of it. And the young people said it was captivity, and asked why I endured that severity and punishment from my servant, or even obeyed her, being myself her mistress. I listened to them and paid attention, and in the end I resolved to love her and esteem what she did, more each day, eventually easily pardoning those excesses which so obviously lead me to virtue and turned me from vice.

38. At this time, which was seven or eight months after I had been in Almazán, the Marqués arrived . . . [28]//

39. My uncle and aunt (who was also my relative, and who had married with [papal] dispensation) arrived from abroad, eight or nine months after our arrival at Almazán, and so great was my contentment with them that I cried for happiness.[29] My uncle showed me, from the first day, very great love, and he noted many things in me which pleased him greatly and with it [pleasure], he told others about them. He stopped there for a very short while, and went on to the court, and I remained with his wife and daughters there in Almazán for two years.[30]

40. My cousin and I learned to write well and read any type of writing and basic accounting, and we did some handwork.[31] And from these exercises we put aside all the time we could, so as to have more to play and go out to the fields and riverbanks of the Duero, which are most pleasant, and with lovely hills and such abundant game, from which [hills] the little birds and deer came out and crossed right before our eyes, and the rabbits passed from one place to another, and the hares jumped out when we least expected it, which is quite common there.

41. Doña María liked to play dolls a lot, but I didn't have the disposition for it,[32] nor did I have the greatest talent in the world for

---

[28] The clean copy ends here, exactly upon the arrival of her uncle, and the draft copy, marred with revisions, continues the narration.

[29] Her aunt and uncle needed papal dispensation to marry because of consanguinity.

[30] *How we pursued Aguilera, just to play and entertain ourselves.*

[31] "Contar," literally 'to count,' here means to do basic accounting, part of their education because noble women often ran large estates (as did Carvajal's mother and her aunt). Her cousin was the Marqués's youngest daughter María, born the same year as Carvajal. María later married Gonzalo de Mesías, the Marqués de la Guardia.

[32] Literally, "I had no phlegm for it," meaning the bodily humor.

componer las casas de ellas. Y luego me iba, dejándola muy enojada porque no quería estar. A las señoras me cuadraba más, y a las monjas, que era nuestro harto ordinario juego, buscando invenciones que sirviesen de coro y rejas, y cantando salmos.

42. *Un día, saliendo yo de mi aposento, doña María se vino de repente a mí, y me empezó a dar muchas puñadas y golpes, mostrando gran cólera contra mí. Y yo miréla atentamente, viéndolo ella, y díjele, "¿Está contenta ahora de haberse descompuesto? ¡Qué linda cosa ha hecho!" Y ella se corrió muchísimo de oírme, y conoció que no era fácil hacerme descomponer y mostrar ira, lo cual ella había pretendido, como me lo decía a mí después, siendo ya mujer, y que le traía envidiosísimamente el ser yo lindísima niña, y alabar mi talle todos tanto, olvidados de ella. Yo no era inclinada a envidia, pero, tres o cuatro veces me entristeció harto este vil vicio, contra otra niña, que le habían dado no sé qué cosas más lindas que a mí. Pero presto se me olvidaba.*

43. No me acuerdo del cuidado que tenía de hacer oración, pero sé que me enseñaba Ayllón tales devociones que no se podían hacer sin harta meditación, en la Pasión especialmente, a que acudía muchas veces y sentía devoción, y no pocas, grande quietud y embebecimiento y honda consideración en aquellos santos y dolorosos pasos. Y debía de querer encaminar a lo mismo a doña María, porque, mucho después, ella repetía, en burla, unas dos o tres palabras con que decía empezaba yo en la oración del huerto, diciéndole, "Considérase el ruidito de la noche y la gran quietud y silencio de aquella parte, y a Nuestro Señor entre tantas angustias, orando," lo cual tenía yo olvidado, y ella no. Gustaba yo harto de libros que me moviesen a horror y temor del infierno, amor y dolor de los dolores de Cristo, y de algunos que enseñaban el modo que se ha de tener en la confesión, a que siempre acudía con consuelo y contento grande que hallaba en el confesarme y en las veces y tiempo, seguía la orden de Ayllón. Paréceme conocía poco de Dios, aunque me daba luz lo que leía. Debía seguir virtud y acudir a las devociones, más  por buena inclinación y la doctrina de Ayllón, que por verdadero amor de Nuestro Señor.

setting up their houses. And so I would go off right away, leaving her very mad because I didn't want to be there. To play ladies was more my style, and nuns, which was our most usual game, searching for things to serve us as choir and grilles, and singing psalms.[33]

*42. One day, as I was leaving my room, doña María came up to me all of a sudden and started to hit me with her fists and arms, clearly quite enraged with me. And I looked carefully at her, so she could see, and said to her, "Are you happy now that you have lost your temper? This is a lovely thing you have done!" And she was very embarrassed to hear me say that, and she realized that it wasn't easy to make me lose my temper and show wrath, which is what she had tried to do, as she told me later, when she had grown up, and the fact that I was such a beautiful girl and everyone admired my figure so, forgetting her, had her full of envy. I wasn't inclined to envy, but three or four times this vile vice afflicted me in some dealings with another girl, for she had been given I don't know what things more beautiful than I had gotten. But I would quickly forget it.*

43. I don't recall the care I took to attain prayer,[34] but I know that Ayllón taught me such devotions that they couldn't be done without quite a bit of meditation, especially on the Passion, to which I turned many times and felt devotion, and not a few [times] great quietude and delight and deep consideration of those holy and painful stations [of the cross]. And I must have tried to steer doña María in the same direction because, much later, she repeated, in jest, two or three words with which she said I used to start in on the prayer from Gethsemane, saying to her, "Consider the little noises of the night and the great quiet and silence of that place, and our Lord amidst so much anguish, praying," which is something I had forgotten but she had not. I really enjoyed books which moved me to horror and fear of hell, love, and pain for the pains of Christ and some which taught the way one should behave in confession, to which I always turned with the consolation and great happiness I found when confessing, and as often and whenever Ayllón instructed. It seems to me that I knew little about God, although what I read enlightened me. I must have followed virtue and attended to my devotions more out of goodness of nature and Ayllón's doctrine than out of true love of Our Lord.

---

[33] Teresa of Ávila recalls playing at hermits with her brother during her childhood (*Life* 1.5). Pretending religious professions was a favorite children's game of the period.

[34] "Tener devoción," literally "to have devotion," with its correlative "tener oración," means to attain some level of spiritual grace through prayer, just as today we use "to get exercise" to mean a certain level of exertion and benefit.

44. Siendo de edad de once años, comulgué la primera vez. Pienso que fue día de Nuestra Señora de setiembre, en la parroquia de San Miguel, que está pegada a la casa del Marqués. Aparejéme con reverencia y devoción, paréceme que lo mejor que supe, y no sé si de aquesto procedió subir con conocido temblor del cuerpo las gradas arriba, de que me acuerdo muy bien, y de pasar algunos ratos con doña María, haciendo gran reflexión sobre la eternidad de pena y gloria. Y con admiración decíamos, "Sobre mil años diez y veinte veces mil, no ha de haber esperar fin; y aquesto viene a ser nada, ni el aumentar un millón sobre muchos. ¡Cosa espantosa!"

. . .

50. Quiso la Marquesa que deprendiésemos latín, en el cual llegamos doña María y yo a poco más de los nominativos, porque pasó el Marqués a Navarra por visorrey de aquel reino y llegado, envió luego por su hija doña Isabel y su yerno (que son éstos marqueses de Caracena que ahora viven), y orden para que consigo llevasen a doña Francisca, su hermana, que ahora es monja carmelita, y a mí.

. . .

53. Antes de mi partida a Navarra, su madre de Ayllón murió, y súpelo yo por carta de don Gutierre, mi hermano, y en algunos días no se lo quise decir, porque me pesaba de afligirla, y buscaba mejor ocasión. En fin lo supo, y le pareció que le convenía acudir adonde había muerto, para recoger la parte que le tocaba de hacienda. Pero decíame que no quería dejarme. Y yo le dije que, si le importaba la ida, no me parecía que la debía de dejar sólo por la pesadumbre que a entrambas había de causar el apartarnos por algún tiempo. Y con esta respuesta, se resolvió a dejarme ir a Navarra y quedarse ella allí. Sentí en extremo dejarla, pero con aquella satisfacción que se halla en hacer lo mejor, sin embargo de mal fundados gustos.

44. Being eleven years old, I made my first communion. I think it was the day of Our Lady in September, in the parish church of San Miguel which abuts the Marqués's house. I prepared myself with reverence and devotion, I believe the best I knew how, and I don't know if that was what made my body tremble overtly as I went up the steps, which I recall very well, and spending some time with doña María, deeply pondering the eternity of pain and glory. And with amazement we would say, "For more than ten times a thousand years and twenty times a thousand, there will be no waiting for an end, and even that amounts to nothing, nor even many times a million. What a frightful thing!"[35]

. . .

50. The Marquesa wanted us to learn Latin, in which doña María and I advanced little further than the nominative case, because the Marqués moved to Navarra as Viceroy of that kingdom and, once he had arrived there, he sent immediately for his daughter Isabel and his son-in-law (these are Marqués and Marquesa de Caracena, who are now living), and an order for her to bring with her doña Francisca, her sister, who is now a Carmelite nun, and me.[36]

. . .

53. Before I left for Navarra, Ayllón's mother died, and I found out about it via a letter from Don Gutierre, my brother, and I didn't tell her about it for a few days because I didn't want to cause her pain, and waited for a better moment. In the end she found out, and thought it best that she go to the place where her mother had died, to collect her portion of the estate. But she said she didn't want to leave me, and I told her that if going was important to her, I didn't think she should not go only because of the sorrow that our being separated for awhile would bring. And with this response, she decided to let me go to Navarra and she would stay there. I felt the separation from her deeply, but with that satisfaction one gets out of doing the best thing possible, in spite of ill-founded desires.

[35] This is probably an echo of Teresa of Ávila's life story, when she recalls of herself and her brother, "We were terrified in what we read about the suffering and the glory that was to last forever. We spent a of lot time talking about this and took delight in often repeating: forever and ever and ever" (*Life* 1.4).

[36] Carvajal greatly understates the results of her Latin studies here, as women were wont to do. As an adult she was famous for her abilities in that language.

54. Y llegada que fui a Pamplona, mi tío me empezó a tener por hija muy del alma, que decía él, y yo a él, por padre muy de la mía, con que se templaba harto la soledad de Ayllón, e iba yo trasladando el amor que a ella tenía, en él.

. . .

67. Mi más ordinaria compañía era la presencia de mi tío, y sentada junto a él pasaba grande parte del día: él en su silla, escribiendo a solas o con sus secretarios o escribientes, y yo en el suelo, raramente queriendo admitir almohada, ni más que las esteras en invierno, con un libro muy espiritual siempre en la mano o debajo del brazo, por casi perpetuo compañero. Los más místicos y llenos de grano me deleitaban mucho, sin cansarme de leerlos cien veces, para atesorarlo en mi memoria, de modo que ella me sirviese de libro en las ocasiones. Y esta era la opinión que en cuanto a libros y lección yo tenía. Y de los demás, aunque buenos, llenos de paja, me daban poquísimo gusto.

68. Y como mi tío era hombre tan grave y amador de honestidad, no había ocasión contra ella, y crecía y fortificábase mi sinceridad. Y yo le miraba siempre con notable respeto y reverencia, como si estuviera delante un cuerpo santo; y a los demás, con aquella sincera vista que se suelen mirar los inanimados. Y parecíanme groseros y fríos y feos, aun los tenidos por más hermosos hombres.

54. And once I arrived in Pamplona, my uncle began to treat me like the very child of his soul, as he said, and I him, as the father of mine, with which the loneliness caused by Ayllón's absence was mitigated, and I begin to transfer the love I felt for her to him.

. . .

## [In Pamplona with the Marqués, 1579-1586]

67.[37] My most usual company was my uncle's and, seated next to him, I would spend a large part of the day: he in his chair writing, alone or with his secretaries or amanuenses, and I on the floor, rarely caring to use a pillow, rather nothing more than the mats in wintertime, with a very spiritual book as an almost perpetual companion always in my hands or under my arm. The most substantial mystical texts pleased me a lot, and I did not tire of reading them a hundred times so I could store them up in my memory such that it would serve me as a book whenever the need arose. And this was the opinion I had of books and reading. And from the other ones, which although good were full of useless stuffing, I derived very little pleasure.

68. And since my uncle was such a circumspect man and a great lover of chastity, there was never any opportunity to offend it [chastity].[38] And I grew and my integrity grew stronger.[39] And I always looked at him with considerable respect and reverence, as if I were before a holy body, and upon all others, I cast that look with which inanimate beings regard each other. And they seemed gross and cold and ugly to me, even those believed to be the most beautiful men.

---

[37] A note on the outside of this folio, in Carvajal's hand, says, "From all this confusion and multitude of things let appropriate things be said so as to put it all in order." Of her move to Navarra at age thirteen, she says in the second draft, "And so I abandoned the principles of grammar and was received by my good uncle with a very singular love." In the margin there, she added this note to herself, "I left Ayllón in Almazán. I shall say how that happened, and how God removed me from her hands and put me in my uncle's" (EA 179).

[38] Carvajal's insistence on the chaste nature of her relationship with her uncle suggests that it could have been otherwise. This passage makes it clear that she had been questioned in detail about her feelings for him. Holy women were expected to be aloof from all interpersonal relationships which might afford them support, while giving endlessly of themselves to others.

[39] Cf. Luke 2: 40, "And the child grew and waxed strong in spirit, filled with wisdom." Carvajal begins to compare herself to Christ for reasons which become apparent as her story progresses.

Y lo mismo de mi tío. Gustaba sólo su compañía y de las visitas de nuestros confesores y personas muy espirituales; y de los demás, aunque fuesen primos, parientes y amigos, me cansaban, y sentía un natural disgusto y dificultad con su conversación y trato, por más modesto que fuese. Y aunque lo disimulaba, les mostraba por los menos siempre una grande sequedad y mesura. Cuando los dejaba de ver por pocos días, fácilmente me olvidaba, y los desconocía cuando los tornaba a ver, aunque lo mismo me acontecía con cualquier mujer de las que más cerca de mí tenía. *Y no por falta de vista, que me la dio Nuestro Señor notablemente buena, ni menos, por tenerla de memoria en lo demás; y para esto me faltaba totalmente. De los vestidos no me podía acordar de los de otros, con la dificultad que digo, sin saber de do[nde] nacía.*

69. Mi tío, cuando dejaba de escribir, o mientras sus escribientes sacaban en limpio lo ya escrito, se ponía luego a hablar en Nuestro Señor conmigo, que, como decía uno de sus hijas, era su pecho fuente manantial de espiritual doctrina, que nunca se agotaba. Y llamábanme a mí su "escuchadora," por ser la que más continua y gustosamente le oía de rodillas, con los brazos sobre el bufete que él tenía delante de sí.[3] Muy ordinariamente leía la Sagrada Escritura y Santos Doctores de la Iglesia, lectura que él mucho amaba.[4]

70. Cuidaba mucho de hacerme tener una hora de oración mental cada día, lo cual yo hacía sobre algún paso de la Pasión, por la mayor parte. Y otras veces la gastaba en meditación de la muerte, pecados, juicio e infierno. No tenía largos discursos ni agudezas de entendimiento, pero ahondaba en el punto que más me movía

---

[3] *Decía algunas veces que era yo su Éster porque, como su tío Mardoqueo la crió a ella en el temor de Nuestro Señor, desde niña, así él me había criado a mí.*

[4] *De oírle leer, sin saber cómo, porque no hacía más de volverlo todo en romance con harta facilidad, desde los 15 años, sin lecciones ni enseñanza alguna, ni preguntar* [ilegible] *en toda mi vida.*

And the same for my uncle.[40]  I enjoyed only his company and the visits by our confessors and very spiritual people. And the others, even though they were cousins, relatives and friends, tired me and I felt a natural disgust and difficulty in their conversation and dealings with them, regardless of how decorous it was. And although I hid it [my disgust], I displayed a great dryness and seriousness toward them. When several days passed without my seeing them, I would easily forget them, and I didn't recognize them when I saw them again, although the same thing would happen to me with any of the women who were close to me. *And not because of bad eyesight, since our Lord gave me remarkably good vision; nor was it because I was thinking of one thing while looking at another, and I never had that problem at all. I could never remember what people were wearing, due to this difficulty I'm describing, without knowing from whence it came.*[41]

69. My uncle, when he stopped writing or while his scribes were copying over what they had written, would start talking immediately with me about Our Lord, because, as one of his daughters used to say, his heart was an abundant fountain of spiritual doctrine that never ran dry. And they used to call me his "listener," since I was the one who most often and with greatest pleasure listened to him on my knees, with my arms on the writing desk in front of him.[42]  He ordinarily read from the Holy Scriptures and Holy Doctors of the Church, texts that he loved greatly.[43]

70. He took extreme care that I should have one hour of mental prayer daily, which I used to do on some station of the cross most of the time. And other times I devoted my meditation to death, sins, judgment, and hell. I didn't engage in complicated reasoning or intellectual wit, rather I would probe the point that most moved me to

---

[40] Meaning she felt the same indifference for her uncle's body. In ¶56, she had specified about her uncle, "He used to say, 'What difference is there between seeing a beautiful woman and a very good diamond?'" (EA 151). She pays him back here with equal objectification.

[41] This is a recondite way to communicate her virtuous visual habits, through which she did not even notice physical details.

[42] *He used to say sometimes that I was his Esther because, as her uncle Mardoc raised her close to him in the fear of Our Lord, so he had raised me.* (See the Book of Esther).

[43] *From hearing him read, without knowing how because I never did anything but translate mentally into Spanish, with great ease [I learned Latin] from the age of fifteen, without lessons or any teaching at all, without having asked [anything] about it my entire life.* She elides her earlier Latin lessons to represent this knowledge as infused, rather than learned. It was considered most exemplary for women to learn Latin from God rather than from grammar.

a amor o temor, lo que me era posible, y allí me detenía. Y mientras hallaba luz y devoción, caminaba con viento próspero; y en faltándome, encallaba la pobre navecilla de mi alma en terribles sequedades, y allí quedaba el espíritu peleando con diversos vagos pensamientos, en que de ordinario padecía mucho, y no menos en desechar el sueño que me apretaba harto, y nunca andaba mi cabeza muy satisfecha de él.

71. Y tomábame mi tío estrecha cuenta de si había tenido mi oración o no, sin olvido, y de si me había dormido. Y yo le respondía con grande puntualidad la verdad sinceramente, y sabía que luego me había de reñir por ello. Y acuérdome que, muy desde los principios, considerando ésta y semejantes cosas, echaba de ver que, si no me resolvía a tratar con toda llaneza y deseo de sólo el gusto de Nuestro Señor, desviando mi corazón por ese camino de aquella torcida senda que lleva por contento y satisfacción de criaturas, a veces blanda y encubiertamente, a veces a grandes ofensas de Dios, presto me hallaría plagada de la sucísima lepra de la hipocresía, para lo cual con mi tío había innumerables y continuas ocasiones. Y a los que le parecían más devotos y espirituales en su casa, mostraba mucho mayor amor y aun más favores. Y de tal manera se sirvió Nuestro Señor que yo conociese estas cosas y aborreciese cuanto olía a hipocresía, que no me puedo acordar haber jamás manchado mi alma con tal vicio, hallándome con corazón libre y muy superior en ello.

72. Y según decía mi tío, tenía falta en disimular demasiado los interiores sentimientos, penitencias, y espirituales ejercicios. Y es cierto, que yo lo hacía así cuanto me era posible, pareciéndome que de lo mucho se debía mostrar lo menos, y de tan poco como yo en mí veía, ninguna cosa, y que siempre que Nuestro Señor no mostrara querer lo contrario, convendría que excediese en gran manera la riqueza interior a la que por de fuera se mostrase. Y nunca le decía nada a mi tío, si no era preguntándome, y entonces muy sinceramente, porque yo iba por camino harto llano de espíritu. Y en cuanto a penitencias, poco más podía yo hacer que lo que él ordenaba, y

love or fear, whatever was possible for me, and there I stopped.[44] And as long as I found light and devotion, I went along at full sail and when that light and devotion did not come to me, the little ship of my soul foundered in terrible drought, and my spirit remained there struggling with varied and vague thoughts, in which I suffered often. And not less [did I suffer] in fighting off a great desire to sleep, and my mind was never very satisfied with it [my spirit].

71. And my uncle asked for a strict accounting of whether I had attained prayer or not, never forgetting to inquire about it, and whether I had fallen asleep. And I answered him with the truth, sincerely and quite precisely, and I knew that later he would scold me for it. And I recall that, from the very beginning, considering this and like matters, it became clear that if I didn't resolve to deal with all frankness and desire for only the pleasure of Our Lord, turning my heart aside from that twisted path that leads through contentment and satisfaction in worldliness, at times gently and secretly, at times in great offense to God, I would find myself quickly tormented by the most filthy leprosy of hypocrisy, for innumerable and continuous opportunities presented themselves with my uncle. And to those who seemed to him to be the most devout and spiritual individuals in his household he showed much greater love and even more favoritism. And Our Lord was served in such a way that I knew these things and I abhorred whatever smelled of hypocrisy, for I cannot remember ever having stained my soul with such a vice, finding myself with a free and very superior heart in this.

72. And, according to my uncle, I had a fault in that I concealed my inner feelings, penitential activities, and spiritual exercises too much. And it is true that I did so whenever it was possible, because it seemed to me that one should reveal the least of what was much, and of what little I saw in myself, nothing. And that as long as Our Lord didn't indicate that He wished the contrary, it behooved me that my inner wealth should exceed that which I showed outwardly in great measure. And I never said anything to my uncle unless he asked me, and then very straightforwardly, because I was headed down an even enough spiritual path. And, as far as penitential practices went, I could do little more than those which he ordered me to do, and I

[44] In Counter Reformation Spain, intellectual pursuit of holy matters was considered inappropriate for lay folk and dangerous for women, who lacked not only education but, so the idea went, the basic mental capacity to undertake such pursuits. Carvajal here follows the advice of authorities such as Luis de Granada, who insist that the purpose of prayer was to move one to fear and love of God (see Rhodes, "Spain's").

obedecíale en ellas, pero no le decía nada hasta que lo preguntaba, que con un "sí" cumplía. Él era tan fervoroso, que quisiera que yo obrara con el mismo fervor, y le dijera por cuán pecadora me tenía, y lo mucho que deseaba hacer por Nuestro Señor, y que le pidiera me mandara hacer tal y tal mortificación y penitencia, y cosas a ese modo. Mas yo no lo podía jamás acabar con mi condición, si ello había de salir de mí misma, que cuando él me decía, "Decid tal o tal cosa," decíaselo por cumplir con la obediencia, que, aunque nunca le hice voto de ella, la tenía en grandísima estimación.

73. Y demás de lo ya dicho, nacía en mí esto de parecerme había gran desproporción entre aquel modo, y ser él hombre seglar, aunque tan santo, y yo también, y en medio del mundo y de continuo trato de él, y que era muy buen camino callar mucho y estar muy presta a obedecer en cuanto no fuese pecado. Y decíale que, con el espíritu que Nuestro Señor le había dado, mirase lo que más conviniese a mi alma dar a Su Majestad, que yo allí estaba para todo con grande rendimiento.

74. Érame de notable contento gobernarme por su consejo, y sin ése, no hacía cosa que fuese de algún momento, ni aun tanto como salir de casa con mi tía o primas casadas, y bajar a la huerta, que era harto retirada de la gente, ni ponerme extraordinario vestido o tocado de fiesta. Y como semejantes licencias tocaban más a mi tía que no a él, y él gustaba

obeyed him in them, but I never said anything to him until he asked about it, and with a "yes" I fulfilled my obligation [to answer him].[45] He was so fervent that he wished me to act with equal fervor and I tell him how much of a sinner I believed myself to be, and how much I wanted to do for Our Lord, and ask him to order me to do such and such a mortification and penance and things like that. But I never could bring myself to do it, if it had to come from within myself, for when he used to say, "Say such and such thing," I would say it to fulfill my obligation of obedience, since, although I never vowed it to him, I held it in most great esteem.

73. And aside from what I have already said, a notion was born in me that there was a great disproportion between his being that way and his being a layman, even though he was so holy, and I [a laywoman] as well and in the midst of the world and in continuous dealings with him, and that keeping silent and being quite ready to obey was a very good path to follow, as long as it was not a sin.[46] And I told him that, with the spirit that Our Lord had given him, he should watch out for what was best for my soul, to give to His Majesty, for I was willing to do anything, yielding completely.

74. To be governed by his advice brought me notable happiness, and without it I didn't do anything of any consequence, not even leave the house with my aunt or married cousins and go down to the grove, which was quite withdrawn from everyone, nor wear any exceptional dress or fancy hair style. And since such permissions were more the responsibility of my aunt than my uncle, and since it pleased

---

[45] She was not silent because she had nothing to say, for in a document describing this period with her uncle and aunt, she wrote, "Nor did I have anyone to whom to open my heart and my great and most loving concerns, nor anyone with whom I could receive any relief or consolation in these matters" (EA 210). Writers such as St. Juan de Ávila (1500-1569) consistently refer to the importance of keeping one's blessings from God to oneself: "true humility asks and desires to hide God's gift" (III: 249). This religious discretion, however, contradicted women's obligation to bare all to their confessors. Carvajal considered her uncle as her "spiritual superior" (¶74), which put them both in a difficult position regarding what she was obliged to tell him. She marks her superiority over her uncle by making it clear that her spiritual intimacies were none of his business and also indicates that she questioned the motives behind his persistent inquiries which, in a layman, were inappropriate.

[46] The virtues attributed to female silence during this period are notorious. Feminist re-evaluation of Judeo-Christian ethics of sin, such as Plaskow's, point out that ethical norms such as the Ten Commandments sustain male experience exclusively and promote self-destructive behavior in females. Women's sins, according to thinkers like Plaskow, are precisely the ones Carvajal describes here: passivity, self-denial, and silence in abusive circumstances.

se las pidiese, procuraba pedirla primero a él, porque [si] me la negaba (como muchas veces lo hacía), no convenía que ella la hubiese dado, porque no cayese en la causa del no ejecutarla yo, que lo tomara muy mal. Y, como digo, en cuanto a gobierno temporal, por ser mujer debía estar sujeta al suyo; por otro cabo, el Marqués era mi superior espiritual, en que lo temporal también se comprendía. Y así, era necesario no pequeño cuidado y destreza para concordar estas dos cosas, cuando ella no estaba ausente en otras tierras, que a veces era por largo tiempo. Y mi gobierno en este caso, poner sus órdenes del Marqués en primer lugar, supuesto que era la superior cabeza de la casa, y más espiritual y de mayor provecho para mi alma, y su dirección permanente y de asiento. Y en las cosas que no lo podía hacer sin nota, callaba el autor y dejaba caer sobre mí lo que a ellos podía parecer falta, por no acomodarse a su gusto, y con todo, a veces sospechaban la causa. En todo cuanto yo me hallaba libre, sin gusto declarado de mi tío, obedecía a la Marquesa, holgando de poder darle contento en cualquier cosa. Y cuando me hallaba con esa libertad, o en cosas menudas, mandándome en un tiempo, presentes entrambos, siempre anteponía lo que ella ordenaba a lo que él, y mi tío, de fuerza había de conocer la urbanidad y conveniencia que en eso había.

75. Y era gran descanso de entendimiento tratar con él por lo bien que calaba las cosas, dándoles desapasionado y verdadero sentido. Hacíame Nuestro Señor misericordia de darme buen discurso y grandes reflexiones en lo que veía y oía, y así, no se me podía escapar del conocimiento la maldad y amargura del mundo, suma bondad y dulzura de Dios, en que iba descubriendo gran campo, y muy más perfecta virtud que la que mi tío se determinaba a aconsejarme. Alabábame muchísimo en presencia y ausencia, mostrando muy continuamente con exageración lo que me amaba y estimaba mi proceder. Y contra la complacencia vana que se pudiera seguir, quiso Nuestro Señor que, desde muy luego me anticipase, conociendo cuán miserable cosa era poner mi confianza en otro que sólo Él mismo, y tanto, como echarla en el asqueroso muladar de la instabilidad de criaturas y facilidad con que se trueca cualquier agradable suceso fundado en ellas. Y acordábame con devoción de aquello, *"Maledictus homo qui confidit in homine;"* y de *"Nolite*

him that I asked him about them, I went to him first, because if he denied me permission (as many times he did), it would have been inappropriate had she told me yes and I was then unable to do what she had told me I could, since she would have taken it very badly. And, as I say, as for guidance in temporal concerns, since I was a woman I should have been subject to her will. On the other hand, the Marqués was my spiritual superior, which also included worldly things. And thus I needed not a little caution and skill to reconcile these two things, when she wasn't away on trips, which was often the case for long periods. And my procedure in this case [was] to put the Marqués's orders first, since he was the highest authority in the household, and most spiritual and of greatest benefit to my soul, and his was the permanent and weighty authority. And in the things for which I couldn't ask his permission without being noticed, I would keep quiet about whom it concerned and let whatever problems might arise from not following his wishes fall on my shoulders, and even then they sometimes suspected the cause. In everything in which I found myself free [to decide myself], without any declared preference of my uncle, I obeyed the Marquesa, delighting in being able to please her in anything. And when I found myself with that freedom, or in minor things, when both were present and in charge of me at once, I always put her orders before his, and my uncle had to recognize the decorum and propriety of this arrangement.

75. And it was a great relief to my mind to deal with him because he probed things so well, giving them objective and truthful meaning. Our Lord showed me the mercy of giving me the ability to speak well and think well about what I saw and heard, and so I could not escape from the knowledge of the world's evil and bitterness, the supreme goodness and sweetness of God, which was opening up to me, and much more perfect virtue than the one that my uncle had set himself to advising me about. He praised me very much in my presence and in my absence in an exaggerated fashion, continually showing how much he loved me and esteemed my ways. And Our Lord willed it that right away I had an understanding beyond my years of the vain complacency that could come upon me [from such praise], knowing what a miserable thing it was to put my confidence in anyone else but Him alone, so miserable as to have confidence in the disgusting dunghill of worldly instability and ease with which anything founded upon it is undone. And I remembered with devotion the words: *"Maledictus homo qui confidit in homine,"* and these: *"Nolite*

*confidere in principibus in filiis hominum, in quibus non est salus,*" deseando no pensase mi tío que, en los pocos años, me dejaba empapar en el favor que me hacía. Y túvose por cosa rara el afición y servicios con que acudí a agradecerle los beneficios que iba haciendo a mi alma, pero de tal manera fue que en mi corazón hallaba yo muy distinto el amor a Nuestro Señor, con conocidísima superioridad. E iba echando raíces en mi corazón un temor fuerte de cuanto podía ser pecado mortal, porque mi tío hablaba muchas veces en cuán detestable cosa era, pintando en extremo bien aquella infelicidad. Y decía muchas veces con gran afecto, "En la mar, hija, no hay suficiente agua para llorar un solo pecado mortal, ni tiempo, en cualquier larga vida, para sentirle." Y según aquello, me parecía que, aun dejando a un cabo la ofensa de Dios, por nuestro muy propio amor y temporal descanso, era más fácil y mil veces mejor dejar de pecar mortalmente, que ponerse en tan grave y dificultosa obligación de dolor y sentimiento. E hice tal aprensión de lo que era pecar así, que ninguna cosa en mi estimación pudiera haber que me hiciera alguna fuerza contra la de este temor santo que hallaba en mi alma. Y así temía, como si verdaderamente, en haciendo un tal pecado, me hubiera de tragar luego allí viva, cuerpo y alma, una horribilísima serpiente, de donde yo venía a despreciar totalmente lo que era sólo pérdida de vida temporal en este caso. Este temor que, en feliz hora, tanto se apoderó de mi corazón, me ha librado de millares de pecados que, sin duda, creo hubiera muy deliberadamente cometido, por la grande miseria y fragilidad que he siempre en mí conocido. ¡Glorificado sea Dios!

76. Y no con menos cuidado me exhortaba mi buen tío a una perfecta obediencia y negación de mi propia voluntad, que decía era contagiosa peste espiritual y fundamento de millones de males y que, de no haberla procurado eficazmente quebrantar y vencer muy a los principios, se tomaban torcidísimos caminos en grandes y chicas materias y, fortificada con la costumbre larga, atravesaba por cualquier razón sabia sin darle oídos. Y que así, los muy voluntariosos no sólo hacen pecados, pero desacreditan sus naturales entendimientos en materias morales y de prudente gobierno. Y de mil modos probaba y quebrantaba la mía.

77. Y cuidando en esto más y más cada día, se resolvió de ejercitarme en modo bien extraordinario y dificultoso a mi natural

*confidere in principibus in filiis hominum, in quibus non est salus,*"[47] desiring that my uncle not think that in those few years I was letting myself become engrossed in the favor that he was showing me. And people found strange the affection and disposition with which I took care to thank him for the benefits he was bringing to my soul, but it happened that, in my heart, I found the love that I felt for Our Lord was quite distinct and obviously superior. And a strong fear of anything that could be a mortal sin took root in my heart, because my uncle spoke often of what a detestable thing that was, describing that misfortune extremely well. And he used to say with great emotion, "There is not enough water in the sea, daughter, to bewail one single mortal sin, nor time in any life, no matter how long it may be, to regret it." And judging from that, it seemed to me that, even leaving aside the offense of God for the sake of our self-love and temporal peace, it was easier and a thousand times better to stop committing mortal sins than to put oneself in such a serious and difficult obligation of sorrow and regret. And I became so apprehensive of what it meant to sin thus, that nothing in my being could force me to make any move against the power of this saintly fear that I found in my soul. And I was as afraid of committing such a sin as of having a most horrible serpent swallow me alive, body and soul, and thus I came to a total disdain of what loss of mere temporal life would be in this case. This fear which, in a happy hour, took such control of my heart, has freed me from thousands of sins which, without a doubt, I think I would have committed quite deliberately, due to the great misery and fragility that I have always known to exist in myself. Glory be to God!

76. And not with any less care did my uncle exhort me to a perfect obedience and negation of my own will, which he said was a contagious spiritual plague and the foundation of thousands of evils, and that, should one not manage to break and conquer it efficiently from the very start, it followed the most twisted paths in great and small things and, fortified by long habit, pierced through any wise reasoning without paying the least attention, and thus those of strong wills not only sin, but disgrace their natural understanding of moral matters and prudent governance. And in a thousand ways he tested and broke mine [will].

77. And watching out for this ever more each day, he resolved to exercise me in quite an extraordinary way, difficult for my natural

---

[47] "Cursed be the man that trusteth in man" (Jer. 17:5); "Put not your trust in princes, nor in the son of man, in whom there is no help" (Ps. 146:3).

humor, teniendo yo entonces catorce años de edad. Había en casa una persona muy sierva de Dios y de suficiente espíritu, secreto y cordura, a la cual ordenó, bajo de obligación de gran secreto, que tomase a su cargo humillarme con mortificaciones y disciplinas. Y a mí me mandó la obedeciese en esas cosas, recibiéndolas como saludable purga, para aumento y fortificación de la salud de mi alma e imitación de los trabajos de Cristo Nuestro Señor.

78. Había un oratorio muy conveniente y secreto, y fuera de él otras partes que lo eran harto, donde ella me ordenaba diversas veces que la esperase. Y entrando, cerradas las puertas con llave, con severo rostro, o grave por lo menos, me mandaba descubrir las espaldas y, quedando desnuda hasta la cinta, con una beatilla presa debajo la barba que llegaba a cubrir el pecho en modo decente, e hincada de rodillas, ofrecía a Nuestro Señor aquel sacrificio, como el más duro y áspero, en mi opinión, que se me podía mandar. Y si antes de empezar a desnudarme no hiciera lo mismo, de lo más íntimo de mi corazón, con fogosísimos actos y afectos de amor de Dios, no pienso que pudiera jamás bastarme el ánimo a hacerme tanta violencia, ni tocar a la primera ropa. Ella llegaba con unas disciplinas de cuerdas de vihuela nada blandas, y me disciplinaba el tiempo que parecía con golpes tan bien dados, que apenas los podía algunas veces sufrir. Y para no mostrarlo exteriormente, me era necesario hacer gran fuerza en las manos, una con otra, o apretando los puños. Y tenía por muy asentada costumbre no hacer nunca ni la más mínima demostración exterior de devoción que otros pudiesen notar, de que yo cuidaba aún más en estas ocasiones, procurando solamente lo que era modestia en todo, porque vergüenza y mortal empacho de verme desnuda érame tan natural que sin alguna duda creo me dejaría el rostro tan pálido y marchito como debiera ya difunta. *La alteración del pecho y dificultad que yo sentía de desnudarme, no podía dejar de causar tal efecto, como digo, en mi semblante y color del rostro.* Y Nuestro Señor, de su mano, liberalísimamente me acudía con una profunda humillación en que se hallaba deshecha mi alma, y mi corazón como quebrantado en pedazos en afectuosísima devoción, de do[nde] manaban copiosas lágrimas suavemente, y como cosa dada de mano de Nuestro Señor, aunque yo no podía bien distinguir si nacían o no de aquella gran fuerza que me hacía para desnudarme y confusión que sentía en estarlo. Pero de cualquiera principio que naciese, sé yo que eran unas lágrimas envueltas en un ternísimo afecto de amor de Dios y excelente

constitution, my being then fourteen years old. There was in the household a devoted servant of God of sufficient spirit, discretion and good sense, whom he ordered, under obligation of great secrecy, to take charge of humiliating me with mortification and flagellations. And he ordered me to obey her in those things, receiving them as a healthy purge for the augmentation and fortification of my soul's health and imitation of the trials of Christ our Lord.

78. There was a very convenient and hidden oratory, and around it other areas that were much so, where she would order me to await her diverse times. And upon entering, the doors being locked shut, with a severe face or at least a serious one, she ordered me to bare my back, and, remaining naked to the waist, with a piece of sheer fabric caught under my chin that managed to cover my chest in a decent fashion, and on my knees, I offered that sacrifice to Our Lord, as the hardest and harshest which, in my opinion, could be asked of me. And if before I began to undress I didn't do the same thing [offer the sacrifice to God] from the most intimate parts of my heart, with most ardent acts and fondness of the love of God, I don't think I ever could have gotten up the courage to do such violence to myself nor touch one piece of my clothing. She would arrive with whips made of guitar strings, not at all soft, and she would flagellate me for however long she thought was right, with such well-delivered blows that I could hardly stand them sometimes. And so as not to show it outwardly, I had to grip my hands together or squeeze my fists. And I had an established habit of never making any outward demonstration of devotion that anyone else could notice, of which I was even more careful on these occasions, procuring only what modesty demanded in everything, because shame and mortal embarrassment at seeing myself unclothed came so naturally to me that I'm sure it left my face as pallid and ashen as it would be if I were dead. *The disturbance in my chest and the difficulty that I felt in undressing myself could not but cause such effect, as I said, in my countenance and in the color of my face.* And Our Lord, for His part, attended me most liberally with a profound humiliation in which my soul found itself undone and my heart as if it were broken into pieces over most affectionate devotion, from which copious tears gently flowed and like that [devotion] which is given by the hand of Our Lord, although I couldn't distinguish well if they originated or not from that great effort that I made to get undressed and the embarrassment I felt about doing it. But from whatever source it originated, I know that they were tears encased in a most tender affection of the love of God and an excellent

modo de humildad, de que me dejaba enriquecida y muy aumentado el desengaño del mundo.

79. Aplicábame muchísimo a todo género de obras de piedad, en cuanto me era posible, y así, procuraba dar buenos consejos a las de casa e interceder con mi tío en favor de otros cuidadosamente, en los casos que creía del servicio de Nuestro Señor. Lastimábame mucho de las necesidades y miserias que veía padecer a los pobres. Deseaba remediarlas y hacía lo que podía, que era poco, en cuando a dar dineros. Y eso suplía, cargando la falta de ellos sobre mi comida, de la cual empecé a sustentar cada día [a] un pobre de los que me parecían más necesitados, de que mi tío gustaba mucho. Y con el tiempo, topando otros que hacían fuerza a mi devoción, fui aumentando el número y no pequeña incomodidad mía. Porque, para darles a ellos bien de comer, muy ordinario me quedaba yo con poquísimo mantenimiento, y para disimularlo, fingía que quería comer caldo, que no se usa en semejantes mesas ni se sirve en ellas sin que se pida. Mi tío gustaba de comerle, y decían que, aun hasta en aquello le parecía, ignorando la causa, que a mí me estaba muy bien. Y de la misma suerte procedía en otras muchísimas cosas de virtud que forzosamente, como ésta, habían de ser en público. Y yo veía claramente que, por la mayor parte, a todos persuadía diestrísimamente lo que quería, con que me conservaba en una muy notable pureza de intención y aumentando el candor y lustre en las obras que hacía.

80. *Y cuanto más sin ser sentida ni entendida pasaba por las cosas de virtud y devoción, aunque no hallaba necesaria obligación de dar ejemplo, mayor y más entrañable gusto y alegría causaban.*

81. Y las misericordias que en esta parte recibía de Nuestro Señor no es fácil decirlas, y mucho menos las que Su Majestad me hacía en materia de sufrimiento de prójimos, en que siempre se sirvió darme grandes ocasiones.

82. Pasando de los quince años todo venía aprisa, y el amor de mi tío y demostraciones de él, no en regalarme, sino en ejercitarme más y más y procurar el aumento de todo, y de tenerme junto a su silla lo más que le era posible. Y así, en habiendo gastado algún tiempo de recreación con sus hijos después de la comida, se iba a sus aposentos, llevándome casi siempre consigo, y, si visitas o negocios no le ocupaban, leía en la Sagrada Escritura o Santos Doctores, o platicaba en espirituales materias grave y espiritualísimamente.

means of humility, which left me enriched and with a much greater understanding of the world's deceits.

79. I devoted myself very much to all types of pious works, to the extent that I could, and so I managed to give good advice to those of the household and to carefully intercede with my uncle in favor of others in the cases that I believed were in the service of Our Lord. The neediness and miseries that I saw the poor suffer pained me greatly. I wished to remedy them and I did what I could, which was little, as far as giving money. And that I supplemented, charging the lack of money to my food, from which I began to sustain a poor individual every day from among those who seemed to me most needy, which pleased my uncle a great deal. And with time, running across others who put pressure on my devotion, I increased the number and my discomfort not a little, because in order to give them food as was necessary, I was left with very little sustenance quite regularly and, to hide that fact, I pretended that I wanted to have broth, which was not done at meals like theirs nor is it served unless one asks for it. My uncle enjoyed having it and they used to say that even in that, it seemed to him, without knowing what I was doing, that I was doing a good thing. And in the same fashion I proceeded in many more matters of virtue which necessarily, like this one, had to be accomplished in public. And I saw clearly that, for the most part, I persuaded everyone most dexterously to do what I wanted, by which means I was able to preserve a very notable purity of intention and increase in the candor and brilliance in the good works that I did.

80. *And the more I passed through acts of virtue and devotion without being heard or noticed, although I was not necessarily obliged to give a good example, the greater and more endearing pleasure and happiness they caused.*

81. And it is not easy to relate the mercies that I received from Our Lord in this area, and much less those which His Majesty granted me in the matter of enduring one's neighbors, in which He was always pleased to give me great opportunities.

82. After I turned fifteen everything came on quickly, [including] my uncle's love and demonstrations of it, not in spoiling me, rather in exercising me more and more and procuring the augmentation of everything, and of having me next to his chair the longest time possible. And so, having spent some time at recreation with his children after eating, he would retire to his chambers, almost always taking me along with him. And, if he didn't have visitors or business to attend to, he would read from the Holy Scripture or Blessed Doctors, or discuss spiritual matters seriously and in a most spiritual

Si eran fiestas, sobre ellas y sus santos misterios, cantando a ratos salmos, en que tenía notable gracia. *Y muchas veces con notable afecto, aquel verso: Venite, filii, audite me; timorem domini docebo vos.* Algunas veces le seguían hijos e hijas, mas poco a poco se iban y le dejaban solo. Y solía él, cuando lo advertía y me veía quedar allí, empezar a cantar, "*Vos estis qui permansistis mecum in tentationibus meis.*"

83. *Era hombre afabilísimo y de apacible trato ordinariamente.*

84. Si venían visitas graves, o tales que no se sufría que me viesen, me ponía en un hueco de ventana, cubierto de las colgaduras; o si era do[nde] alguno de sus oratorios o librería estaba a mano, entrábame allá. Y en yéndose, alzaba él mismo la voz y llamábame. Y si escribía, sentábame con mi libro junto a él y leía, como ya dije.

85. Cuando iba fuera de casa y era fuerza dejarme en los aposentos de la Marquesa, muchas veces me persuadía, o a quedar en el oratorio que allí él tenía, llevándose él la llave, o a que me fuese a mi propio aposento, sin quedarme en el camino con mis primas y criadas de casa, la cual, siendo en muchas cosas de ejemplar virtud, especialmente en recato y honestidad, no bastaba a satisfacer su deseo, por aquel tan ferviente que tenía de que mi trato y conversación de criaturas se trocase en la de los ángeles y santos celestiales, procurando no sólo preservarme de pecados graves, sino también de los ordinarios y ligeros que de tal compañía se me podían ofrecer.

86. La Marquesa no se aplicaba a exhortar a estas cosas, ni a más que a lo que tocaba a ser mujeres honradas y cuerdas, aunque ella era muy penitente, devota, y retirada de su marido, hijas y gente de casa. Pasaba su tiempo escribiendo y negociando porque, además de los negocios de su estado y vasallos y cosas de la casa que el Marqués dejaba totalmente a su cargo y disposición, era tan procuradora de pobres y de que tuviesen, los años secos, el pan barato, y de

fashion. If it was a holiday, about it and its holy mysteries, singing psalms at times, in which he had considerable talent. *And many times with noteworthy affection, that verse, "Vent, filii, audite me; timorem domini docebo vos." At times, his sons and daughters followed him, but little by little, they departed and left him alone, and when he realized it and saw that I was still there, he used to begin to sing: "Vos estis qui permansistis mecum in tentationibus meis."*[48]

83. *He was a very agreeable man and usually even-tempered.*

84. If important visitors arrived or of the type for which my being seen was inappropriate, he put me in the sill of a window, covered with the curtains or, if it was where one of his oratories or libraries was close by, he put me in there. And, when the company left, he himself would raise his voice and call me. And if he was writing, I would sit with my book next to him and read, as I said before.

85. When he was away from the house and it was necessary to leave me in the apartments of the Marquesa, he persuaded me many times either to remain in the oratory that he had there, with him taking the key with him, or that I go to my own room, without stopping along the way to spend time with my cousins or the household servants, (who [the Marquesa], being of exemplary virtue in many things, especially in prudence and modesty, was insufficient to satisfy his desire) because of that so fervent [desire] that he had that my dealings and conversation with earthly creatures be exchanged for that of angels and celestial saints, procuring not only to preserve me from grave sins, but also from the ordinary and inconsequential ones in which I could have incurred being in that company [of my aunt, cousins, and servants].[49]

86. The Marquesa did not spend her time exhorting to these things, nor to anything beyond being virtuous and sensible women, although she was very penitential, devout, and withdrawn from her husband, daughters, and the people of the household. She spent her time writing and conducting business because, besides the matters of her estate and vassals and things of the household, which the Marqués left completely in her charge and at her disposition, she was so attentive to the poor and to their having, in dry years, cheap bread, and to

---

[48] "Come, ye children, hearken unto me: I will teach you the fear of the Lord" (Ps. 34:11). "You were the one who remained with me during my temptations" (I cannot identify the source. It may not be biblical, and in any case is heavy with implication.)

[49] The syntax is jumbled, which often occurs when Carvajal implies a critique of her uncle. This is a loud echo of Teresa of Ávila's locution in which God told her, "No longer do I want you to converse with men but with angels" (*Life* 24.5).

cuantas obras piadosas o convenientes a virtud le parecía que podía encaminar en el lugar o provincia do[nde] se hallaba, que le venían a sobrar ocupaciones. Y trataba y escribía a todos los concernientes, corregidores, venticuatros, mercaderes, patrones de hospitales y cofradías, y obispos y otras dignidades eclesiásticas. Éste era todo su entretenimiento, campos y fiestas, en que raramente me acuerdo haberla visto, a importunación de su marido. Asistíamos con ella a los divinos oficios en las iglesias de la advocación de las fiestas o monasterios, todo el entero año, con puntualidad. Llevábanos a los hospitales, en que yo nunca faltaba, empleando muchas tardes de las fiestas en eso y llevando algún refresco a los pobres como cestos de manzanas camuesas, granadas o naranjas dulces, y hacía que las fuésemos repartiendo de cama en cama.

. . .

95. Salíase mi tío a una aldea dos leguas de Pamplona, de lindos campos y huertas, algunas primaveras y parte del verano. Y porque no había parte conveniente para oratorio, se había hecho al cabo de un larguísimo corredor, que caía sobre las huertas de la casa. Allí iba yo, después de acostados todos, a hacer mis disciplinas. Una noche, mi tío y sus hijos estaban al fresco en este corredor, y él paseándose, rezaba sus Horas o Rosario, bien desviado de todos. Y yo lo estaba, haciendo mi examen, de pechos sobre  las barandas, con un alto almendro delante. Y de repente, me pareció que había visto una sombra grandísima, tan alta como el almendro o mayor, blanca como la nieve

carrying out as many pious works or whatever virtue demanded that she felt she could handle in the place or province where she was living, that she eventually had too much to do.[50] And she dealt with and wrote to all of the concerned parties, mayors, councilmen, merchants, patrons of hospitals and confraternities, and bishops and other ecclesiastical dignitaries. In this work consisted her only entertainment, relaxation, and festivities (which I recall seeing her attend rarely, and at her husband's insistence). We attended the divine office with her on the occasions when saints' days were consecrated in churches or monasteries, without fail throughout the year. She used to take us to hospitals, where I never failed to go, spending many holiday afternoons doing that and bringing some treat to the poor, such as baskets of pippins,[51] pomegranates or sweet oranges, and she would make us distribute them from bed to bed.

. . .

95. My uncle used to go to a village that was two leagues from Pamplona, with lovely countryside and gardens, sometimes in the spring and part of the summer. And because there was no convenient place to have an oratory, one had been made at the end of a very long corridor that ran above the gardens of the house. I used to go there, after everyone was asleep, to flagellate myself.[52] One night, my uncle and his daughters were out in the fresh air of this corridor and he, strolling along, was praying his hours or rosary, well removed from the others. And I was likewise removed, doing my examination [of conscience], my chest against the railing, with a tall almond tree before me. And suddenly I thought I had seen a huge shadow, as tall as the almond tree or taller, and somewhat clear, white as snow and

[50] Carvajal tellingly contrasts the self-serving, obsessive piety of the Marqués with the Marquesa's administration of the estates and devotion to practical concerns of the poor who lived under her jurisdiction. Her husband's itinerant career and obsession with his personal development left his wife saddled with enormous responsibilities, which may be behind some of the dryness of character Carvajal repeatedly attributes to her. Abad treats the Marquesa with complete contempt, probably because she was more business woman than maternal figure (*Epist.* 51; *Mis.* 48). However, Carvajal provides substantial evidence of her aunt's efficiency and thoughtfulness and there is implicit admiration and understanding in the picture of her painted here.

[51] Pippins are a variety of sweet apples.

[52] The literal translation is "to take my disciplines," a concept similar to today's ideas about "working out," meaning something strenuous believed to be healthy and easily taken to unhealthy extremes.

y algo lúcida, delante de mis ojos, con que fue muy alterada y movida mi sangre, y quitéme de allí para ir a acostarme. Y llegando a pedir la mano a mi tío para besársela y tomar su bendición (como las hijas de personas tales lo usan en España, en noche y mañana, y las sobrinas tan cercanas como yo, criadas en casa, se tratan y tienen por hijas, y el padre y la madre, dándoles la mano, les echa su bendición), no sé qué se vio en mi semblante, que me preguntó que qué tenía. Yo excusaba el decirlo pero, mandándolo, supo que me había turbado aquella imaginación. Y él era muy amigo de quebrantar miedos y mortificar a quien los tenía, y díjome, "Yo quiero que volváis allí otra vez, de la manera que estábades antes." Respondíle que yo creía que había sido solamente cosa de mi imaginación, pero que me había turbado tan extrañamente que no podía aún librarme de la turbación. Y que así temía que tornaría a representárseme la misma sombra, y podría dañar demasiado mi corazón. Él dijo que había de volver allá y asióme del brazo para llevarme, y yo hice alguna fuerza por detenerme. Y esto era tan nueva cosa en mi obediencia, que decía él después, que había sido indicio muy claro del gran mal que yo sentí. Y es así cierto que, en sólo pensar de ir, sentí gran desaguamiento y desmayo. Fui, viendo que era su resuelta voluntad, y en llegando, se me representó al momento lo mismo que primero. Perdí totalmente la color, y cayéronseme los brazos sin fuerza, y apenas me parece que podía estar en pie. Mi tío empezó recio y con prisa a decir, "No temas, hija, que yo vi lo mismo que tú."

96. Fuímonos de allí, y yo acudí a tener alguna oración. Y al cabo de dos o tres horas, me vine a sentir con fuerza y ánimo no demasiado. Mi tío se había acostado y pensado en el negocio, y resuéltose en mandarme ir al retiramiento que estaba hecho al cabo del corredor, y que tomase allí una disciplina. Y era, como digo, de extraordinaria largura, y la puerta al principio de él. Había de pasarle todo a lo largo. Envióme a llamar y ordenó que lo hiciese así. Y sin réplica alguna, quedando toda la casa reposando en sus camas, con

somewhat bright, in front of my eyes, which agitated and altered my blood,[53] and I left that place to go to bed. And upon arriving to ask my uncle for his hand to kiss and receive his blessing (as the daughters of such people do in Spain, in the evening and in the morning, and the nieces as closely related as I, raised in their house and treated and held as daughters, and the father and mother, giving them their hand, bless them), I don't know what was evident in my appearance that led him to ask me what was the matter with me. I avoided saying it, but he ordered me to do so and found out that I had been upset by what I had imagined. And he was a great one for overcoming cowardice and mortifying those who were cowardly, and he said to me, "I want you to go back there again, in the same way you were there before." I responded that I believed it had been merely something imagined, but it had upset me so strangely that I still couldn't free myself from the perturbation. And so I was afraid that the same shadow would appear again to me, and could harm my heart in excess.[54] He said I had to return there and grabbed me by the arm to take me there, and I resisted. And this was something so out of character with my usual obedience, that he said afterward that it had been a most clear indication of the great pain I felt. And it is true that upon merely thinking about going, I felt totally drained and faint. I went, seeing that it was his unshakable will, and upon arriving, the same thing appeared to me as soon as I got there. I completely lost my color and my arms fell helpless at my sides and I believe I could hardly stand up. My uncle began to say loudly and in a hurry, "Do not fear, daughter, for I saw the same thing as you."

96. We left that place and I went to have some prayer. And after two or three hours, I began to feel not too much stronger and braver. My uncle had gone to bed and had thought about what had happened and he resolved to order me to go to the removed quarters at the end of the corridor and flagellate myself there. And it was, as I said, extraordinarily long [the corridor], and had the door at the beginning. I would have to walk down the entire thing. He had me called for and ordered me to do it and, without replying anything, with everyone else in the house resting in their beds, with a

---

[53] Meaning that it shocked her so much that one of her humors was set off balance.

[54] Carvajal here wrote "alma" 'soul,' then blackened it out to replace it with "heart," thereby lessening the obvious relationship between the shadow and Satan in favor of a physiological explanation. Her uncle's determination to have her conduct a holy exercise on the spot was in part due to his belief that she could thereby overpower the evil spirit they both saw.

una candela en la mano, fui, e híceme tanta fuerza a cumplir esta obediencia, cuanta sabe sólo Dios. Y cuando llegué al mismo puesto de mi temor, se me erizaron los cabellos y me moví toda yo. Y ofreciéndolo a Nuestro Señor, sin volver los ojos, pasé aprisa y puse mi relojillo de arena de cuartos e hice una disciplina, a mi parecer de media hora, que ésa solía ser mi más ordinaria tasa. Allí sentí consuelo grande y con que se confortó mi corazón, y volví sin pavor, con quietud a cuanto me puedo acordar.[5]

97. Otras veces me probaba en estas cosas de miedo, enviándome sola a partes oscuras, y en el oratorio del cuarto de la Marquesa me dejaba sola cerrada y se llevaba él la llave fuera de casa. Y hartas veces era bien oscuro cuando tornaba, y se le solía algunas olvidar que estaba yo allí, hasta ya tarde que, viendo que lo era, tocaba a la puerta. Y si acaso pasaba alguna criada, lo iba a decir y si no, aguardaba que lo oyesen. Cuando la Marquesa estaba en casa y lo acertaba a saber, decía, "¿Es posible que está sola allí? Anda luego a abrir." Y daba su llave, que la tenía maestra como la de mi tío, para toda la casa, y era ella por extremo medrosa aun de estar a solas de día en un aposento. Yo procuraba muchas veces, de mío, sin decirlo a mi tío, ir a partes solas y sin luz y hacer oración allí, por deshacer los temores, que yo tenía por vergonzosa cosa en quien trataba de espíritu.[6]

98. Entre los quince y dieciséis años, conocía ya mucho a Nuestro Señor, con luz para distinguir lo perfecto de lo imperfecto. Y como andaba metida entre tanta mortificación, alegrábame mucho de que no podía tocar a pensamientos de casamiento. Y si alguno raramente

---

[5] *Era antes de esto del corredor cuando me encerró una prima y lo [supo] el Padre Ortiz. Del sufrimiento, y lo que sentía que mi tío se enojase con ellos por mí, y me iba de allí por no poderlo sufrir, que no podía sufrir en mi tío cosa que tirase a hacer gran falta en obra o cosa semejante, por lo que amaba el alma de los que quería bien.*

[6] *De la calentura que me dio el día de San Lorenzo, meditando en la ventana en sus llamas, y la pena de mi tío.*

candle in my hand I went, and forced myself so much to comply with this proof of obedience that only God knows how much. And when I arrived at the same place where I had my scare, my hair stood on end and my entire self shuddered. And offering it all to Our Lord, without turning my eyes, I walked along quickly and set my little fifteen-minute hour glass and took my scourge, for what seemed to me to be half an hour, since that was my usual dosage. I felt a great consolation that and one with which my heart was comforted, and I returned without panic, tranquil, as far as I can remember.[55]

97. At other times he tested me in such things related to cowardice, sending me alone into dark places, and he used to leave me shut up in the oratory in the Marquesa's room and he would take the key out of the house [with him]. And many times it was quite dark when he returned, and he used to forget sometimes that I was in there until late when, realizing what was going on, I knocked on the door. And if a servant happened to pass by, she went to tell someone, and if not, I waited until somebody heard me. When the Marquesa was at home and she found out about it, she would say, "Is it possible that she is alone in there? Go and open it right away." And she would provide her key, since she had the master [key] like my uncle's for the entire house, and she was extremely timorous about being alone in a room even during the day. Many times I managed, on my own without telling my uncle, to go to solitary places without light and pray there, to undo my fears, which I believed were shameful things in someone who dealt in spirituality.[56]

98. By between age fifteen and sixteen, I knew Our Lord deeply, with enlightenment to distinguish the perfect from the imperfect. And since I was involved in so much mortification, I was delighted that I couldn't deal with thoughts of marriage.[57] And if an offer arose

[55] *It was before this episode of the corridor that a cousin locked me up and Father Otiz found out. On the suffering, and how sorry I was that my uncle got mad at them because of me, and that I was planning to leave because I couldn't stand it, that I couldn't stand that my uncle should commit a fault in his behavior or anything similar, because I so loved the souls of those I cared for.* Beneath the veneer of smooth praise for her uncle, there runs a steady thread of violence.

[56] *On the fever I got on St. Lorenzo's feast day, meditating in the window about his [experience in the] flames, and my uncle's sorrow.* The need for women to be prudently fearless is one of the outstanding themes in the writings of Teresa of Ávila, who insists that God "is a friend of courageous souls" (*Life* 13.2).

[57] She blacked out "se," which would have meant that her uncle was pleased that she could not marry, and replaced it with "me," to refer to her own happiness. Young girls were generally married after their first menses. Intense physical mortification might have caused Carvajal to experience amenorrhea, which would have kept her out of the marriage market.

se me ofrecía, me parecía que solamente pudiera escoger tal vida, en el modo que de algunos santos lo había leído, que hicieron voto de virginidad ellos y ellas, y vivieron como hermanos, apartados en diversos aposentos con notable virtud y ejemplo. Pero este pensamiento, como de aire, tan presto como se asomaba se deshacía. Mi tío decía siempre que quería que me casase, porque aquel estado tenía necesidad de personas que diesen en él grande ejemplo de santidad, y él creía que yo haría aquello.[7] Yo le oía con mi mesura ordinaria, sonriéndome un poco a veces, sin decir nada, porque me parecía que el decirlo no era hacerse, y que no era menester anticiparme a rehusarlo sin tiempo y que era más cordura dejar pasar tales pláticas en silencio, como cosa de burla y de que yo no hacía caso. E interiormente, con actos, fortalecía el amor y estima de la virginidad.

. . .

100. Acostumbraba a ponerme silicio de cerdas cuando mi tío lo ordenaba, que nunca le faltaba cuidado en tales cosas, y otras veces, a mi elección. Las cuaresmas era tres días en semana: martes, jueves y sábados, y los otros días había disciplina.

. . .

103. Desde antes de los quince años, empecé a hacer ásperas disciplinas, siempre en las espaldas, por opinión de mi tío, y traíalas tales que raramente me faltaba dolor. Una vez hice una disciplina con una de cerdas blancas llena de escobillas, harto curiosa, que yo pensaba ser harto más blanda. Y pareciéndome que quedaba algo maltratada,

---

[7] *Admirábame de que mi tío, con tan gran entendimiento y espíritu, no echaba de ver que no se podía seguir y pretender fruto* [ilegible] *de la doctrina de perfección y mortificación que me enseñaba, que eso fuera coger del olmo peras. Y con todo, callaba sin decirle nada.*

on rare occasions, it seemed to me that I could only choose such a life under the conditions in which some saints had chosen it, with both the man and the woman taking a vow of virginity, and living like brother and sister, in separate rooms, with noteworthy virtue and example.[58] But this thought, like air, went as quickly as it came. My uncle always used to say that he wanted me to marry because there was a need for married people to provide great examples of sanctity, and he thought that I would do that.[59]  I heard him with my usual restraint, smiling at times without saying anything, because it seemed to me that saying it was not doing it, and that I didn't need to rush to refuse to do it ahead of time, and that it was wiser to let such talk go along without comment, like a joke, to which I didn't pay any attention. And inwardly, with actions, I strengthened my love and estimation of virginity.

. . .

100. I got used to wearing a hair shirt of bristles when my uncle ordered me to, for he never lacked diligence in such things, and other times, by my own choice. During Lent it was three days a week: Tuesday, Thursday and Saturday, and the others I flagellated myself.[60]

. . .

103. Since before I was fifteen, I began to practice some harsh flagellation exercises, always on my back, on the recommendation of my uncle, and I had it [my back] such that rarely did it not hurt. I once flagellated myself with a scourge made of white bristles full of thistles, quite remarkable, which I thought would be much softer than it was. And since it seemed to me that I had wound up a bit

---

[58] These saints were noble or royal women, such as Bridget, Catherine of Genova, and Margaret of Scotland. Carvajal elides the detail that most of these couples initiated their married life with a sexual relationship which they later renounced.

[59] *I was astounded that my uncle, with his great understanding and spirituality, didn't see that one can't follow and reap fruit . . . [ms. illegible] from the doctrine of perfection and mortification that he was teaching me, that such a thing would be to pick  pears from an elm tree, but notwithstanding, I kept quiet without saying anything.*

[60] This exaggerated regimen under her uncle's supervision contrasts starkly with the modest penitential exercises Carvajal prescribes for the members of her Society (Schedule ¶32).

puse una toalla delgada, de algunos dobles, por que no me manchase la sangre la camisa y vestido, y lo viesen después las criadas. Y al  otro día, estaba tan pegada que la hube de dejar así. Y apostemáronseme las espaldas tanto que, estando en sermón, día de Santo Tomás de Aquino, se me pasó casi todo en vehemente dolor. Y a la noche, llegando de repente una criada a tirar de la una manga de mi jubón para acostarme, le sentí tal que, sin ser en mi mano, di un gran gemido. Pero, en fin, no supieron la causa, y no pudiendo casi revolverme en la cama ni levantar los brazos, hube de recurrir a tratar de ello con aquella persona, mi amiga, de quien mi tío fiaba mis mortificaciones, [ilegible] que qué tenía porque parecía no estar buena. Y cerradas en un aposento con[veniente], probó a quitar la toalla, y no pudiendo sin llevar pedazos de la carne tras ella, en que sentí dolor tan fuerte que parecía que me tiraban de entrañas, sin decir nada, ayudada de mi remedio de apretar los dientes y puños, cortó a pedazos la toalla con unas tijeras. Y preguntando ella después, por rodeos en secreto a un médico, qué se haría en tal caso, le dio unos parches de ungüento con que sentí gran alivio, y chuparon toda la materia, que era mucha, y al cabo de algunos días quedé sana. Ella temía que no fuera posible sin venir a manos de cirujano, porque estaba honda la materia, y así nunca acababa de admirarse de que hubiesen bastado los parches, y yo pasado sin calentura. Fue este remedio tal que me aprovechó otras veces, aunque solamente otra vez llegué a estar tan mala. Verme así era mi consuelo, pareciéndome que en aquello, en fin, tomaba alguna venganza de mis desagradecimientos, y me ofrecía y sacrificaba en alguna manera al dulcísimo y divino Señor Nuestro crucificado.

hurt, I put on a thin towel, folded a few times, so my blood wouldn't stain my blouse and dress and the servants would see it later. And the next day it was so stuck to me that I had to leave it like that. And the towel became so embedded in my back that I listened to almost an entire sermon on the day of St. Thomas of Aquinas in vehement pain, and that night, when a servant suddenly arrived to pull off one of the sleeves of my bodice to put me to bed, I felt such pain that, without being able to control it, I gave a loud cry. But, in the end, they never found out why, and since I couldn't turn in bed or raise my arms, I had to go to that person, my friend, whom my uncle had entrusted with my mortification exercises, [who asked me] what was the matter because I didn't look very well. And with both of us enclosed in an appropriate room, she tried to get the towel off, and not being able to without yanking off pieces of skin with it (which pained me so that I thought my insides were being pulled out, without saying anything, helped by my practice of gritting my teeth and squeezing my fists), she cut the towel into pieces with some scissors.[61] And later asking a doctor, in a roundabout secret way, what should be done in such a case, he gave her some patches of salve that much relieved me, and absorbed all the infection, which was considerable, and after a few days I had recovered. She was afraid that it wouldn't work out without [my] having to go to a doctor because the infection was so deeply embedded and so her amazement never ceased that the patches had sufficed and that I had recovered without a fever. This cure was such that it served me on other occasions, although I was in such a bad state only one other time. To see myself like that was my consolation, seeming to me that in such behavior, in the end, I took some manner of vengeance on my ingratitude, and I offered myself and sacrificed myself in some way to the most sweet and divine Lord of ours, crucified.

---

[61] This episode echoes Passion literature typical of Carvajal's age, in which Christ's bloodied garments are ripped from his body, taking skin with them (Luis de Granada, *Libro*, I: I.1.6).

a) Tras lo de la lana, pondré de la calentura del día de San Lorenzo

b) Semana entera de azotes y ultrajes y frío, y confusión que esto me causaba desde cerca de los 16 años

c) *Cantábame mi tío un oficio de santa, delante de mí y de sus hijas, por santo entretenimiento. Y yo estaba muy serena y con todo, sonriéndome un poquito a veces, como si se hiciera de otra persona.*

. . .

## [redacciones fragmentarias]

120. Y la primera cuaresma, siendo ya de catorce años, poco más, mi tío me dio una disciplina de seda blanca toda ella, curiosa y delicada, y me aconsejó que me disciplinase con ella, pienso que los viernes no más por entonces. Y pareciéndome que era la disciplina muy blanda, cogíle a doña Francisca, mi prima, un abrojo que ella tenía y juntéle a ella.

. . .

124. Y habiendo en su casa una persona muy sierva de Dios y de suficiente espíritu, secreto y cordura, me ordenó que, siempre que ella me mandase ir al oratorio que para esto había en parte conveniente, y quisiese allí darme alguna disciplina por su mano de rodillas delante del altar y las espaldas descubiertas, la recibiese humildemente, porque esto sería una muy saludable purga para mi alma. Yo, como siempre, respondía que haría lo que él me mandaba puntualmente. Y así, muy ordinario, especialmente en cuaresma, témporas y adviento y vigilias

**[The final folio of this draft section contains this list of matters Carvajal planned to address in her final revision:]**

a) After the business about the wool, I will put the part about the fever on the day of St. Lorenzo

b) An entire week of whippings and outrageous offenses and cold, and the embarrassment that this caused me from around age 16

c) *My uncle used to sing the office of a female saint in front of me and his daughters, as a holy entertainment. And I was very serene and smiled a bit throughout the whole business at times, as if it were about someone else.*[62]

## [From the third manuscript packet, details about her penitential exercises]

120. And the first Lent, at the time when I was fourteen or so, my uncle gave me a scourge all of white silk, unusual and delicate, and advised me to flagellate myself with it, I think only on Fridays right then. And since the scourge seemed very mild to me, I took a thistle from the one belonging to Doña Francisca, my cousin, and attached it.

. . .

124. [63]And there being in his [my uncle's ] household a devoted servant of God of sufficient spirit, discretion and good sense, he ordered me that, whenever she should command me to go to the oratory which there was for this purpose in a suitable place and should want to whip me some herself, on my knees before the altar and my back exposed, I should humbly receive it, because this would be a very healthy purge for my soul. I, as always, would respond that I would do what he ordered me to without fail. And thus quite often, especially during Lent, days of fasting,[64] Advent, and the vigils before

---

[62] It is unclear whether these two sentences describe the same event, or two different things she planned to develop later.

[63] This paragraph is an early version of material Carvajal reworked in ¶¶'s 77-78.

[64] The Spanish word, "témpora," means the period set by the Catholic Church for fasting at the beginning of the four seasons, carried out on Wednesdays, Fridays, and Saturdays.

solemnes, por prepararme, de las grandes fiestas, era llevada a aquel género de sacrificio, para mi natural condición de los más ásperos que se pudieran hallar. Y acabada la disciplina, muchas veces me mandaba con mucho señorío que le besase los pies, y yo, postrada en el suelo, se los besaba. Pero en esto no hacía yo nada, ni en sufrir golpes de una disciplina de cuerdas de vihuela, nada blanda, tan bien dados que apenas podía sufrirlos. Y para no mostrarlo exteriormente, me era necesario hacer gran fuerza en las manos, apretando los puños cuando no estaban atadas, no de modo que se impidiese el cerrarlas, o hacer fuerza una sobre otra, si la soga las tenía juntas.[8] Todo mi sentimiento y dificultad estaba en el extraño empacho que sentía de desnudarme y, según la alteración que sentía en el pecho y violencia que me hacía en ello, creo que se podía conocer en la color de mi rostro demudado y marchito. Y muchas veces me pareció que no pudiera sentir más la misma muerte, y más cuando se resolvía en que la disciplina fuese de los pies a la cabeza, con una toalla puesta por la cinta, de la manera que se pinta un crucifijo, y atada a una columna que para eso había hecha a propósito, y los pies en la tierra fría, y una soga de cáñamo a la garganta, con cuyos cabos se ataban las muñecas y manos a la columna. Algunas veces pude saber cuántos eran los golpes de la disciplina, porque los contaba la misma persona de modo que yo lo oía. Y acuérdome de que eran a veces ciento y a veces cincuenta o más, y nunca a mi parecer eran menos. Y pienso que de ciento pasaban hartas veces pero no lo puedo certificar, por falta de memoria que de eso tengo. El dolor, como dije, no era poco, ni el frío que se metía en los huesos en los días muy fríos del invierno, por serlo la tierra mucho. Y a todo vencía la confusión y vergonzoso empacho que sentía, con una alma muy rendida y un corazón muy deshecho y humillado en la presencia de Nuestro Señor. Y acordándome de Cristo cuando se vio así por mí y tanto más maltratado y con tan diferente ánimo de los que lo hacían y tan públicamente avergonzado, parecíame que me fuera consuelo muy extraordinario verme así atada delante un juez infiel y delante un pueblo incrédulo e ingrato, esperando sentencia de muerte, e imaginábame como si estuviera en tal ocasión. Y con ser tan seca y dura en materia de lágrimas naturalmente, en viéndome así desnuda, poco o mucho, y humillada cuanto me era posible, me daba Nuestro Señor tan abundantes lágrimas, que parecían arroyos mis ojos. Y si me los mandaba levantar en alto, como lo hacía muchas veces, no casi podía mirar, de ciega de lágrimas. Y ordinariamente estaría por

---

[8] *Ojo. Para los 15 años, la soga, etc.*

the high holidays, to prepare myself, I was led to that manner of sacrifice, for my nature among the harshest that could be imagined. And, the whipping being finished, many times she ordered me very haughtily to kiss her feet, and I, prostrate on the ground, kissed them. But in this I did nothing, nor in enduring the blows of a scourge made of guitar strings, not at all bland, so well delivered that I could hardly stand it. And so as not to show it outwardly, I had to exercise a great effort in my hands, squeezing my fists, when they were not tied in such a way that I could not close them, or push one down over the other, if the rope was holding them together.[65] All my worry and difficulty was in the peculiar shame that I felt when I undressed, and, judging by the unease I felt in my chest and the violence that the whole thing accomplished in me, I think was visible in the altered and faded color of my face. And many times it seemed to me that I wouldn't feel death itself any more, and more so, when she resolved that the discipline would be from my feet to my head, with a towel around my waist such as is painted on a crucifix, and tied to a column that there was, constructed specifically for this purpose, and my feet on the cold ground, and a hemp rope at my throat, with whose ends my hands and wrists were tied to the column. Sometimes I could tell how many blows there were in the session because the very person [delivering them] counted them in such a way that I heard it. And I recall that sometimes there were one hundred and at times fifty or more, and it seems to me that they were never less. And I think they exceeded a hundred many times, but I can't be sure of it, due to the lack of memory that I have about that. The pain, as I said, was not little, nor the chill that entered my bones on the very cold days of winter, because the floor was very cold. And the confusion and shamed embarrassment that I felt outdid it all, with a soul quite overcome and a heart quite undone and humiliated in the presence of Our Lord. And recalling Christ when he saw himself thus for me and so much more mistreated and with such a different soul than those who were doing it to Him and so publicly shamed, it seemed to me that it was a quite extraordinary consolation to see myself tied up thus before an infidel judge and before an incredulous and ungrateful people, awaiting the death sentence, and I imagined that I was in such a situation. And since I am so dry and hard in what provokes me to tears, upon seeing myself thus, unclothed, a little or a lot, and as humiliated as I could be, Our Lord gave me such abundant tears that my eyes seemed like streams. And if she ordered me to

---

[65] *Attention. At age 15, the rope, etc.*

lo menos media hora desnuda, y muchas veces una, y creo que más. Y cuando era tiempo muy frío venía a sentir el cuerpo como insensible por un poco de tiempo, y en las manos quedaba aquello por largo rato, que con dificultad podía vestirme, acabada la disciplina. Y me era forzoso muchas veces poner el corchete del cuello de la ropa para tapar el jubón desabrochado, porque no tenía en los dedos fuerza para poner los botones, hasta que sobre la lumbre, poco o poco, se iba cobrando, sin osar llegar a mucho fuego, por no tullirme con los extremos de calor y frío. Salía del oratorio con el mismo corazón que dije, deshechísimo, y deseando poder seguir las pisadas de Cristo.

125. Y no se puede fácilmente creer el cuidado de mi buen tío en que yo fuese humillada y quebrantada con este género de penitencia.[9] Y así, ordenaba algunas veces que me llevasen desnuda y descalza, con los pies por la tierra friísima, con una cofilla en la cabeza que recogía el cabello solamente, y una toalla atada por la cintura, una soga a la garganta, que algunas veces era hecha de cerdas de silicio y otras de cáñamo, y atadas las manos con ella, de unos aposentos a otros, como a malhechora, hasta un último oratorio pequeño que estaba al cabo de ellos. Era habitación cerrada y fuera del concurso de la casa y parte muy secreta. Y delante de mí, tirando blandamente de la soga, iba una de las personas siervas de Nuestro Señor que he dicho, y a veces me decía palabras de humillación y abatimiento.

126. Un día de la conversión de San Pablo, me acuerdo, siendo de quince o dieciséis años, que la otra sierva de Nuestro Señor me mandó, con el imperio que siempre lo hacía, bajase a un oratorio bajo muy secreto que había, después de la hora de comer, y que me aparejase para recibir una disciplina de las ordinarias, que era de rodillas y descubiertas las espaldas, con una toalla prendida debajo la barba que me cubría el pecho. Y esto era una como dorada vergüenza y templadísimo modo para mí. Y habiendo descargado con alguna fuerza la mano, lo cual conocí en el ordinario dolor que sentí, me dijo que le besase los pies, y yo lo hice, y me vestí. Y no sé cuántos días después, mandándome la otra persona que me

---

[9] *Después halló mi tío [a] otra persona, de las mismas de casa, a propósito para esto. Y a veces lo ordenaba a la una, a veces a la otra. El pie sobre el pecho me trabajó mucho. El día de la Conversión de San Pablo, por los bofetones.*

raise them up [eyes], as she did many times, I could hardly see, being so blinded by tears. And I would usually be disrobed for at least half an hour, and many times an hour, and I think more. And when it was very cold I eventually felt that my body was numb for a little while and in my hands that [sensation] remained for a long time, for I could dress with difficulty once the flagellation was finished. And many times I had to fasten the hook on the neck of my dress to hide my unbuttoned undergarment, because my fingers didn't have the strength to do the buttons, until by the fire, little by little, it [my strength] returned, without [my] daring to get too close to the fire so as not to become paralyzed by the extremes of hot and cold. I would leave the oratory with the same heart that I described, completely undone, and desirous to follow in the footsteps of Christ.

125. And the care my uncle took to see that I was humiliated and broken with this sort of penance cannot be easily believed.[66] And thus he would order at times that they lead me unclothed and barefoot, with my feet on the extremely cold floor, with a cap on my head that only held my hair, and a towel tied to my waist, a rope at my neck, which sometimes was made of bristles and others of hemp, and my hands tied with it, from one room to another, like an evil-doer, until arriving at the last small oratory that was at the end [of the passage]. It was a locked room and removed from the rest of the house and in a very secret part. And in front of me, pulling lightly by the rope, went one of the servile women of Our Lord of whom I have spoken, and at times she uttered words of humiliation and shame.

126. Once on the day of Saint Paul's conversion I recall, being fifteen or sixteen, that the other servant of Our Lord ordered me, with the haughtiness with which she always did it, to go down after the mid-day meal to a lower, very secret oratory there was, and that I prepare myself to receive one of the ordinary flagellations, which was on my knees and with my back exposed, with a towel caught beneath my chin that covered my chest. And this was like a gilded shame and a very moderate type for me. And once she had unleashed her hand somewhat forcefully, which I recognized by the ordinary pain I felt, she told me to kiss her feet and I did so, and got dressed. And I don't know how many days later, when the other person ordered me to go

---

[66] *Later my uncle found another person from among the same women of the house-hold to serve in this, and at times he would order one [to flagellate me], at times the other.* Just under this: *The foot over my chest worked me over greatly*; then, *The day of the Conversion of St. Paul, for the hard slaps.* There was evidently much more ritual-ized violence involved in these "exercises" than Carvajal's final draft reveals.

fuese a aparejar para otra disciplina, yo lo hice. Y cuando puso los ojos en mis espaldas, díjome que me tornase a vestir, porque aquellas espaldas no estaban para recibir más azotes que los que tenían señalados en sí, y que se admiraba de que Juana, que así se llamaba la otra, hubiese llegado a maltratarme tanto. Y volviendo yo a tomar mi vestido, vi uno de mis hombros, por la parte que pude alcanzar de paso con la vista, con varias señales y ramalazos muy azules.

127. Una mañana, me acuerdo que vino a mí, estando yo en la cama.[10] Y había dormido muy mal aquella noche, porque mi cama era hecha entonces sobre un mate de verano, que está hecho de unas cinchas anchas, creo que de cáñamo delgado, o no sé qué cosa friísima. Y yo, cuando estaban todos ya durmiendo, muchas noches arrollaba mi colchón, que era sólo uno, a los pies, y quedábame sobre las cinchas, y no sé si con manta debajo o sin ella, de modo que, antes que nadie lo viese a la mañana, tendía mi colchón. Y aquel frío de las cinchas me trabajaba toda la noche notablemente, Y estando yo descuidada, por ser muy temprano, vino, como digo, a mí, y cogióme de repente sobre las cinchas. Pero no dijo nada, sino mandóme levantar. Y desnuda, con sólo un lienzo por la cintura hasta las rodillas, como otras veces he dicho, y con la soga a la garganta y manos atadas, llena de frío e incomodidad, me llevó a un oratorio cercano, que él y el paso estaba solo. Y a puertas cerradas y habiéndome disciplinado, me hizo echar en el suelo, donde me disciplinó de los pies hasta los hombros. Y no sé con qué palabras de menosprecio, me puso uno de sus pies sobre el pecho, en medio de él. Y como tenía un zapato de dos suelas, grosero, y debió descuidarse en cargar demasiado, sentí grande pena dentro del pecho y en todo lo interior de él, tanto, que si no acertara a levantarle presto, me pareció podía recibir mi salud notable daño. La otra de estas dos . . .

[fin del fragmento]

---

[10] *Desde mi cama me llevó* [ilegible]

prepare myself for another flagellation, I did so. And when she laid eyes on my back, she told me to get dressed again because that back was not ready to receive any more whippings than those that were already evident on it, and [she said] that she was astounded that Juana, for this was the other woman's name, had gone so far as to mistreat me so much. And when I was going to pick up my dress, I saw one of my shoulders, the part that I could see by looking in passing, with several very blue marks and welts.

127. One morning, I recall that she came to me when I was in bed.[67] And I had slept very badly that night because my bed was then on a summer mat, which is made of wide ropes, I believe of slender hemp, or I don't know what very cold thing. And many nights, when everyone else was sleeping, I would roll up my mattress, of which there was only one, to my feet, and get on top of the ropes, and I don't know if I put a blanket underneath or [if I slept] without it, such that, before anyone saw in the morning, I would unroll my mattress.[68] And that cold from [sleeping on] the hemp ropes worked me over a great deal the whole night. And when I wasn't paying attention, since it was so early, she came, as I said, to me, and caught me on the ropes. But she didn't say anything, rather she ordered me to get up, and unclothed, with only a cloth from my waist to my knees, as I have said other times, and with the rope around my neck and my hands tied, filled with cold and discomfort, she took me to a nearby oratory, for there was no one in it or the hallway. And behind closed doors and having whipped me, she made me lie down on the floor, where she whipped me from my feet to my shoulders. And with I don't know what words of disdain, she put one of her feet on my chest, in the middle of it. And since she had on a shoe with a double sole, thick, and she must have been careless about how much pressure she should exert, I felt a great pain in my chest and in all of its interior, so great that had she not raised it quickly, I thought my health would be seriously damaged. *Her foot on my chest worked me over greatly.* The other of these two . . . [fragment ends here, left unfinished].[69]

---

[67] *She got me out of bed* [illegible]

[68] Bed frames during this period had ropes where modern beds have wooden slats. Sleeping without a mattress was then a common penitential exercise.

[69] The fourth set of pages contains ¶¶128-132, recounting events in Pamplona already described.

Habiendo puesto por escrito todos cuantos votos y obligaciones semejantes tenía hechos en todo el discurso de mi vida, hoy, viernes, a 20 de octubre de 1600 años, excepto los de importancia que quedan escritos en mi poder, los di al Padre Maestro Esteban de Ojeda, Rector que es al presente en este colegio de la Compañía de Jesús de Madrid. Y habiéndolos tenido algunos días en su poder y considerado lo que en este caso más convenía hacer, dispensó con todos los dichos votos y obligaciones, dejándome libre de ellos, a mi ruego y petición, en virtud de los privilegios que para esto tiene como superior en la dicha Compañía, y de tal manera los dispensó absolutamente, que no me queda ninguna obligación, y dice no tengo que acordarme de ellos ya jamás. Y el P. Maestro Juan de Cetina, y el P. Cristóbal de Collantes, Padres de la misma Compañía y teólogos muy aprobados en ella, me afirmaron que, con la dicha dispensación, cumplía suficientemente, y que no tenía que me acordar más de los dichos votos. Y con esto rompí los papeles en que tenía hecha memoria de ellos.

L[uisa]

# *Vows* [1]

Having put in writing all the vows and similar commitments that I had made during the course of my life, today, 20 October 1600, except those of importance whose copies I have in my possession, I gave them to Father Master Esteban de Ojeda, presently the Rector of this Imperial College of the Society of Jesus of Madrid. And after keeping them in his possession for several days and having considered what was the most appropriate procedure in this case, he dispensed with all of said vows and commitments, leaving me freed from them, at my request and petition, by virtue of the privileges granted him in said Society to effect such measures, and in such a way dispensed with them absolutely so that they by no means oblige me, and he says I never again need think of them. [2]   And Father Master Juan de Cetina, and Father Cristóbal de Collantes, Fathers of the same Society and among its most accepted theologians, affirmed that, with said dispensation, I met my obligation sufficiently and that I no longer had to keep said vows in mind. [3]   And with that I ripped up the papers on which I had written them down to remind myself of them.

L[uisa]

[1] Carvajal's vows evolved to suit her needs and desires. The only other vow she specifies having taken before these is a secret promise to do anything asked of her for the love of God, in imitation of St. Francis, which she took just after arriving in Pamplona. I follow Abad's transcription (EA 238-45), correcting errors. Father Hernando de Espinosa, SJ, had a sealed set of the four vows which follow, copies used as evidence in the Cause for her beatification and now in her papers at the Encarnación. Also in the convent are autograph copies from Carvajal's own collection.

[2] The fact the Ojeda had a signed copy of her vow of poverty explains why Walpole requested that the Jesuits pay Carvajal's debt of 160 *reales* when she died: they were in possession of the documents permitting them access to her money.

[3] Juan de Cetina was a preacher and confessor of the Imperial College in Madrid, where Cristóbal Collantes taught the guidance of conscience (Abad, EA 239, nn. 2-3).

## *Voto de pobreza*
### Año 1593

1. Yo, Luisa de Carvajal, a mayor gloria de Dios Nuestro Señor, de quien misericordiosamente he recibido afectuosísimo deseo de agradarle en cuanto me ha sido posible, hago firme promesa y voto de perpetua pobreza delante Su Divina Majestad, de todo mi corazón, y entera y verdadera renunciación en Jesucristo Nuestro Señor, y en mi superior en su nombre, del dominio y propiedad de dinero u otra cosa que se pueda tener por mía, o se haya de gastar por mi elección, o en el sustento de mi vida, sin excepción alguna, lo cual estará siempre sujeto a la ordenación, parecer, y consejo de mi superior. Y, con su licencia, podré disponer religiosamente, excusando siempre toda superflua y vana correspondencia y cualquier mezcla de conocida imperfección que en ello se advierta. Y con esa misma licencia, cobraré cualquier deuda que se me deba y el precio de nuestras labores, y lo que, de gracia o limosna, se me diere, y lo podré tener el tiempo y en el modo que a mi superior le pareciere.

2. De todo lo cual podrá salir el gasto y conservación de las cosas siguientes, habiéndome sido concedido por él el uso de ellas de limosna:

3. Alguna porción moderada en enfermedad y salud, conforme a la diferente necesidad de entrambas cosas. El vestido ordinario que traigo, que es el que religiosamente debo traer, sin admitir en él mezclas contrarias a espíritu ni cosa alguna que tire a estilo mundano.

4. Cama y alhajas convenientes a esta profesión, y las demás menudencias convenientes, sin salud o con ella, y lo que costare curarme estando indispuesta, y cuanto conviniere gastar con mis compañeras, estando en casa o despidiéndose de ella.

5. Aderezos de oratorio y de la Misa, con llaneza y decencia conveniente, y limosna de las Misas que se quisieran decir en él, y las demás imágenes y devociones convenientes para la casa, y cercos de reliquias, no más costosas que de latón dorado,

## *Vow of Poverty*
### Year of 1593

1. I, Luisa de Carvajal, to the greater glory of God our Lord, from whom I have received a most affectionate desire to please Him as much as possible, make a firm promise and vow of perpetual poverty before His Divine Majesty, with all my heart, and complete and true renunciation, unto Jesus Christ Our Lord and unto my superior in His name, of the control and possession of money or other things which might be called mine, or which must be spent as I see fit, or for the sustenance of my life, without any exception whatsoever, which will ever be subject to the disposition, opinion, and counsel of my superior. And, with his license, I shall religiously dispose of it, always refusing any superfluous and vain influence and any admixture of manifest imperfection which might be found therein. And with this same license, I shall collect whatever debt might be owed me and for the price of our handwork, and that which, from grace or alms, might be given me, and I will be allowed that license for the length of time and by whatever means that my superior might determine.[4]

2. From out of which will come the expense and maintenance of the following items, with their use as alms having been conceded to me by him.

3. A moderate sum in sickness and in health, in conformity with the differing needs of both conditions. The ordinary clothing I wear, which is that in which I should religiously attire myself, without admitting admixture of that which is contrary to the spirit nor anything similar to a worldly style.

4. Bed and bedding appropriate to my profession, and other appropriate details, in a state of illness or health, and whatever it might cost me to be indisposed, and however much should be appropriate to spend with my companions, being in this house or [preparing to be] leaving it.[5]

5. Adornments for the oratory and the Mass, with appropriate simplicity and decency, and alms for the Masses which I might desire to have said therein, and the other images and appropriate devotions for the house, and reliquaries, no more expensive than gilded tin,

---

[4] This clause gave Carvajal permission to administer the finances of her *beaterio*, or house of holy women, accepting alms and payment for the needlework they did to earn money.

[5] The reference is to the dowries that Carvajal provided for women desiring to enter convents, as she did for Inés de la Asunción.

y las demás penitencias, y traer todas las reliquias que mi superior quisiere.

6. Los libros convenientes a mi mayor edificación y consuelo y de mis compañeras, y los cuadernos y libros que se trasladaren por dinero, excusando siempre lo superfluo y poco necesario, y los recados de escribir que se gastaren. Y, si conviniere guardar papeles u otras cosas debajo de llave, lo haré con licencia de mi superior.

7. Todos los muebles convenientes al servicio de la casa, y renovación de ellos siendo necesaria, y alquilar cualquiera que yo quisiere con licencia de mi superior, y hacer cualquier edificio que conviniere hacer. Y podré alquilar cualquiera casa cuando mi superior lo quisiere.

8. Y en los caminos que hiciere, gastaré todo lo que conviniere al mayor recato y seguridad mía y de mis compañeras.

9. Y en cuanto al voto y promesa, cuya señal es una cruz, podré libremente acudir a su mejor y más cumplido efecto, sin embargo de cualquiera obligación de conciencia en que mis votos me hayan puesto, a la dicha obligación repugnante. Y, procurando en ella la dirección de mi superior, con su bendición y licencia podré gastar todo el dinero necesario, aunque sea por mi mano.

10. En todo lo sobredicho y semejantes materias que se fueren ofreciendo, procuraré la dirección de mi superior, y sus licencias podrán ser en particular o general, y por el tiempo que él juzgare conveniente más al servicio de Nuestro Señor.

and other penitential items, and any other relics which my superior might desire.[6]

6. Books appropriate for my greater edification and consolation and that of my companions, and folders and books which I might order copied in exchange for money, always excepting anything superfluous and little necessary, and whatever costs of copying or dictation might be incurred. And, if it should be appropriate to store papers or other items under lock and key, I shall do so with the permission of my superior.

7. All furniture appropriate to the functioning of the house, and its renovation should it be necessary, and any rental fees that I should like, with the permission of my superior, and the building of whatever might be appropriate. And I shall be able to rent any house whenever my superior should so determine.[7]

8. And in whatever travels I might undertake, I shall spend whatever should be necessary for the greatest modesty and security of my person and my companions.

9. And as regards the vow and promise marked with a cross,[8] I shall be able to seek its best and most complete accomplishment freely, in spite of any obligation of conscience in which my vows might have placed me which might contradict said obligation. And, seeking the guidance of my superior in its carrying out, with his blessing and license I shall be able to spend whatever money necessary, even if I should do so on my own.

10. In all of the above materials and similar circumstances which might present themselves, I shall seek the guidance of my superior, and his leave may be for particular or general items and circumstances, and for whatever length of time he shall judge most appropriate for the service of Our Lord.

---

[6] These details indicate how steeped in formalistic ritual Carvajal's piety was, so much so that she budgeted funds for material objects of piety, such as relics. Her enthusiasm for Catholicism's physical components, such as her oratory, is typical of post-reformation Catholicism. Such heavily conditioned "poverty" contrasts starkly with Teresa of Ávila's severe insistence for her nuns: "Let them live always on alms and without any income" (*Constitutions* 9).

[7] This detail and those following, particularly regarding the conditions of travel, suggest that Carvajal was planning her trip to England when she made this vow. Her freedom to rent whatever house she saw fit made it possible for her to contract the country house she did, in Spitalfields, initially (so she insisted) to protect herself from the foul air of London, but also used as a Jesuit hideout.

[8] There is a cross marked next to her vow of martyrdom (EA 241, n. 5).

11. Si mi superior estuviere en diferente lugar, ahora sea de paso o asiento, o en cualquier parte remota, y sin culpa ni negligencia mía hubiese dilación en escribir o recibir respuesta, podré, en el ínterin, gobernarme conforme yo entendiere ser servicio y gloria de Nuestro Señor.

12. Si con el tiempo se ofrecieren escrúpulos o dudas en estas materias que aquí no se previenen ni declaran, se da facultad a mi superior para que, a mi petición y ruego, pueda hacer la declaración que en su conciencia le pareciere más conveniente al servicio y gloria de Nuestro Señor y mayor aprovechamiento de mi espíritu.

13. Todos los votos de pobreza, más y menos estrecha, que tengo hasta aquí hechos, y los que en cualquiera manera tocan a materia de hacienda, están dispensados y conmutados en lo contenido en este papel, [habiendo primeramente comunicado con mi confesor muy en particular las obligaciones de cada uno de ellos]. Y declárase que, en cualquier tiempo que me viniere alguna herencia o cosa semejante, estaré obligada a disponer de ello sin dilación alguna, señalando, por mi misma devoción, la obra pía que me pareciere de mayor gloria de Nuestro Señor.

## *Voto de obediencia*
### Año de 1595 [Escribióse de nuevo el de 1600]

1. Hallándome obligada con inmensos beneficios que de la mano de Dios Nuestro Señor he recibido, humildemente le ofrezco y entrego esta libre voluntad mía que Él fue servido de darme, con voto y promesa que hago, a Su Majestad, la más firme que me es posible, de obedecer, todos los días de mi vida, a los mandatos y ordenaciones de la persona que en su lugar y nombre santísimo yo eligiere por mi superior y guía, obligándome a esto de mi parte en cualquier modo y forma que ser pueda, sin que mi superior lo admita, en caso que él no lo admitiese.

11. Should my superior be in a different place [than I], whether temporarily or permanently, or in any removed location, and through no fault of mine there should be a delay in writing or receiving answers [to my queries], I shall be able, in the interim, to govern myself in conformity with whatever I understand to be the service and glory of Our Lord.

12. If in time, scruples or doubts related to these materials should arise which are not foreseen or declared here, authority is given to my superior so that, at my request and petition, he may declare whatever his conscience might dictate to him as most appropriate for the service and glory of Our Lord and of greatest benefit to my spirit.

13. All the vows of poverty, more and less strict, which I have made until now, and those which deal in any way with my estate, are disposed of and commuted to the contents of this paper, [with my having first communicated with my confessor in detail regarding the obligations of each one[9]]. And it is declared that, at any time when I might receive an inheritance or something similar, I shall be obliged to dispose of it without any delay whatsoever, choosing, in accordance with my own devotion, the pious work which seems to be to the greatest glory of Our Lord.

### *Vow of Obedience*
### Year of 1595 [Newly written in 1600][10]

1. Finding myself obliged by immense benefits which from the hand of God Our Lord I have received, I humbly offer and deliver unto Him this free will of mine which He was served to give me, with a vow and promise I make, to His Majesty, as firmly as I can, to obey, all the days of my life, the directives and ordinances of the person in His holy place and name whom I choose as my superior and guide, obliging myself to this on my part in any way and form I can do so, without my superior accepting it, in the case that he should not.[11]

---

[9] Abad notes that this clause appears only in the autograph copy of the vow (EA 241, n. 6).

[10] There are three autograph copies of this vow, one of which states, "This paper was written in the year 1600." In this document, Carvajal aggressively negotiates the delicate business of men's supervision of her activities.

[11] This condition was necessary because the Jesuits did not accept such vows of obedience (Abad, EA 242, n. 1). Carvajal had a Franciscan superior as well as a Jesuit.

2. Debajo de esta misma fuerza quedo obligada a hacer cada año nueva elección de superior por Pascua de Espíritu Santo, en el mismo del año pasado, o en otra cualquiera distinta persona, presente o ausente, como más parezca convenir al bien de mi alma.

3. Y si acaeciere que mi superior muriese dentro del mismo año, nombraré [a] otro que supla por él hasta que llegue la Pascua, en la cual se volverá a hacer de nuevo la elección.

4. Y para su mejor efecto, antes que llegue este santo día, podré hacer alguna humilde oración a Nuestro Señor, pidiéndole que yo, en el elegir y obedecer, y mi superior, en me guiar y gobernar, acertemos a hacer su dulcísima e inestimable voluntad lo más perfectamente que nos sea posible.

5. Y teniendo pensado qué persona será más conveniente, sin respectos particulares ni gustos del amor propio, la elegiré con devoción en la divina presencia, y desde ese punto la respetaré, como dada de su soberana mano, todo el tiempo que tuviere la dicha superioridad.

6. Las faltas que causare su ausencia, cuando la hubiere, se podrán suplir por cartas y otros semejantes medios, y con licencias particulares o generales en todas aquellas cosas que conviniere darlas.

7. Y en caso que hubiese forzosas dilaciones en escribir y dar cuenta de mí, o en recibir sus respuestas, podré, en el ínterin, gobernarme conforme a lo que yo entendiere ser de mayor servicio y contentamiento de Nuestro Señor.

8. Y declárase que, si en este voto y obligaciones de él hubiere cosa que requiera interpretación, o con el tiempo se ofrecieren dificultades y dudas que aquí no se hayan prevenido, las podrá allanar todas mi superior, ordenando lo que fuere más conveniente al servicio de Nuestro Señor y bien de mi alma, no mudando ni alterando en nada las cosas aquí declaradas y expresas.

2. As part of these same constraints, I remain obliged to newly elect a superior every year around Pentecost, either the same one as the previous year or whomever else, present or absent, as should be most fitting for the good of my soul.[12]

3. And should it happen that my superior should die within the same year, I shall name another who will take his place until Pentecost, at which time the election will take place again.

4. And for its greatest effect, before the arrival of this holy day, I will be able to pray humbly to Our Lord, asking that I, in electing and obeying, and my superior, in guiding and governing me, might succeed in doing His most sweet and inestimable will as perfectly as is possible for us.

5. And having thought about which person will be most appropriate, without regard to individual concerns nor the pleasures of self-love, I shall select that person with devotion in the divine presence, and from that point on I shall respect that selection as one decided by His sovereign hand, throughout the time that he will exercise said charge.

6. The faults that his absence might cause, whenever that may occur, may be compensated for with letters and other similar means, and with single or general permission in all those things for which such permission ought to be sought.

7. And in the case that there should be inevitable delays in writing and my accounting for myself, or in receiving his replies, I may, in the interim, govern myself according to that which I understand to be to the greatest service and delight of Our Lord.

8. And it is declared that, if in this vow or his obligations there arise something needing interpretation, or should difficulties and doubts arise with time which are not here addressed, my superior will be able to resolve them, ordering whatever might be most appropriate for the service of Our Lord and the good of my soul, without changing or altering in any way the things declared and expressed here.

---

[12] Pentecost, celebrated on the seventh Sunday after Easter, marks the descent of the Holy Spirit upon the Apostles; hence the Spanish "Pascua del Espíritu Santo." The election explained in this paragraph not only gave Carvajal the freedom to choose her superiors, but to hire and fire them as well, as it were. The right for religious women to determine their own confessors and superiors was a hotly contested issue during this period, and in ¶11 Carvajal underscores the difference between her status and that of women obliged to other types of obedience.

9. Y en cuanto a los votos principales a que estoy de presente obligada y como parece por los papeles de ellos, no podrá jamás mi superior quitarme ninguno en virtud de éste, ni obligarme a que yo lo quiera, ni que pida conmutación ni dispensación alguna.

10. Habiéndome sido conmutados y dispensados todos los votos que en cualquiera manera tenía hechos de esta materia, quedo de aquí adelante, a gloria de Nuestro Señor, con obligación de guardar lo contenido en este papel, excepto lo que toca a instrucción.

11. Todo lo cual servirá de ayuda contra los estropiezos e inconvenientes que con el tiempo se pueden ofrecer a quien ha de tener un solo y absoluto superior.

## *Voto de mayor perfección*
### 1595

1. Después de experimentadas no pocas dificultades de las que se suelen atravesar en el camino de la virtud, me vine a hallar con notable ánimo y esforzadísimos deseos de seguirla a costa de cualquier trabajo y cuidado mío, e iba hallando cada día tan superior mi corazón, que me pareció podía estrechar las obligaciones de mi conciencia más de lo que lo estaban. Y así hice el voto siguiente:

2. Humillada en un profundo abismo en la dulcísima presencia de Dios Nuestro Señor por lo que le debo y espero de su inmensa benignidad, hago firme promesa y voto de hacer siempre, en todas las cosas, lo que yo entendiere ser de más perfección ante sus divinos ojos, en la manera que en mí esto puede ser posible.

9. And as regards the principal vows to which I am presently sworn and as appears in the papers containing them, my superior will never be able to take away any one of them by virtue of this [vow], nor oblige me to so desire, nor request their commuting or any dispensation [to alter them].[13]

10. With all my previous vows of any kind which I ever made before in this area having been rescinded for me, I remain from now on, to the glory of Our Lord, with the obligation to carry out what is contained on this paper, except that which touches upon instruction.[14]

11. All of which will serve as an aid against the difficulties and inconveniences which might arise in time for the person who must have a single and absolute superior.

*Vow of Greater Perfection*[15]
1595

1. Having experienced not a few of the difficulties which those on the path of virtue tend to come upon, I found myself with notable spirit and most powerful desires to follow it [virtue] at the cost of any trial and care for me, and I was finding my heart so much improved every day that it seemed to me that I could further tighten the obligations of my conscience. And thus I took the following vow:

2. Humiliated in a profound abyss in the most sweet presence of God Our Lord due to what I owe Him and what I hope for from His immense kindness, I make a firm promise and vow to do always in all things that which I understand to be most perfect before His divine eyes, in the manner in which this may be possible for me.

---

[13] ¶¶ 8-9 contain important clauses which relativize Carvajal's obedience substantially, insisting on the primacy of her other vows over her vow of obedience to any superior's desire to see her renounce or modify them. She surely had in mind her vow of martyrdom, which several of her superiors did indeed want rescinded, but which Walpole defended as a matter of conscience. The penultimate paragraph and the several conditions Carvajal places on this vow (for example, her freedom to choose her superior and to switch superiors annually) show a marked influence of Jesuit casuistry and are purposefully ambiguous. Carvajal declares obedience at the same time she pries the door open to remarkable freedom.

[14] Neither Abad nor I know what she refers to in this last clause; it is probably a reference to Jesuit conditioning of obligations.

[15] There are three copies of this vow in Carvajal's papers, one of which evidences many corrections. Another bears the heading "Año de 1598," which Abad calls "the real date." It is likely that Carvajal actually made the vow privately before 1595, described it in writing in 1595, and composed this document as a means of updating her vows in 1598.

3. Y por evitar escrúpulos, y que el entendimiento de esta obligación quede más llano, la divido en dos puntos:

4. El primero contiene todas aquellas cosas que, por ser menudas o de paso, requieren breve y no muy considerada resolución. Y en todas ellas quiero que se entienda que podré hacer de presente aquello que, fácilmente y con verdad, se me representare entonces ser conveniente y conforme a razón, según la obligación de perfección del dicho voto.

5. El segundo toca a todo cuanto fuere de más asiento y diere más tiempo y lugar a su determinación, en lo cual es mi intento que, en cualquiera cosa de éstas en que yo no sepa juzgar cuál sea la mayor perfección que debo seguir y sobre ello me hallare dudosa e indeterminable, representando el caso a mi superior, he de tomar y seguir su parecer, durante la duda e irresolución mía, y no de otra manera.

6. Y desde que hice este voto, nunca he sentido con él pesadumbre, ni inquietud, ni estrechuras de escrúpulos, antes gran consuelo y contentamiento de haberle hecho, y deseo de cumplirle con todas mis fuerzas.

## *Voto de martirio*
### Jesús, Año de 1598

1. Viendo que los impetuosos y delicadísimos afectos de dar la vida por Cristo Nuestro Señor, siguiendo sus dulcísimas pisadas, uniéndome estrechamente con Él por este medio, tenían en gran manera apretado mi corazón y penetrado de una gravísima herida. Ya que no estaba en mi mano satisfacer a su deseo, quise acudirle con el alivio que pude, haciendo el voto que sigue:

2. Yo, Luisa de Carvajal, lo más firmemente que puedo, con estrecho voto prometo a Dios Nuestro Señor que procuraré, cuanto me sea posible, buscar todas aquellas ocasiones de martirio que no sean repugnantes a la ley de Dios, y que siempre que yo hallare oportunidad semejante, haré rostro a todo género de muerte, tormentos y riguridad, sin volver las espaldas en ningún modo, ni rehusarlo por ninguna vía, y que cada y cuando me viere en ocasión tan venturosa, me ofreceré, sin ser buscada.

3. And to avoid scruples, and so that the understanding of this obligation be clearer, I divide it into two points.

4. The first contains all those things which, because they are small or ephemeral, require quick resolution without much consideration. And in all these [things] I wish it to be understood that I may do right away that which, easily and in truth, comes to me as appropriate and in conformity with reason, according to the obligation to perfection of said vow.

5. The second deals with all that which runs deeper and takes more time and reasoning to determine, in which it is my intention that, in any of these things in which I might not know how to judge which is the greater perfection that I should follow, and about which I might be doubtful and indeterminate, upon explaining the case to my superior, I must take and follow his opinion, for however long as I have doubts and am unresolved, and [should proceed] in no other way.

6. And since I made this vow, I have never felt weighted down by it, nor restless, nor pressured by scruples, rather greatly consoled and happy for having done it, and I desire to fulfill it with all my power.

## *Vow of Martyrdom*
### Jesus, Year of 1598[16]

1. Seeing that impetuous and most delicate inclinations to give my life for Christ Our Lord, following in His most sweet footsteps, joining myself closely to Him through this means, had my heart greatly pressed and penetrated it with a most critical wound. Since I no longer had means to satisfy its desire, I wished to provide it with such relief as I might, by taking the following vow:

2. I, Luisa de Carvajal, as firmly as I am able, with a strict vow promise God Our Lord that I will procure, to the extent possible, to seek out all those opportunities of martyrdom which are not repugnant to the law of God, and that whenever I find such opportunity, will face all manner of death, torments, and rigors, without turning my back on them in any way or refusing them in any way, and that when and if I should find myself in such a fortunate situation, I shall offer myself without having to be sought out.

---

[16] This extraordinary vow freed Carvajal's destiny from the hands of her superiors and placed it squarely in God's, whose will was indistinguishable from her own. The autograph copy bears no date; the copy that Ojeda submitted as part of his testimony for Carvajal's beatification, presumably the copy Carvajal turned over to him on 22 Oct. 1560, is dated 1598.

3. El haber hecho este voto ha sido para mí de gran gusto y contentamiento, cuanto espero lo será la posibilidad de ejecutarle. Y, en el ínterin, me consuelo con él entrañablemente, deseando, aunque tan miserable, sobre todas las cosas, que en ésta y en las demás se cumpla en mí perfectamente la inestimable voluntad de Dios.

3. Taking this vow has been a great pleasure and happiness to me, as I hope will be the possibility to carry it out, and, in the interim, I am deeply consoled by it, desiring above all things, though despicable as I am, that in this and in all else the inestimable will of God be accomplished in me.

## Poetry: Introduction

According to Manual Serrano y Sanz, writing in 1903, Luisa de Carvajal is "undoubtedly the most illustrious religious poet of those who flourished in Spain during the sixteenth century; into her verses, removed from all conventionalism, she let flow her intense mystical fervor and her desire to suffer continually for Christ, whom she had ever before her eyes" (I: 234). His estimation reveals the traps into which remarkable poetry like Carvajal's can lead, traps often poised to spring on works by women: concentration on themes and images (such as suffering and selflessness) to the exclusion of formal and artistic components, and the assumption of an isomorphic relationship between the poet and her poem. While much less universalizing than more well-known poetry of her time, Carvajal's verse is deeply indebted to the European erudite poetic tradition, and her texts provide evidence that she had John of the Cross, the Bible, Petrarch, and Jorge de Montemayor before her eyes as well as Christ.

Like much of her autobiographic prose, much of Carvajal's verse is disturbing. As Cruz observes, "while spiritual moving, Carvajal's metaphysical conceits and intense images of physical pain are often disquieting to modern sensibilities" ("Chains" 98). Just as her recollections of the abuse inflicted upon her by her uncle jump out at the modern reader from her spiritual life story, so this pain is the most startling feature of her poems. Carvajal's poetic corpus best illustrates El Saffar's belief that "Luisa channeled her experience of pain and humiliation into the image of Christ's suffering, finding through his example justification and value in her own sense of bodily and emotional ravaging" (77). Carvajal's ideas about the positive value of painful suffering challenge many who would sympathize with her today. Studies such as Helen Luke's, of passionate and compassionate suffering in the monastic context, are helpful as tools for understanding Carvajal's exaltation of agony.

Psychological interpretations are plausible explanations for the vivid and unusual relief given to suffering in Carvajal's verse. At the same time, it is important to mention that most if not all of her poetry is believed to have been written during her years in Madrid, which was precisely the period during which Carvajal was most deeply

settled into the performance of a gender-specific and extremely lim-
iting religious role, that of the self-denying female ecstatic, a role she
eventually abandoned. During those same years, she was petitioning
for permission to go to England, and the political efficacy of verse
such as hers, with its loud echoes of hagiographic martyr accounts,
should be factored into its evaluation.

Much of Carvajal's verse is written in the pastoral anecdote, meaning she uses the contrived, idealized figure of the literary shepherdess
to represent her poetic characters. Pastoral literature was fashionable
in Spain after the 1543 publication of Garcilaso de la Vega's famous
Eclogues, followed by Jorge de Montemayor's pastoral romance *Los
siete libros de la Diana* (1559). Like much pastoral literature, Carvajal's
is a lightly encoded representation of specific individuals: her own
poetic persona, "Silva," uses the letters of "LVISA," employing the
Latin semivowel "v"; "Nise" is generally believed to represent Inés de
la Asunción, Carvajal's companion of thirteen years; Amari represents María Hurtado de Mendoza, the third daughter of Carvajal's
uncle, who was Carvajal's age.

Religious poets such as John of the Cross appropriated the pastoral anecdote for religious expression, capitalizing on the rural features of the Song of Songs in particular to express the solitary searching for love expressed in both the religious and secular pastoral tradi-
tions. Like the saint whose poetry she admired greatly, Carvajal employs the biblical motif of Christ the good shepherd. Although John
of the Cross's poetry was not published during Carvajal's lifetime,
she did have a manuscript copy of it in Spain.[1]

The medieval metaphors of service and war, upon which many
of Carvajal's poems are based, are drawn from Spain's rich tradition
of chivalresque literature, which was initiated with the famous romance *Amadís de Gaula* by Garcí Rodríguez de Montalvo (published
in 1508, it was one of the books that drove Cervantes's Don Quijote
crazy). These aggressive metaphors enjoyed renewed popularity during the Counter Reformation, when many were set to the service of
religious motifs, and Carvajal employs them widely to reinforce her
expression of submission and victory. The political and philosophi-
cal inversions with which she plays in many poems, such as the notion that to be a slave is to reign (Poem 14, ll. 31-35) or, in the
following sonnet, that to live is to die (Poem 15, ll. 1-4), are examples of a popular baroque technique which seventeenth-century

---

[1] In a letter of Dec. 1607 she asks Inés de la Asunción to send it to her in
London (*Epist.* 235).

theorists of poetry called "concordant contrasts," paradoxes meant to illuminate the irresolvable conflicts of human existence. They do not necessarily attest to literal desires to die and suffer, and their interpretation should be tempered with awareness of the vogue they enjoyed in the poetic discourse of Carvajal's time.

Carvajal's poetry is punctuated with stylistic flourishes that signal her membership in the educated elite that enjoyed access to the classics. This is a group which, during the late sixteenth century, began to imitate Latin syntax in Spanish poetry as a means of composing verse whose meaning could be penetrated by only the most intellectually privileged. The most challenging of these techniques is Carvajal's frequent employ of hyperbaton, the breaking of normal syntactic order, which forces the reader to enter the poem and reorganize it to draw meaning from it. Respecting this important poetic technique means leaving the reader of the English text to wrestle with the word order as must the reader of the Spanish, and whenever possible I have done so. The concept of difficulty and suffering to attain an objective is fundamental in Carvajal's works, whether displayed through her poetic syntax or her English mission itself. The forced and unnatural flow of some of her verse, then, not only displays her understanding of poetic styles of her day, but reinforces a salient feature of her writings. When English syntax cannot tolerate the inversions possible in Spanish, I respect the English requisites; for example, l. 38 of Poem 46, reads in Spanish, "del Duero profundas aguas," which in English literally means "of the Duero deep waters." In such cases I normalize the syntax ("deep waters of the Duero") but try whenever possible to respect the limits of the line composition.

No autograph copies of Carvajal's poetry are known today. Muñoz, who published 48 of her poems in his 1632 *Vida* of Carvajal, presumably worked from authorized copies or the originals. Importantly, he indicates that the rubrics, which include what are now used as the poems' titles, were written by Carvajal (531).[2] Juan Nicolás de Faber published a previously unknown poem by her in his 1821 *Floresta de rimas antiguas castellanas* (I: 82), but since then no others have surfaced. I base my edition and translation on Abad's transcription (*Epist.* 427-52), but modify his punctuation. I have edited the prose explication of "On a Harsh Journey" from the autograph manuscript.

---

[2] The detail is significant because a poem's title and rubric profoundly condition its reading, as Williamsen has indicated.

3

*Romance espiritual de Silva*

*De afectos interiores de amor de Dios*

     ¡Ay, si entre los lazos fieros
que a mi gloria aprisionaron
por mi libertad, yo viera
enlazar mi cuello y manos!
5     Pero, si es atrevimiento,
porque esos son sacrosantos,
e indigna toda criatura
de adornos tan soberanos,
concédeme, Amor, siquiera
10    (pues en dar no eres escaso)
algunas dulces prisiones
que les parezcan en algo.
Dulces las llamo, porque,
en ley de amor, sus amargos
15    son tan dulces, que la vida
se suele dar por comprarlos.
¡Oh cuán mil veces dichosa
aquella do ejecutados
mil sangrientos sacrificios
20    y abrasados holocaustos,

3

*Silva's Spiritual Ballad*[1]

*On Inner Feelings of Love for God*

Ah, if among the fierce bonds
that imprisoned my glory
in exchange for my freedom, I should see
my neck and hands entwined!

5 But, if to so desire is over bold,
for those are sacrosanct,
and unworthy any creature
of such sovereign adornment,
concede to me, Love,

10 (for in giving you are not miserly)
even some sweet imprisonment,
similar to them in some way.
Sweet I call them because,
in the law of love, their bitter afflictions

15 are so sweet that one tends to give
one's life to purchase them.
Oh a thousand times fortunate
that life during which, a thousand
bloody sacrifices and burnt holocausts

20 having been carried out,

---

[1] The *romance* is the traditional Spanish ballad form consisting of an indeterminate number of eight-syllable lines which rhyme in the last accentuated vowel of the even lines only. John of the Cross is the most famous mystical poet to adapt extant *romances* to religious themes, but it was a very popular verse form among Spanish poets of the early modern period. I follow Olivares and Boyce, who suggest that Carvajal likely did not divide her *romances* into regular stanzas (513).

se te ofrece, Cristo mío,
en lo posible mostrando
cuán imposible es que quede,
en ningún modo ni caso,
25    su fuerte amor satisfecho,
ni el tuyo inmenso pagado!

it offers itself to you, my Christ,
showing by what is possible
how impossible it is for that strong love,
in any means or circumstance,
25      to be satisfied,
or your immense love repaid!

## *Introduction:*
## Prose explication of "On a Harsh Journey"

*T*his document, one of several loose folios in Carvajal's papers, explicates one of her poems in a rather pedantic fashion. Although she attached brief prose explications to five other poems, this one was left separated from the text it describes. In another loose prose document, which begins "Being very young when my parents died," she describes writing the verses during a period of great trial in Madrid, when she was weakened by an illness during which, she says, she believed she was going to die. In the margin of the "Being very young" folio, she wrote "27," presumably indicating her age at that time, which would date the poem at 1593.

Rarely did poets compose prose renditions of their poetry during this period, since the very point of the verse was poetic expression. John of the Cross was required by his superiors to explicate his because of their dangerously provocative nature. Carvajal may have been asked to explain her poem by a superior for the sake of documentation, but it is more likely that she did so moved by a desire to make herself understood, since the rubrics she wrote to introduce almost all of her other poems indicate an intention to illuminate her reader. These explications are important because they indicate that she imagined a public for her writings, since she herself obviously had little need for such elaboration.

The amorous concepts on which the poem itself is based are not only the founding principles of courtly love (still in vogue in the early modern period), but they are also fundamental in the relationships among love, passion, and suffering in Christian theology, relationships which inform the poetic language of all seventeenth-century Spanish courtly verse. Carvajal's persistent references to solitude and loneliness, illness and closeness to death, are typical of women's religious writings during this period, particularly those of Teresa of Ávila, whose *Works* had been published in 1588. Peculiar to Carvajal are the unusually violent concepts she employs to represent her spiritual quest, concepts typical of the Baroque period but remarkably intense in her writings. Thus Cruz specifies that Carvajal's imagery of wounds, chains, and shackles was uncommon in the sixteenth century (98). Also noteworthy in this poem is the overt self-consciousness of the spiritual process Carvajal presents, evident in the way she describes herself manipulating her memory, for example. Such mirroring and the objectification of abstractions are not only Baroque markers, but also reflections of the Jesuit methods of self-examination practiced by the poet.

The text of the poem was surely meant to follow the prose introduction, although the manuscript has since been cut off after the last sentence in prose, perhaps because the version that followed was unacceptable to either its author or one of her readers. I re-append the poem.

[*Explicación en prose de "Por un áspero vïaje"*]

Ihs, Ma.

1. En este romance que empieza "Por un áspero vïaje," refiere Silva cifradísimamente cuanto había pasado por su alma en el discurso de su vida, de lo cual se ayudaba en sus desconsuelos, cuando, viéndose en todo extremo afligida con los desvíos y casi perpetuas ausencias de su Señor y su Dios, se le representaban sus pecados y faltas, con que el alma daba en desmayo extraño. Y anímase volviendo a sí misma y alentado el ánimo caído, porque no hallaba en nadie este consuelo. Y dice en sustancia, "¿De qué te afliges, Silva, como si lo que has pasado y en lo que te has puesto no fuera por tu Señor, pues sabes que, en ley de amor, el padecer y atravesar dificultades por el que se ama se estima por galardón, redundando una gloria en el alma que basta a templar las penas más rigurosas que pueden padecerse?"

2. Y porque ella así lo experimentaba con la memoria presente, prosigue adelante renovando las pasadas, y se dice así, como fue su Señor el que pudo tanto con su corazón y como fue Él a quien ella buscó pisando la tierra agreste, y a cada paso espinas, que en este camino tiene buen cuidado Satanás de sembrarlas, para asombrar a los que buscan a Cristo, haciéndoseles agrio y dificilísimo, por el cual entraron sus divinos pies primero, por buscar a la que amó. Y llegó tan adentro, metiéndose tan en lo fragoso, que quien hubiere de llegar a hallarle allí a Él ha menester llevar el pecho bien encendido de su amor para salir con ello.

3. Y fue Silva sola con sólo el amor, como refiere, porque no quiso Dios que hubiese otro medio, ni que hallase en nadie de esta vida ayuda, ni consejos, ni amparo. Y dice que perdió el miedo a las fieras, con la costumbre de oírlas bramar, y que aun las acometía con el esfuerzo del amor. Que son estas fieras aquellas tres que dice San Juan: concupiscencia de ojos, concupiscencia, etc., que es a do[nde]

## [*Prose explication of "On a Harsh Journey"*]

Ihs, Ma. [Jesus and Mary]

1. In this ballad, which begins "On a harsh journey," Silva explains, in a most encoded fashion, all that had passed through her soul during the course of her life, which helped her in her grief when, finding herself afflicted to all extremes with the detours and almost perpetual absence of her Lord and God, her sins and faults rose up to her, at which point her soul fainted oddly away. And she encourages herself, turning into herself and cheering her fallen spirit, for she found this consolation in no one else. And in essence, this is what she says: "Why are you afflicted, Silva, as if what you have endured, and the situation in which you find yourself, were not for your Lord? For you know that, according to the law of love, suffering and enduring difficulties for the beloved is to be esteemed as a boon, redounding to glory in the soul sufficient to temper the most rigorous pains that can be suffered."

2. And because she experienced it thus in the presence of her memory, she continues on, renewing past recollections, and thus says how it was her Lord who was able to do so much in her heart, and how it was Him whom she sought by treading rugged ground, with thorns at every step, for on this path Satan is very careful to sow them, so as to frighten those who seek Christ, making the way bitter and difficult, along which His divine feet first passed to find her whom He loved. And she arrived so far inward, entering so much into that which is impenetrable, that whoever should arrive there to find Him must needs have a heart well ignited with His love to emerge from it.

3. And Silva was alone with love alone, as she explains, because God did not wish it to be any other way, nor that she find any help, council, or shelter from anyone in this life. And she says that she lost her fear of wild beasts, as well as the tendency to hear them roar, and she even took them on with the power of love. For these are those three beasts of which St. John speaks: visual concupiscence, concupiscence, etc.,[1] in which is represented all

---

[1] "For all that is in the world, the lust of the flesh, and the lust of the eyes, and the pride of life, is not of the Father, but is of the world" (1 John 2.16).

se cifra todo lo que tácita o descubiertamente hace guerra al alma que busca a su Amado, de las cuales se producen y salen otras mil bestias fieras a espantarla con sus aullidos, como se experimenta, si hay luz y entendimiento para conocer las cosas espirituales.

4. Y en estas almas es a do[nde] el enemigo hace cuanto le dejan hacer desde el cielo, que las siente briosas. Y aunque las tema, arrójase temerariamente, por lo en que estima sacarle a Dios una entre mil de entre las manos.

5. Asimismo dice esa alma cuántas prendas tiene ya en este negocio, y que, pues ha habido ánimo hasta allí, no es justo desmayar un punto, y que mayores cosas ofreció y a mayores se determinó, cuando le dio su fe.

6. Y suspirando, como pecho que se va desahogando, forjados los suspiros o gemidos del dolor que la oprime y acaba, por aquella representación y sospecha ya dicha, de si la olvidaba su amado Señor, tomó por resolución, sobre la que se tenía, de entrar con ánimo tras de sus divinas pisadas por cruz y muerte y deshonras, etc., hasta encontrarse con Él, de manera que pueda decir, *"Tenui eum,* etc." como la esposa santa, viendo en sí cumplido aquel deseo que ella tenía cuando decía, "¿Quién me dará aparte, hermano mío, que te halle yo fuera y allí me pueda estrechamente abrazar contigo, que ya nadie me despreciaría? Temeraríanme mis enemigos y no se osarían atrever como hasta allí, y yo te hallaría fuera a do[nde] nadie me estorbase." Que a tal puesto no pudo jamás, ni con mucho, llegar el mundo, ni la carne, ni el demonio, enemigos crueles de mi bien y felicidad, si no da el alma muchos pasos atrás, o desde allí se despeña por soberbia, como Lucifer, desde tanta altura de gracia.

7. Y en razón de hallarle así, dice que se sacrificará a Él, por pasar cuanto en este camino se atravesare, con ánimo y brío, puesta toda su confianza en quien la puso siempre, con que va bien seguro.

that which tacitly or openly declares war upon the soul that seeks its Beloved, from which another thousand wild beasts are produced and projected to frighten it with their howls, as one experiences if one has light and understanding to recognize spiritual things.

4. And it is within these souls that the enemy accomplishes all that heaven permits him to do, for he resents their being high spirited. And though he might fear them, he boldly throws himself at them, due to the value he places upon stealing one among a thousand from God's hands.

5. Likewise that soul says how many tokens of love it already has in this pursuit and that, since it has been valiant up to that point, it is not right that it become the least disheartened, and that upon pledging its faith to Him it offered greater things and set itself to greater acts.

6. And [the soul] sighing, like a breast finding relief, with laments or moans forged in pain that oppresses and kills it over that notion and suspicion already mentioned, of whether or not her beloved Lord had forgotten her, resolved, above and beyond the resolution already made, to fall courageously into His footsteps along the way of the cross, death, and dishonor, etc., until finding herself with Him, so that she could say, "Tenui eum, etc."[2] as did the holy spouse, seeing accomplished in herself the desire that she had when she said, "Who will take me aside, my brother, that I might find you without and could embrace you closely there and not be despised?"[3] My friends would be in fear of me and would not dare approach me there, and I would find you outside where none would get in my way. For to such a place the world could never get close, nor the flesh, nor the devil, cruel enemies of my good and happiness, unless the soul goes many steps backward, or throws itself down out of pride, like Lucifer, from the heights of grace.

7. And because of finding Him thus, she says that she would sacrifice herself to Him, so as to endure anything that might arise along this path with spirit and courage, with all of her trust placed in Him in whom she always placed it, with whom she travels safely indeed.

---

[2] "Tenui eum, nec dimittam" ("I held him and would not let him go," Song 3:4).

[3] This is an interesting adaptation of Song of Songs 8:1-2, which reads, "Oh that thou wert as my brother, that sucked the breasts of my mother! when I should find thee without, I would kiss thee; yea, I should not be despised. I would lead thee, and bring thee into my mother's house, who would instruct me; I would cause thee to drink of spiced wine of the juice of my pomegranate."

4

*Romance espiritual de Silva*

*en que de paso va tocando
lo sucedido en su espiritual camino*

   Por un áspero vïaje,
   mirando con vista humana,
   caminaba una pastora,
   el alma de amor llagada.
5  Con lágrimas en los ojos
   con sí misma razonaba,
   diciendo, "Silva, si huiste
   y dejaste la cabaña,
   bien sabes que lo causó
10  aquella belleza extraña
   que un día consideraste
   en el que te robó el alma,
   y te tiró aquella flecha
   en su amor enherbolada,
15  que en tal extremo te puso
   que luego, determinada
   te viste a dejarlo todo
   cuanto fuera de él se halla.
   Y el solícito cuidado
20  que en tu pecho se encerraba;
   a modo de ardiente fuego
   las entrañas te abrasaba.
   Y en busca de tu Pastor

4

*Silva's Spiritual Ballad [1593]*

*in which, along the way,
she describes her spiritual path*

On a harsh journey
gazing with human sight,
a shepherdess was walking,
her soul wounded by love.
5     With tears in her eyes
she was reasoning with herself
saying, "Silva, if you ran away
and abandoned your hut,
you know well the reason was
10    that singular beauty
which you esteemed one day
when it robbed your soul
and shot you with that arrow
dipped in its love
15    which placed you in such extremes
that in that instant you found yourself
determined to abandoned everything
that is found outside of it.[4]
And the attentive care
20    locked itself within your breast;
like a burning fire
it consumed your entrails.
And in search of your Shepherd

---

[4] These lines recall Teresa of Ávila's famous vision of an angel piercing her heart with an arrow (*Life*, Ch. 30), as does Carvajal's Poem 46, ll. 51-54.

saliste por la montaña
25  porque tuviste por cierto
que en lo agrio de ella habitaba.
Sola, con sólo el amor
que a solas te acompañaba,
pisaste la agreste tierra
30  de espesas zarzas poblada.
Y metida tan adentro
de esta soledad tamaña,
a oír los fuertes bramidos
de fieras acostumbrada
35  quedaste, y [a] acometerlas
con libertad denodada,
la flor de la mocedad
marchita y desfigurada,
perdido el lozano talle
40  en la amorosa demanda,
y lo vistoso y lucido
que al morir vano agradaba.
Y entre ti y tu dulce Bien,
hecha ya ley asentada,
45  con mil solemnes promesas,
y dándole la palabra
de que siempre serás suya
y te tendrás por su esclava,
y que será tu blasón
50  verte por él aherrojada,
a romper dificultades

you went out on the mountain

25      because you were certain

that in its untamed folds He resided.

Alone, with love alone

which accompanied you alone,

you tread the wild earth

30      thick with dense brambles.

And once so deep within

such a huge solitude,

you became accustomed

to hearing the wild beasts'

35      loud howling and to attacking them

with intrepid freedom,[5]

the flower of youth

faded and disfigured,

your robust figure lost

40      in the loving quest,

gone all things bright and colorful

which used to please a vain gaze.[6]

And between you and your sweet Dearest

the ordained law having been enacted

45      with a thousand solemn promises

and giving Him your word

to be ever His;

and you will be as His slave,

and your blazon will be

50      to see yourself shackled by Him,

to overcome difficulties

[5] Wiesner-Hanks observes, "'Freedom' to them [women] meant the ability to participate in public life" (3).

[6] As Schulenburg indicates, the negation of physical beauty was a basic means of virginal defense (60).

de continuo aparejada,
Y ahora, sólo un pensamiento
te trae tan desanimada,
55    y de tristeza cubierto
el corazón y la cara."

    Estas cosas dice Silva,
y grandes suspiros daba
apremiada del dolor
60    que la consume y acaba,
el cual causó parecerle
que su Pastor la olvidaba,
y que cuanto ha referido
no debe estimarse en nada,
65    que nada puede llegar
a lo que se halla obligada.
Y procurando alentarse,
este remedio tomaba:
de no acordarse de sí,
70    y emboscarse en la montaña
más áspera y más fragosa
en busca de aquel que ama,
embebida toda en él,
y a él toda sacrificada,
75    esperando Silva en quien
puso toda su esperanza.

and be ever prepared for more.
And now just one thought
has you so dejected
55 and with heart and face
covered with sorrow."

These things Silva says
and sighed deeply,
rewarded with a pain
60 which consumes and finishes her,
which caused her to believe
that her Shepherd had forgotten her,
and that all things she just told of
should not be at all esteemed,
65 for nothing can attain
that to which she is obliged.
And attempting to rouse herself,
she decided upon this remedy:
not to think of herself
70 and to immerse herself in the harshest
and densest mountain
in search of Him whom she loves,
completely absorbed by Him
and to Him completely sacrificed,
75 Silva [is] hoping for the one in whom
she put all hope.

5

### *Quintillas espirituales de Silva*

*En que se muestra el sentimiento que tiene de no acertar a dar
gusto a su Señor. Quéjase amorosamente de esto y pídele
su divina ayuda, representándole las razones que hay para
esperarla de su divina mano*


    No pudiendo remediar
    la causa de mi dolor,
    me es forzoso preguntar,
    "¿Hasta cuándo, mi Señor,
5    tanto mal ha de durar?"

    "¿Cuándo he de ser socorrida?,
    que me veo en grande estrecho,
    de mil partes combatida,
    de amor abrasado el pecho,
10    y de tu ausencia afligida.

    "Pues el no haber acertado
    a amarte, luz de mis ojos,
    como debes ser amado,
    ¡cuántos millares de enojos
15    y amargura me ha costado!

    "Y ver que te descontenta
    quien por ti el vivir no estima,

5

*Silva's Spiritual Stanzas*

*In which is shown the sorrow she feels for not succeeding in pleasing her Lord. She complains lovingly about this and requests His divine assistance, showing Him the reasons there are for her to expect it from His divine hand*


Unable to remedy
the cause of my pain,
I am forced to ask,
"Until when, my Lord,
5      must so much ailment continue?"

"When will I be succored?
For I find myself in dire straits,
assailed from a thousand sides,
by love my breast burnt,
10      and afflicted by your absence.

"Indeed, how many thousands of irritations
and how much bitterness has it cost me
not to have succeeded
in loving you, light of my eyes,[1]
15      as you ought to be loved!

"And seeing that the one who, for your sake,
does not esteem living, displeases you,

[1] García-Nieto points out that the phrase "light of my eyes" appears regularly in the poetry of Fernando de Herrera (1549-1597), a renowned figure of the Sevillan poetic school (ed. *Poesías*, 70 n. 12).

tanto el dolor acrecienta,
que me mata y me lastima
20    y me acaba y me atormenta.

"De mí muy más recatada
ando que de un bravo toro
y, como sobreenterrada,
sobre mí viéndome, lloro,
25    sin hallar descanso en nada.

"Vuelve esos ojos, mi Aurora
y bien de mis bienes todos,
al corazón que te adora,
que, estrechado en tantos modos,
30    sangre en lugar de agua llora.

"Y dame, Rey soberano,
cómo pueda contentarte,
que siempre me saldrá en vano
el procurar agradarte
35    si no me acude tu mano.

"¿Hasta cuándo, mi alegría,
has de mostrar que olvidada
tienes a quien trocaría
la más alta y sublimada
40    dicha por tu compañía?

"Porque aunque en esto no hubiera
para mí más que ser tuya,
fuera de ti, el resto diera

increases the pain so much
that it kills me and wounds me
20     and finishes me and torments me.

"I am much more cautious
with myself than with a fierce bull
and, like one buried to great depths,
above myself, seeing myself, I cry,
25     without finding rest in anything.

"Turn back your eyes, my Aurora
and goodness of all my goods,
unto the one who adores you,
who, pressed in so many ways,
30     blood instead of water weeps.

"And give me, sovereign King,
the means to satisfy you,
for I will ever strain futilely
to try and please you
35     lest your hand assist me.

"Until when, my Joy,
must you show that forgotten
is she who would exchange
the most exalted and sublime
40     fortune for your company?

"For although in this there were nothing
for me, except to be yours,
except for you, I would give all the rest

          por ti solo, o me destruya
45        esa mano justiciera.


          "Y si acaso dilatar
          quisieres de mi gemido
          la pena, sin me escuchar,
          dime, mi gloria, te pido,
50        ¿hasme hasta el fin de olvidar?


          "¿Quién (¡ay fiero pensamiento!)
          osará darte acogida
          en sí ni un solo momento?
          ¡Porque verdugo a la vida
55        serás, y al alma tormento!


          "Mucho menos riguroso,
          sin duda alguna, sería
          del infierno tenebroso
          sufrir mil años, que un día
60        de pesar tan espantoso.


          "Provocado a desecharme
          te hallarás, Señor, si a mí
          a solas quieres mirarme;
          pero, mirándome en Ti,
65        no podrás dejar de amarme.


          "Ya sabes, dulce Bien mío,
          que con mano poderosa
          en un campal desafío

for you alone, or be destroyed
45    by that avenging hand.


    "And if perhaps you should choose
to prolong the pain
of my moans, without heeding me,
tell me, my Glory, I beg you,
50    must you leave me forgotten to the end?


    "Who (oh vicious thought!)
would dare to shelter you
in one's self for a single moment?
For the executioner of life
55    you will be, and torment to the soul!


    "Much less rigorous
it would be, without a doubt,
to suffer a thousand years
of the infernal gloom rather than one day
60    of such heavy grief.


    "Provoked to abandon me
you will find yourself, Lord, if
you wish to look at me alone;
but, looking at me in you,
65    you will not be able to stop loving me.


    "You already know, sweet Goodness of mine,
that with a mighty hand
in a daring battle

te venció Amor y animosa-
70     mente cobró señorío.


"De tu justicia ha tenido
en mi favor mil victorias,
y si tu pecho encendido
tiene, en todas sus historias
75     se hallará bien referido.


"La real grandeza en grosero
sayal trocando, a buscarme
como un pobre ganadero
saliste, que por cobrarme
80     dieras tú tu reino entero.


"Y hallándome que aherrojada
estaba en dura cadena
y ya a muerte condenada,
en ti libraste mi pena
85     por verme de ella librada.


"Y en bienes, vida, y honor,
hasta desnudo expirar,
te hizo ejecutar Amor
porque quisiste pagar
90     por mí de todo rigor.


"Y porque más restaurado
mi reino y cetro perdido
quedase, vituperado

Love conquered you and
70      valiantly gained sovereignty.

     "Over your justice Love has had
a thousand victories in my favor,
and if it has your breast ignited,
in all its tales
75      it will be well referred to.

     "Exchanging royal grandeur
for a vile, coarse cloth to seek me,
like a poor herdsman
you set out, since to gain me
80      you would give your entire kingdom.

     "And finding me bound as I was
in the irons of harsh chains
and already condemned to death,
you charged my pain to yourself
85      to see me freed thereof.

     "And to the point of being naked,
in goods, life, and honor,
Love had you executed,
because you wished to pay
90      for me to the utmost letter of the law.

     "And in order that, more fully restored
my kingdom and scepter, once lost,
would endure, yours was

fue el tuyo y tan abatido
95    que viniste a ser pisado.


      "Pagaron con mil espinas
mi soberbia altiva y vana
tus bellas sienes divinas,
que son (¡bondad soberana!)
100   trazas de amor peregrinas.


      "Él fue quien, aportillada
en ti la muralla fuerte,
dejó con una lanzada
y, con no más que una muerte,
105   hasta Dios llana la entrada."

vituperated and so beaten down
95     that you were eventually trod upon.

"Your lovely, divine temples
paid with a thousand thorns
for my haughty and vain pride,
temples which are (oh supreme goodness!)
100     remarkable signs of love.

"Love was the one who, the mighty wall
having been pierced in You,
left, by means of a single blow,
and with nothing more than one death,
105     the entrance to God wide open."[2]

[2] The hyperbaton, which rises to an intense crescendo in this final stanza, unpacks into the following: "Love was the one who, with you having pierced the mighty wall [of the flesh], left the entrance to God wide open by means of a single blow, with nothing more than one death."

6

*Romance espiritual*

*del testamento de Silva*

Sintiendo Silva de amor
gravemente el alma herida,
y que jamás acostumbra
a herir que deje con vida,
con vida que fuera de Él
vivir pueda un solo día,
empezó a hacer testamento,
y con prisa disponía
de todo lo que hasta allí
esperaba o poseía.

Manda el alma a su Pastor,
a cuyo imperio rendida
está, porque en buena guerra
la ganó estando cautiva,
y al cuerpo con "S" y clavo
un precepto le ponía:

6

*Spiritual Ballad*

### about Silva's Last Will and Testament

[1]Silva, feeling her soul
gravely wounded by love,
which never has the custom
of wounding unless mortally,
5    with a life which, without Him,
can be lived but for one day,
began to write her will,
and with haste she disposed
of everything which until then
10    she hoped for or possessed.

She sends her soul unto her Shepherd,
to whose rule she has yielded,
because in fair war
He won her when she was a captive
15    and upon her body, with an "S" and a nail,
he branded a precept:[2]

---

[1] Carvajal actually wrote her will in 1604, in Valladolid, but she had been contemplating it long before. This ballad mocks the complex laws of inheritance that cost her years of legal struggles, specifically satirizing the *mayorazgo*, the passing of the paternal estate intact to the eldest son. As the poet's treatment of the chaotic world intensifies, she employs intensifying techniques such as anaphora and suggests instability by such means as combining polysyndeton with asyndeton in close proximity. Carvajal anticipates by some years the acute disillusion with the world that eventually dominated Spanish poetic composition in the Baroque period.

[2] The Spanish word "esclavo," 'slave,' originally denominated a white slave of Slavic blood, captured and sold by Catalans in the Middle Ages. Carvajal's etymology derived from the "S" and "clavo" [nail] with which slaves were actually branded. She is among the first Spanish poets to fixate on the lexicon of slavery as a vehicle of upper-class poetic expression.

de que al ama, su señora,
sujeto y sin rebeldía
obedezca humildemente,
20 y él así lo prometía.
  Nombrado ha por heredero
de su loca fantasía
al mundo porque de él hubo
esta hacienda tan de estima,
25 y el mayorazgo heredado
de aquella prosapia antigua
que suele rentar cada año
dos milliones de fatigas:
las unas sobredoradas
30 y llenas de amargo acíbar,
y las otras plateadas
y por de dentro vacías.
Deja a los ricos avaros
el muy rico oro de Tíbar,
35 y a los Señores y Grandes
de vanidad una sima,
y el bajo amor fementido
que a las almas tiraniza,
a los corazones viles
40 que sobre sí le entronizan.
  Las galas manda a las damas
y toda la bizarría:
guantes, ámbar, y pebetes,

that the body unto the soul its lady,
subjected and without rebellion,
would humbly render obedience,
20    and the body thus did promise.
          She has named as heir
of her foolish fancy
the world, for this estate
so esteemed came thereof,
25    and the entailed estate, inherited
from that ancient lineage
which annually draws as interest
two thousand miseries,
some of which are gilded
30    and full of bitter aloe,
and others silver plated
and hollow within.
To wealthy misers she leaves
the Tiber's very rich gold,
35    and to the Lords and Grandees
she leaves a sinkhole of vanity,
and lowly, traitorous love
that tyranizes souls
to the base hearts
40    which enthrone it above themselves.
          She sends her fancy clothes to the ladies
and all her trinkets:
gloves, amber, and joss sticks,

cazoletas y pastillas,
45     fiestas, banquetes, jardines,
faustos, pompas, cortesías.
Entre aquéllos a quien toca,
por no hacerles injusticia,
quiere que se les reparta
50     todo en juro de por vida,
y en esperanzas sin fruto
y en la flor desvanecidas.
Y, en quimeras y designios,
trazas, lisonjas, mentiras,
55     intereses, pretensiones,
temores, melancolías,
correspondencias y amigos
compuestos de mil falsías,
mejora en el tercio y quinto
60     a la gente más lucida.
A los discretos y honrados
que tienen por granjería
el tratar con esta hacienda
y rica mercadería,
65     y al ya nombrado heredero,
deja lo que se le olvida
para que lo dé a quien sabe
que más su amistad codicia.

bowls and beads,[3]
45     festivities, banquets, gardens
splendors, pomp, courtesies.
Among those to whom it is befitting,
so as not to do them an injustice,
she wishes that all this be distributed
50     all by means of a lifelong perpetuity
and fruitless hopes
and withered in the prime of life.
And, in illusions and plots,
designs, bribes, lies,
55     interests, pretensions,
fears, melancholy,
paired relationships and friends
made up of a thousand falsehoods,
she does most excessively favor
60     the most magnificent people.
To the tactful and honored,
who find it is a splendid investment
to deal in this estate
and valuable merchandise,
65     and to the afore-named heir,
she leaves whatever she has left out
so that said heir give it to whomever
it knows most covets its friendship.[4]

---

[3] García-Nieto notes that amber, joss sticks, little bowls and beads were all items used to scent the air (ed. 77, n. 34), similar to today's aroma therapy kits. Amber was also used by Spanish noblewomen specifically to scent gloves, rendered high luxury items by said treatment; Carvajal made gifts of these gloves to English-women she wanted to impress. Perfumes were important items in a cosmetic inventory because bathing was then believed to be unhealthy.

[4] "It" because she had declared her heir to be the world (l. 23).

Y vuelta Silva al Pastor
70   de cuyo amor quedó herida,
le dijo, "Bien de mi gloria,
recibe a Silva, que expira,"
y en sus manos dejó el alma.
Y el Pastor la recibía
75   y con solemnes exequias
Él mismo la deposita
en un glorioso sepulcro
que dentro en su pecho había,
dejando el de sumo olvido
80   que para Silva tenía
el vano mundo engañoso
edificado a gran prisa.
Y el Pastor, muerto de amores,
puso a su esposa querida
85   una letra soberana
que su memoria eterniza,
que dice, "Silva, cual Fénix,
en mil llamas encendida,
yace dichosa y feliz
90   en mí, del mundo escondida."

And Silva said, having turned to the Shepherd
70  whose love had left her wounded,
she said, "Goodness of my glory,
receive Silva, who is dying,"
and in his hands she left her soul.
And the Shepherd received her
75  and with solemn funeral rites
deposits her Himself
in a glorious sepulcher
which there was within his breast,
abandoning the one of absolute oblivion
80  which the vain, deceitful world
had built for Silva
in great haste.
And the Shepherd, having died of love
for his beloved spouse, composed
85  a sovereign epitaph
which renders her memory eternal,
which says, "Silva, like the phoenix,
lit up in a thousand flames,
lies fortunate and happy
90  in me, hidden from the world."

14

*Romance a Cristo Nuestro Señor*

*Del amor que tiene a las almas*

Vuelve tu rendida Silva,
de ansia amorosa apremiada,
los tristes ojos cansados
que no hallan descanso en nada,
5    en busca de tu hermosura,
que cual flecha enherbolada
hizo en mi corazón suerte,
dejando el alma allanada.
Y en señal de posesión
10    pacífica y asentada,
en su más alto homenaje
la real bandera plantada
del amor, con la divisa
más heroica y señalada
15    que hubo en todos sus trofeos
de memoria eternizada,
y en una divina letra
tu condición declarada,
que dice: "Yo a los soberbios
20    hago guerra ensangrentada,
y a los humildes perdono,
gente a mi ley ajustada."
    ¡Oh Amor! Gran fuerza es la tuya,
fuerza, en fin, no limitada,
25    que no osara otra ninguna

14

*Ballad to Christ Our Lord*

*on the Love He has for Our Souls*

Urged by anxious love,
your yielding Silva turns
her sad, weary eyes,
that find no rest in anything,
5      in search of your beauty,
which, like a poisoned arrow,
hit its target in my heart,
leaving my soul pacified.
And [leaving], as a sign of possession,
10    peaceful and steady,
in its highest homage
the royal standard of love
set, with the most heroic
and illustrious motto
15    that there was among all its trophies
of eternal memory,
and in a divine hand
your declared condition
it states: "I wage bloody war
20    against the arrogant
and pardon the humble,
people who live in accordance to my law."
Oh Love! Your power is great,
power, indeed, unlimited,
25    such that no other would dare

intentar, de escarmentada,
esta difícil empresa,
que estaba a ti reservada,
y a mi dichosa ventura,
30    digna de ser celebrada.
Porque ser tu prisionera
y ser tu esclava aherrojada
es reinar, sin duda alguna
y verdad averiguada.

attempt, being forewarned,
this difficult undertaking
which was destined for you
and for my happy fate,
30    worthy of renown.
For to be your prisoner
and to be your fettered slave
is to reign, without a doubt,
and is proven truth.

## 15

*Soneto espiritual de Silva*

*de sentimientos de amor y ausencia profundísimos*

¿Cómo vives, sin quien vivir no puedes?
Ausente, Silva, el alma, ¿tienes vida?
Y el corazón aquesa misma herida
gravemente atraviesa, ¿y no te mueres?
5　　Dime si eres mortal o inmortal eres.
¿Hate cortado Amor a su medida
o forjado, en sus llamas derretida,
que tanto el natural límite excedes?
Vuelto ha tu corazón cifra divina
10　　de extremos mil Amor, en que su mano
mostrar quiso destreza peregrina,
y la fragilidad del pecho humano
en firmísima piedra diamantina,
con que quedó hecho alcázar soberano.

15

*Silva's Spiritual Sonnet*

*on most profound feelings of love and separation*

How do you live, without whom you are unable to live?[1]
With your soul absent, Silva, do you have life?
And that same wound your heart
heavily traverses and you do not perish?
5     Tell me whether you are mortal or immortal you are.
Has Love cut you to his measure
or forged you, melted in his flames,
that you so exceed natural limitations?
Love has turned your heart into a divine cipher
10  of a thousand extremes, in which his hand
desired to show rare dexterity,
    and the fragility of the human breast
into firmest stone as solid as diamond,
with which it became a sovereign castle.

---

[1] The antecedent of "whom," Christ, is understood, but its absence makes the phrase ungrammatical.

18

*Soneto espiritual de Silva*

*Al Santísimo Sacramento*
*En que habla el divino Verbo inmenso con el alma*
*que le está recibiendo de las manos del sacerdote*

De inmenso Amor aqueste abrazo estrecho
recibe, Silva, de tu dulce Amado,
y por la puerta de este diestro lado
éntrate, palomilla, acá en mi pecho.
5      Reposa en el florido y sacro lecho
y abrásate en amor tan abrasado
que hasta que el fuerte nudo haya apretado,
no sea posible quede satisfecho.
Mira cómo te entrego, amiga mía,
10    todo mi ser y alteza sublimada.
Estima aqueste don que amor te ofrece.
Tendrás en mí gloriosa compañía
y entre mis mismos brazos regalada,
gozarás lo que nadie no merece.

18

*Silva's Spiritual Sonnet*

*To the most holy sacrament*
*In which the immense divine Verb speaks with the soul*
*receiving it from the hands of the priest*

Of immense Love this tight embrace
receive, Silva, from your sweet Beloved,
and through the door of this right side
come in, little dove, here to my breast.
5      Repose in the flowery, sacred bed
and burn in love so enflamed
that until the mighty knot be tightened
it is not possible that Love be satisfied.
See how I hand over to you, my companion,
10     all my being and exalted majesty.
Esteem this boon that love offers you.
You will have in me glorious company
and, within my very arms regaled,
delight in that which no one deserves.[1]

---

[1] García Nieto points to the influence of John of the Cross's poetry on this sonnet, evident in mystical symbolism of the dove (the soul), the bed (Christ's breast) and other erotic images (ed. *Poesías* 108)

22

*Romance espiritual de Silva*

*Refiere el esfuerzo con que un alma que ama a Cristo Nuestro*
*Señor se determina a buscarle e irse a Él y, pospuesta*
*toda dificultad, se ofrece a los innumerables trabajos, desamparos,*
*y peleas que se le interpusieren, como bravo mar que, atravesado*
*delante de los ojos, pretende enflaquecer la fortaleza del ánimo,*
*aunque en vano, cuando el amor divino tiene tomada la posesión.*
*Y dice que, así como el fuego del alquitrán se aumenta con el agua,*
*así el amor de Dios recibe gran acrecentamiento con las saladas*
*aguas de las adversidades y enemigas impugnaciones.*
*Llama sirenas del mar a las prosperidades encantadoras*
*y gustos halagüeños de mortífero veneno.*

     Amor, el pecho animoso
de Silva consideraba,
que, cien mil dificultades
rompiendo, al mar se arrojaba.

5       Las apacibles riberas
trueca por aguas saladas,
y contrastando las ondas
con ímpetu, atrás quedaban,
que es de acero, aunque parece
10     de materia delicada.
No teme las tempestades
del mar, ni sus olas bravas,
que van las del corazón
más furiosas y alteradas,

22

*Silva's Spiritual Ballad*

*Telling of the effort with which  a soul that loves Christ Our
Lord determines to seek Him out and go to Him and, leaving behind
all difficulties, offers itself up to the innumerable trials, helplessness
and struggles that might intervene, like a wild sea which, stretched
in front of one's eyes, presumes to weaken the spirit's strength,
although in vain, when divine love has the soul in possession.
And it says that, just as a tar fire flares up with water,
so the love of God is greatly augmented with the salty
waters of adversity and impugnation.
It calls sea sirens all bewitching prosperity
and pleasing delights of lethal venom.*

 

Love was considering

Silva's spirited breast,

who, overcoming a hundred thousand

difficulties, threw herself into the sea.[1]

 

5   She exchanges agreeable shores

for salty waters,

and countering the waves

energetically, behind they remained,

for she is of iron, though she seems

10   made of delicate substance.

She fears not the tempests

of the sea, nor its savage waves,

for those of her heart

are more raging and agitated,

---

[1] Carvajal uses "pecho animoso," 'spirited breast,' as a metonym for herself
and it is the literal subject of ll. 1-10. Since she abandons it in l. 11 (the breast
would not have a heart, but she would), I translate the subject of all verbs as "she."

15 y el fuego hace al elemento
húmedo grandes ventajas,
cuando como el de aquitrán
se acrecienta con el agua.
No la encantan las sirenas
20 con su voz fingida y falsa,
porque la tiene el Amor
toda absorta y traspasada,
cuyos cuidados destierran
todos los demás del alma.
25 Y Silva, sólo el que lleva
(que de sí no se acordaba),
es de cuándo podrá verse
en alta mar engolfada,
porque desde allí hasta el puerto
30 adonde su Bien la aguarda,
casi siempre se camina
viento en popa y mar bonanza.
Y el Dios de Amor, admirado,
que de estarlo muestras daba,
35 del prodigioso suceso
el fin dichoso aguardaba.

15    and fire has great advantages

over the humid element,[2]

as when the flame of lit tar

rises up with water.

Sirens do not enchant her

20    with their feigned and false voice,[3]

because Love has her

completely absorbed and transfixed,

[Love] whose cares exile

all others from the soul.

25    And the only one that Silva bears

(for she was unheedful of herself),

is for when she will see herself

surrounded by the high seas,

because the distance from there to the port

30    where her Dearest awaits her,

is almost always traveled

with the wind and smooth sailing.

And the God of Love, amazed

at the prodigious event,

35    for He gave signs of being so,

awaited the happy end.[4]

---

[2] The reference is to water, one of the four elements.

[3] Of the sirens, figures from classical mythology (specifically *The Odyssey* XII), Covarrubias's 1611 dictionary offers a fanciful definition, "Poets feigned that they were sea nymphs, the top half of their bodies being enticing women, the lower half being fish, and that with the softness of their song they hypnotized sailors, and, climbing up onto their ships, ate them" (897). More typical is the myth that their song lured sailors to jump into the sea and drown. Either version makes these figures an apt symbol for worldly temptations, and in her application Carvajal rejects the traditional association between the Sirens and women's enticing, deadly allure to men.

[4] The beginning and ending of this poem enclose Silva's quest in a male gaze, interesting because early modern women (and modern women) frequently represent themselves as visual objects; see John Berger's *Ways of Seeing*.

31

*Romance espiritual de Silva*

*en que refiere el tiempo y modo con que fue Nuestro Señor ganando
el alma y robando la voluntad para sí,
con lo demás que a esto sigue*

Madre, siendo niña
me prendió el Amor;
con cadenas de oro
presa me dejó.
5    Pensé se burlaba,
y Él se me rió
y me dijo, "Silva,
yo soy tu Señor."
No sentí su fuego
10    aunque abrasador;
después de mayor,
ahora bien le siento
que la burla y juego
veras me salió!
15    Ya no soy de nadie
sino del Amor,
que con fuertes lazos
así me enlazó;
y son sus lazadas
20    de tanto primor,
que atando desatan,
y bien lo sé yo.

## 31

*Silva's Spiritual Ballad*

*which tells of the time and way in which Our Lord won
her soul and stole her will for Himself,
with other events that followed thereafter*

> Mother, when I was little[1]
> Love seized me;
> with chains of gold
> He left me captive.
> 5 I thought He was joking
> and He laughed at me
> and said to me, "Silva,
> I am your Lord."
> I didn't feel His fire
> 10 although it was scorching;
> now that I am older,
> I feel it perfectly well,
> for the jest and the game
> turned out to be in earnest!
> 15 And now I belong to no one
> except to Love,
> who with powerful bonds
> so bound me,
> and His love knots are
> 20 so exquisite,
> that upon binding, they release,
> and I know it well.

---

[1] The poetic setting of a young girl complaining of love to her mother dates back to the earliest lyric poetry on the Iberian peninsula, the *jarchas*, from the eleventh century.

Con su S y clavo
señalada estoy,
25 señales de gloria
con que me adornó.
Volvió a mí sus ojos,
y de ellos salió
fuego vivo, ardiente,
30 que a Silva abrasó;
abrasóle a Silva
alma y corazón.
Y arcos imagino
que sus ojos son,
35 porque una saeta
de ellos despidió.
Asestóla al alma,
y en el blanco dio;
quedé tan herida
40 que muero de amor,
y el dolor que siento
es grave dolor.
Templarle, mi madre.
nadie podrá, no,
45 que único remedio
de él es mi Señor;
sólo sanar puede
la mano que hirió.

With His "S" and His nail
I am marked,
25    tokens of glory
with which He adorned me.
He turned His eyes to me,
and from them leapt
live, ardent fire
30    that inflamed Silva;
the fire inflamed Silva,
soul and heart.
And I imagine
that His eyes are bows,
35    because he released
an arrow from them.
He aimed it at my soul
and hit the target;
I was left so wounded
40    that I am dying of love,
and the pain that I feel
is a grievous pain.
Ease it, my Mother.
no one can, no,
45    for its only remedy
is my Lord;
only the hand can cure
that made the wound.

## 35

### *Romance espiritual de Silva*

*Declara el señorío y fuerza de amor, considerada en el mismo Jesús,
y cuáles han de ser los pechos en que Él ha de tomar posesión y
vivir de asiento*

<br>

Absoluto Dueño
del pecho rendido,
que todo lo allanas,
siendo obedecido
5    con tal diligencia,
que jamás ha habido
rey que se te iguale
en cuantos han sido;
que eres Rey de reyes,
10    y Dios, aunque niño;
conquistas las almas
por modo no visto.
Tu arco certero
jamás en vacío
15    despidió sus flechas,
ni erró ningún tiro.
Y el pecho a que asestas
siempre es escogido,
animoso y sabio,

## 35

### *Silva's Spiritual Ballad*

*It sets forth the dominion and force of love pondered in Jesus Himself, and how those hearts must be that He will possess and in which He will repose*

[1]Absolute Lord
of the yielding breast,
who resolves all
upon being obeyed
5     with such diligence
that never has there been
a king to equal You
among all the kings of time;
for You are King of kings,
10    and God, although a child;
you conquer souls
by a means unknown.
Your well-aimed bow
never into a void
15    released its arrows,
nor erred any shot.
And the breast at which you aim
is always select,
brave and wise,

[1] Like Poem 31, this is a *romancillo*, a "little ballad," consisting of a six-syllable line that rhymes in the final two vowels of the uneven lines. The poem intensifies and socializes the calming order of God as assured in Teresa of Ávila's famous verses, "Nada te turbe" ("Let nothing trouble you," III: 386). Carvajal's light-hearted play on Jesus's and Cupid's comparative features as gods of love makes this poem particularly successful.

20     constante y de brío,
porque te desplace
el que es abatido,
cobarde, indiscreto,
y en el amar tibio,
25     que, aunque pequeñuelo,
eres muy sabido
y, aunque delicado,
de nadie vencido.

20      constant and courageous,
for you are displeased
by the one who is dispirited,
cowardly, tactless,
and lukewarm in love,
25      for, although small,
you are very well learned
and, although delicate,
conquered by none.

43

*Soneto espiritual*

*de afectos de amor encendidísimo*
*y deseos de martirio*

Esposas dulces, lazo deseado
ausentes trances, hora victoriosa,
infamia felicísima y gloriosa,
holocausto en mil llamas abrasado:
     di, Amor, ¿por qué tan lejos apartado
se ha de mí aquesta suerte venturosa,
y la cadena amable y deleitosa
en dura libertad se me ha trocado?
     ¿Ha sido, por ventura, haber querido
que la herida, que al ama penetrada
tiene con dolor fuerte, desmedido,
     no quede socorrida ni curada,
y, el afecto aumentado y encendido,
la vida a puro amor sea desatada?

43

*Spiritual Sonnet*

*on the Affection of a most enflamed love
and desires for martyrdom*

Sweet manacles, coveted noose,
trials now gone, victorious hour,
delightful and glorious infamy,
holocaust burnt in a thousand flames:
    tell me, Love, why has this fortunate fate
drifted so far from me,
and the pleasant and pleasureful chain
turned into harsh freedom for me?
    Has it been, perhaps, due to my having desired
that the wound of my penetrated soul,
with strong, excessive pain
    be neither treated nor cured
and that, with increased and ignited affection,
life be unbound to pure love?

## 44

*Soneto espiritual de Silva*

*Para una señora grave, a quien ella amaba mucho y deseaba verla
muy ocupada en cosas espirituales, porque era muy para ello,
y no derramada en ocupaciones y correspondencias humanas,
aunque con buen fin*

¿Cómo, di, bella Amari, tu cuidado
estimas en tan poco, que, olvidada
de Quien con tanto amor eres amada,
te empleas en el rústico ganado?
5        ¿Háte la vana ocupación comprado?
¿Qué nigromántica arte embelesada
te trae, y de tu bien tan trascordada?
¡Ay, alevosa fe!, ¡ay, pecho helado!
        Vuelve, Amari; repara que perdiendo
10        vas de Amor el camino; digo, atajo.
Y ése que llevas, ancho y deleitoso,
        suele mañosamente ir encubriendo,
entre las florecillas y debajo
de verde hierba, el paso peligroso.

44

*Silva's Spiritual Sonnet*

*For an important lady, whom she loved greatly and desired to see
very devoted to spiritual things, for she was quite inclined to it,
and not spent in worldly occupations and affairs,
although for good causes*

Tell me why it is, lovely Amari, that you esteem
your own care so little that, forgetful
of the One who loves you with so much love,
you busy yourself with your rustic herd?
5  Have you been bought by futile activity?
What arts of necromancy hold you
spellbound and forgetful of what is good for you?
Ah, treacherous faith!, Ah, frozen breast!
  Look back, Amari; observe that you are straying from
10 the path of Love; I mean, the narrow path.
And that one you are on, wide and pleasureful,
  often cleverly disguises,
among little flowers and beneath
the green grass, the perilous way.

45

*Liras de Silva*

*a los divinos ojos de Nuestro Señor*

Al alma que te adora
vuelve los ojos claros, Cristo amado,
que más que en sí, en ti mora,
y todo su cuidado
5   en sólo tu mirar está cifrado.

Ojos restauradores
de vida, que la dan de amor matando,
absolutos señores
de cuanto están mirando,
10   inmensa majestad representando;

puro y vivo traslado
de todo el bien que encierra el alto cielo,
que tras el delicado
disfraz de humano velo,
15   hacen rico y dichoso a todo el suelo;

sacros soles dorados,
cuya amable presencia poderosa
los males desterrados
deja, y su victoriosa
20   luz deshace la niebla tenebrosa;

45

*Silva's Liras*

*to Our Lord's divine eyes*

[1]Unto the soul that adores you
turn your bright eyes, beloved Christ,
which more than in itself, in you dwells,
and all its attention
5    is fixed on your gaze only.

Eyes restorative
of life, which give the soul love by killing,
absolute lords
of all they behold,
10    representing immense majesty;

pure and vivid image
of all the good that heaven bears
which behind the delicate
disguise of a human veil
15    bring wealth and abundance to all below;

sacred golden suns
whose agreeable, powerful presence
leaves evils banished
and their victorious
20    light clears the sinister fog.

[1] The *lira* is a poetic composition of high renaissance culture, formed by two 11-syllable lines and three heptasyllabic lines that rhyme aBabB. Invented by the Italian Bernardo Tasso (1493-1569), it was introduced into Spanish poetry by Garcilaso de la Vega (1501-1536).

rara y suma lindeza,
y el *Nihil ultra* de la excelsa mano,
adonde con destreza
juntó un mirar humano
25    con un mirar divino y soberano;

depósitos divinos
do está toda mi gloria atesorada;
espejos cristalinos,
vista dulce, agraciada
30    dorado día, aurora arrebolada;

jardines celestiales,
ameno paraíso deleitoso,
luceros orientales,
refugio venturoso,
35    puerto en la tempestad maravilloso:

en esos ojos bellos
todo su bien librado el alma mía
tiene, y colgada de ellos
vive, que no podría
40    de otro modo vivir ni un solo día.

En cuanto me ha importado,
¿qué para mí no son, o no hayan sido?,
¿o qué en ellos buscado
de bien he, o pretendido,
45    que vano o engañoso haya salido?

Decid, luces serenas,
¿quién de ese dulce revolver mirando

rare and extreme loveliness,<br>
and the *Nihil ultra*[2] of the sublime hand,<br>
where a human gaze<br>
dexterously joined with<br>

25     a gaze divine and sovereign;

divine storehouses<br>
in which all my glory is amassed;<br>
crystalline mirrors,<br>
sweet, pleasing sight,<br>

30     gilded day, crimson dawn;

celestial gardens,<br>
pleasant, delightful paradise,<br>
eastern morning stars<br>
blessed refuge,<br>

35     wondrous port in a storm:

in those beautiful eyes<br>
all the goodness of my soul<br>
is delivered and lives dependent<br>
on them, where otherwise it<br>

40     could not live even a single day.

Of all that has mattered to me,<br>
what are they not for me, or have not been?<br>
Or what good in them<br>
have I sought, or aspired to,<br>

45     that has turned out vain or deceitful?

Tell me, serene illuminations,<br>
who turned into noose and chains<br>

---

[2] Latin for "beyond which there is nothing."

lazos hizo y cadenas,
con que el alma enlazando,
50 sutilmente la van aprisionando?

Las hazañas famosas
de Amor, y sus victorias no imitadas
siempre más venturosas
fueron y señaladas,
55 desde ese Alcázar Real ejecutadas.

De tanta hermosura
la fuerza intensa, aún no experimentada
con dichosa ventura,
en mirarla ocupada
60 viene a quedar suspensa y transportada.

Y habiendo Amor robado
mi corazón, que en nada resistía,
le vi que, remontado
por el aire subía,
65 y en tus ojos con él se me escondía,

por alcaide celoso,
en medio el pecho, en su lugar dejando
un afecto fogoso,
que en llamas abrasando
70 le está, y el homenaje a Amor guardando.

the act of gazing upon that sweet glance
such that, ensnaring the soul,
50      they subtly, slowly imprison it?[3]

Love's famous deeds
and inimitable victories
were ever more fortunate
and distinguished
55      being executed from that Royal Palace.

Of such beauty
the intense power, not yet tested,
with happy fortune
engaged in gazing upon it
60      is eventually suspended and transported.

And, with Love having stolen
my heart, which resisted not at all,
I saw He was soaring
up through the air
65      and in your eyes hid my heart on me,

like a vigilant castellan,
leaving in its place in the core of my breast
an ardent affection
which is burning it in flames,
70      and guarding the watchtower for Love.[4]

---

[3] Such turns of phrase, which employ violent images to represent loving acts, are the hallmark of Carvajal's style.

[4] *Homenaje* here has a military meaning: "the greatest tower of a fortress or stronghold, where the castellan or keeper solemnly swears fidelity, according to the law" (*Tesoro* 642).

## 46

### *Romance espiritual de Silva*

Silva a Nise, entre otras cosas
que con ella en gusto hablaba,
determinó de contarle
una que, aunque fue soñada,
5  no era poco misteriosa,
a su Señor aplicada:

"Bien conoces," dijo, "a Amari,
Amari mi prima hermana,
iguales en la amistad,
10  en los años y crianza;
no en las suertes, porque han sido
de todo en todo contrarias.

"Soñaba, pues, que yo y ella,
de nuestra antigua morada
15  salíamos una tarde,
del gran calor apremiadas,
— al tiempo que el claro Febo
apriesa se desviaba
del horizonte, y la noche
20  clara, fresca y sosegada,

46

*Silva's Spiritual Ballad*

[1]Among other things that Silva
spoke with pleasure about to Nise,
was something she decided to tell her
which, although she had dreamt it,
5    was not a little mysterious,
when interpreted with thoughts of her Lord.

"You know Amari well," she said,
"Amari my cousin,
with whom I share friendship,
10    age, and our youthful past;
although not our fates, for they have been
completely opposite in every way.

"I dreamt, then, that she and I
from our former dwelling
15    went out one day,
driven by the great heat,
  — at the time of day when Phoebus
was quickly steering away
from the horizon, and the night,
20    clear, cool, and calm,

---

[1] Dream works are relatively common among early modern women poets, who find in this poetic tradition a means to amplify the significance of their experiences and opinions by endowing them with cosmic attendance. See, for example, Marguerite de Navarre's *Dialogue en forme de vision nocturne* and Sor Juana Inés de la Cruz's *Sueño*. In Carvajal's poem, Amari represents María Hurtado de Mendoza, Carvajal's cousin and companion of youth, who married the Marqués de la Guardia and lived the secular life of a noblewoman; hence the contrast Carvajal draws between her own life and María's.

sucediendo, al alto cielo,
su vistosa y turquesada
color, de cien mil diamantes,
con arte y primor bordaba —,
25    a las riberas umbrosas
de fresca hierba adornadas,
adonde me parecía
que, junto a nuestra cabaña,
gozando del fresco viento
30    conmigo Amari en pie estaba.
Y de la callada noche
y soledad convidadas,
con un profundo silencio
los ojos consideraban,
35    a veces el prado ameno,
de anchura y belleza extraña,
a veces, las cristalinas
del Duero profundas aguas,
donde, como en claro espejo,
40    dentro de ellas se mostraba
la luz de una gran estrella,
en todo trasordinaria,
la cual en un punto vimos
que el puesto desamparaba,
45    y, como rayo ligero,
del cielo en la tierra daba.

following, unto the high heavens,

its bright and turquoise-shaded

color, of a hundred thousand diamonds,

was artfully and delicately embroidering —,[2]

25      to the shady riverbanks,

adorned with cool grass,

where it seemed to me

that, next to our hut,[3]

enjoying the cool wind,

30      Amari was standing beside me.

And, by the hushed night

and solitude invited,

with a profound silence

our eyes considered,

35      at times, the agreeable meadow,

wide and of extraordinary beauty,

at times, the crystalline,

deep waters of the Duero

where, as if in a clear mirror,

40      within them was displayed

the light of a great star

in every way beyond the ordinary,

which we saw suddenly

abandoning its place

45      and, like a weightless lightning bolt,

heading from heaven to earth.

---

[2] Phoebus is the sun. Unraveling the hyperbaton, these lines render: "and the clear, cool, and calm night following [the day] was artfully and delicately embroidering its bright and turquoise-shaded color unto the high heavens of a hundred thousand diamonds."

[3] "Cabaña," 'hut,' is the standard dwelling place of literary shepherdesses and shepherds, although Carvajal obviously refers to her uncle's place in Almazán, by which the Duero river flowed.

Y apartada un grande trecho,
de la tierra levantada,
divina gloria influyendo,
50     se acercó de un salto a entrambas.
Y absortas en tal suceso,
al tercer asalto, asestaba,
Nise, en medio de mi pecho,
y dentro de él se me entraba.
55     Su luz del todo ocultando,
quedó en el pecho encerrada;
y no sé a cuál de las dos
dejó más maravillada
y atenta a la superficie,
60     con la pastoril zamarra
cubierta, que de cortina
sirvió y sirve a gloria tanta.

"En esto desperté y vime
del caso y historia rara
65     lejos, y en sólo mi Bien
el alma toda ocupada,
cuya ausencia me traía
de lo demás olvidada.
El sueño pasó por sueño;
70     y, estando bien descuidada,
me vino, Nise, un recado

And a great distance away,
lifted from the earth,
infusing divine glory,
50  it approached us both in one leap.
And enrapt in such an event,
upon the third leap it aimed,
Nise, at the center of my breast,
and entered within me.[4]
55  Hiding its light completely,
it remained locked in my breast;
and I know not which one of us
it left most amazed
and attentive to the surface
60  covered by pastoral garb
which, as a curtain,
served and serves so much glory.

"At this point I awakened and found myself
from the incident and odd story
65  removed, and my soul completely occupied
in only my Dearest,
whose absence left me
in oblivion of all else.
The dream passed as a dream;
70  and being quite unprepared,
a message came to me, Nise,

---

[4] Women mystics of the Christian tradition often employ such images of penetration by the divinity to express union, using what twentieth-century readers call phallic terms. Such, for example, would be Teresa of Ávila's famous encounter with an arrow-bearing angel: "I saw in his hands a large golden dart and at the end of the iron tip there appeared to be a little fire. It seemed to me this angel plunged the dart several times into my heart and that it reached deep within me" (*Life* 30:13).

que mi Señor me enviaba,
diciendo que aparejase
mi pecho para morada
75 suya, porque desde luego,
por suya la señalaba.
Y ya ha dos años cumplidos
que, casi cada mañana,
cuando de su Alcázar sale
80 y acá a nuestra sierra baja,
en este albergue pajizo
de la que más que a sí le ama
entra, y le deja hecho cielo
y hecha también diosa el alma."

that my Lord sent to me,
telling me to prepare
my breast as His dwelling,
75    because in that instant,
He was marking it as His.
And now, two full years later,
almost every morning,
when He emerges from His Castle
80    and comes down here to our lowly hills,
into this straw dwelling
belonging to her who loves Him more than herself,
He enters, and leaves it transformed into heaven,
and rendered likewise a goddess her soul."

*Compañía de la soberana Virgen María, Nuestra Señora*

*Instrucción espiritual*

1. Viendo, mis caras hermanas, que Dios Nuestro Señor os ha traído (como parece) a mi compañía, con deseos de entregaros del todo a Él en la manera de vida más religiosa que os sea posible mediante su divina asistencia, que espero suplirá mis deméritos, he resuelto ordenaros aquí un modo de proceder y distribución de tiempo que procuraréis ejecutar con la mayor puntualidad y exacción que os permitiere el corto número de personas y estrechura de casa y otras dificultades que, como veis, no poco nos impiden. Para todas las que se os opusieran, idos disponiendo con gran dilatación de ánimo y resignadísimo corazón en la Majestad de Dios, pidiéndole con clamores, de día y de noche, su santísimo amor y gracia tan eficaz que venga a serle vuestra vida y muerte, pura y aceptable ofrenda a su mayor gloria y salvación de las almas de vuestra patria, necesitada de espirituales ayudas en el grado que sabéis. ¡Ojalá rematásemos nuestro camino con violenta y dichosa muerte por la confesión de la santa fe católica!

2. Antes de pasar adelante, quiero brevemente exhortaros a un estrecho vínculo de caridad y amor con que deseo os unáis, de suerte que no se pueda hallar más que un corazón entre todas, despidiendo, muy al principio, con toda diligencia cuanto pudiere entibiaros. Y para alentaros a ésta y otras heroicas virtudes, acordaos de aquella edad dorada de quien nos quedó escrito: *Multitudinis autem credentium erat cor unum, et anima una.* De donde redunda y nace notable hermosura de exteriores acciones: *"Ecce quam*

## Society of the Sovereign Virgin Mary, Our Lady[1]

### Spiritual Instruction

1. Seeing, my dear sisters, that God Our Lord has brought you (as it seems) into my company, desiring to turn yourselves over completely to Him in the most religious way of life possible for you through His divine presence, which I hope will compensate for my faults, I have resolved to set forth here a means of proceeding and a schedule that you will endeavor to carry out as precisely and exactly as possible, given your small number and the limitations of the house and other difficulties which, as you have seen, impede you more than a little. In all the difficulties that set themselves before you, proceed with great expansion of your souls and a heart most resigned to the Majesty of God, begging Him with cries by day and night for His most holy love and grace, so efficient that He come to be your life and death, a pure and acceptable offering to His greater glory and the salvation of the souls of your country, needy of spiritual assistance to the degree that you are aware. Would that our road might end with a violent and fortunate death for the confession of the holy Catholic faith!

2. Before going on, I wish briefly to exhort you to the close bond of charity and love with which I desire you be united to each other, such that there be but one heart among you all, releasing with all diligence, from the very beginning, anything that might temper it. And to encourage you to this and other heroic virtues, recall that golden age of which the following was left us in writing: "*Multitudinis autem credentium erat cor unum, et anima una.*"[2] From which a notable beauty of our outer actions redounds and is born: "*Ecce quam*

---

[1] This document shows a marked structural similarity to Teresa of Ávila's Constitutions (III, 319-33). The first section, however, in which Carvajal addresses her "dear sisters" directly, breaks with her earlier vow to address everyone formally (see Intro. to Letters), while signaling the intimacy she had attained with her companions.

[2] "And the multitude of them that believed were of one heart and of one soul" (Acts 4:32).

*bonum et jucundum habitare fratres in unum.*" Y pues los católicos de Inglaterra se hallan en el estado de los de la primitiva Iglesia en cuanto a persecución de fe, imiten sus sagrados ejemplos, unión y suma paciencia en inmensos trabajos y dificultades, que así se fue aumentando y ensanchando la santa Iglesia católica.

3. Y porque con dificultad se conservará esta conformidad de ánimos y gran perfección sin particular cabeza y gobierno, a cuya voluntad se reduzcan las demás, de suerte que pueda enderezar hasta las más menudas acciones vuestras, conviene que, en nombre y lugar de la soberanísima Virgen María Nuestra Señora, que será vuestra más dulcísima y especial Superiora y Madre de misericordia, tengáis siempre señalada entre vuestras hermanas una de más aprobada virtud, prudencia y edad conveniente a quien obedecer, amar y respetar en todo. Y confiad que la invisible dirección de la Santísima Virgen guiará la dirección visible a mayor gloria de Dios.

4. Elegida superiora, lo primero a que acudirá sea a señalaros confesor y espiritual padre, suyo y vuestro, de asiento, si ya no le tuviereis cual conviene, a quien daréis muy particular cuenta de vuestras conciencias y espíritu con toda llaneza y verdad. Respetadle y obedecedle, no como a hombre, sino como a quien Dios os ha puesto en su lugar. Ya sabéis la importancia de esto y el desmedro y peligro en que pone el alma lo contrario.

5. Adorné con no menos rico y dichoso nombre vuestra pobre congregación, llamándola "Compañía de la soberana virgen María Nuestra Señora," el cual nombre y título se conservará siempre. Su imagen tendréis en eminente lugar en el altar del oratorio y encima del de la superiora, en todos los que le tocan, y ella dejará su primer puesto vacío, en señal de la suma reverencia y respeto debido a esta celestial Señora.

6. Vuestro traje debía ser muy religioso. Y ahora es fuerza que sea templado, con lo que pide haber de salir necesariamente fuera de casa, a tantos ojos, enemigos de demostraciones religiosas, pero mezclada esa prudencia con espíritu y ejemplo santo, evitando

*bonum et jucundum habitare fratres in unum.*"[3] And since the English Catholics find themselves in the state of the primitive Church as regards the persecution of the faith, imitate their holy examples, their oneness and patience in immense trials and difficulties, for in this way the holy Catholic Church grew and expanded.

3. And because you will maintain this conformity of wills and great perfection with difficulty without a single head and leadership, to whose will that of the others might submit, such that she can rectify even your most minuscule actions, it behooves you to have, in the name and place of the most sovereign Virgin Mary Our Lady, who will be your most sweet and special superior and Mother of Mercy, ever chosen from among your sisters one of the most unanimously proven virtue, prudence and appropriate age, whom you might obey, love, and respect in all things. And trust that the invisible direction of the Most Holy Virgin will guide your visible direction to the greater glory of God.

4. A superior having been elected, let the first thing to which she attend be the selection of a confessor and spiritual Father for herself and for you, a prudent man, in the event that you should not already have someone appropriate, to whom you will render a most complete account of your conscience and spirit with all straightforwardness and truth. Respect him and obey him, not as a man, but rather as one whom God has put in His place. You already know how important this is and how any other arrangement can deteriorate and endanger the soul.

5. I adorned your poor congregation with no less a rich and fortunate name, calling it "The Society of the Sovereign Virgin Mary Our Lady," which name and title will be ever preserved. You will maintain Her image in an eminent place on the altar of the oratory and above that of the Mother Superior, in all places which are Her due, and she [the Mother Superior] will leave Her first seat vacant, as a sign of the maximum reverence and respect due to this heavenly Lady.[4]

6. Your dress should be very religious. And for the time being, it must necessarily be moderate, since you must go out of the house, to the sight of so many eyes, enemies of religious demonstrations, but with this moderation being mixed with holy spirit and example, care-

---

[3] "Behold how good and how pleasant it is for brethren to dwell together in unity!" (Ps. 133:1).

[4] Meaning that the Virgin was symbolically occupying the seat in the oratory usually reserved for the Mother Superior.

del todo, con cuidado, cualquier pequeña cosa que tire a vanidad o curiosidad.

7. La poca firmeza con que se puede asentar nuestro modo de vida en tan turbulento e inconstante mar como es el presente estado de Inglaterra, me ha hecho dudar algo en cuanto a los votos de obediencia, pobreza, y castidad. Y, en fin, juzgo que no es bien defraudaros del gran mérito que os pueden causar, y ni pienso estaréis quietas sin ellos, ni sé cómo podrán ser bien reducidas voluntades varias a conformidad de vida perfecta con menos eficaz freno que el voto de estrecha obediencia. A la pureza del alma y cuerpo os habéis mostrado inclinadas con suma estima y amor. Y en cuanto a la santa pobreza, os deja ya convidadas el evangelista San Lucas, prosiguiendo a lo que os apunté, sin casi poderse dividir, a mi parecer. Dice así: "*Multitudinis autem credentium erat cor unum, et anima una; nec quisquam, eorum quae possidebat aliquid suum esse dicebat, sed erant illis omnia communia.*" Y primero, en el capítulo 2: "*Omnes etiam qui credebant, erant pariter, et habebant omnia communia; possessiones, et substantias vendebant, et dividebant illa omnibus, prout cuique opus erat.*" Y advertid que entre ellos había gran número sujeto al yugo del matrimonio y puestos en dificultades de persecución de fe. Y, sobre todo, se animaban con los consejos evangélicos, en que se sirvió Cristo Nuestro Señor declararnos su mayor gusto y contentamiento.

8. Sobre aqueste presupuesto, sin temor, y con gran confianza en la majestad de Dios Nuestro Señor, haréis los tres votos: de estrecha obediencia, pobreza sin propio, y castidad, añadiendo un cuarto voto de muy especial obediencia y reverencia, aliende y demás de la que es debida de los fieles católicos, a la Santidad del romano pontífice Paulo V y a todos sus sucesores, canónicamente elegidos en la apostólica silla de San Pedro. Es bien hacer mayor esfuerzo y resistencia contra las herejías de nuestro tiempo, en aquella parte do ellas se esfuerzan más a batir la muralla de la santa Iglesia católica.

fully and completely avoiding even the smallest thing that might lean toward vanity or fussiness.

7. The little stability with which our way of life can be established in such a turbulent and inconstant sea as is the present state in England has made me have doubts regarding the vows of obedience, poverty, and chastity. And, in the end, I have decided that it is not good to deny you the great merit they can bring you, and neither do I believe you will be settled without them, nor do I know how a variety of wills can be reduced to conformity with the perfect life with a less effective bridle than the vow of strict obedience. You have shown yourselves to be inclined to purity of soul and body with great esteem and love. And as for holy poverty, the evangelist St. Luke invites you thereto, following that upon which I remarked above almost without point of distinction, in my opinion. He says, "*Multitudinis autem credentium erat cor unum, et anima una; nec quisquam, eorum quae possidebat aliquid suum esse dicebat, sed erant illis omnia communia.*" And earlier, in Chapter 2: "*Omnes etiam qui credebant, erant pariter, et habebant omnia communia. Possessiones, et substantias vendebant, et dividebant illa omnibus, prout cuique opus erat.*"[5] And note that among them there were many subjected to the yoke of matrimony and in difficulties arising from the persecution of the faith. And above all, they cheered each other with evangelical counsel, through which Christ Our Lord was served to reveal his greatest pleasure and contentment to us.

8. On this supposition, without fear, and with great confidence in the majesty of God Our Lord, you will take three vows: of strict obedience, poverty without individual goods, and chastity, adding a fourth and very special vow of obedience and reverence, above and beyond that required of all faithful Catholics, to the Holiness of the Roman pontificate Paul V and all of his successors, elected by canonical process to the apostolic seat of St. Peter.[6] One does well to make the greatest effort and resistance against the heretics of our time in that place where the most vigorous effort is made to batter the walls of the holy Catholic Church.

---

[5] "And the multitude of them that believed were of one heart and of one soul; neither said any of them that ought of the things which he possessed was his own; but they had all things common"; "And all that believed were together, and had all things common. And sold their possessions and goods, and parted them to all men, as every man had need" (Acts 4:32; 2:44-45).

[6] This loud echo of the fourth Jesuit vow had particular relevance in England, where the authority of the Pope was the major distinction between the Catholic Church and the Anglican.

9. Vuestra vida ha de ser en común, y ninguna ha de poseer cosa en particular como propia, sino el uso de las que hubiere necesidad, concedido por la superiora, a cuyo arbitrio queda el juzgar cuánta sea la necesidad de cada una, habiendo primero oído con grande benignidad lo que de sí le quisieren decir. Y de sí misma, cuidará siempre de cuanto advirtiere tocar la salud y consuelo de todas. No os parezca la vida común dura, porque no os halláis en formadas casas de religión de tierras católicas. Considerad el ejemplar que os he puesto delante de los ojos. Ni [os parezca dura] el vivir con gran pobreza, del todo arrojadas en los brazos de la divina providencia. Si amáis de veras a Dios, que por vuestro amor se hizo pobre, y bajó hasta el más ínfimo grado de necesidad y desprecio, antes seguiréis sus pasos codiciosamente, y el ánimo y gallardía de los que os van delante condenará cualquier tardanza vuestra, y [la] hará insufrible, por temor de no caer en aquella severa reprensión de Moisés al pueblo de Israel: "*Generatio perversa et infideles filii.*" Tomaréis el consejo del apóstol San Pedro: "*Christo igitur passo in carne, et vos eadem cogitatione armamini.*" Armados con este pensamiento contra toda deslealtad a Dios. Y sobre esto velaréis con cien ojos atentos, para no consentir que en vuestro corazón entre ni salga cosa de tal calidad, aunque os costase contento y vida, que por Dios nada se pierde, antes se trueca en mejor.

10. Pondréis el posible cuidado en andar en presencia de Nuestro Señor ordinariamente, por ser manantial de grandes bienes. Y creed que, al paso que aprovecharéis en esto, crecerán vuestras espirituales riquezas. Amaréis y estimaréis en mucho los ratos retirados de oración, procurándolos fuera de las horas que están señaladas, pero no de manera que hagáis ni un solo punto falta a la obediencia ni a la caridad de las hermanas, ni a otra cosa alguna de las que se han de hacer en casa, en que podáis ayudar y estén a vuestro cargo. Emplearéis el tiempo de la oración bien, aunque os cueste trabajo y dura pelea contra pensamientos vagos, que, como sanguijuelas, chupan toda la sustancia y fuerza que en este santísimo ejercicio ha de recibir el alma, y la debilitan y secan notablemente.

11. No os paguéis de ternuras y gustos poco macizos y sólidos, mas cuando la devoción sensible os desampare, súplalo

9. Your life should be communal, and none of you should possess anything individually as her own, rather for the use of whomever might need it, conceded by the Mother Superior, whose judgment determines how great each one's need is, having first listened with great kindness to whatever they might care to tell her about themselves. And on her own she will be on the lookout for whatever might be appropriate for the health and consolation of all. Let communal life not seem harsh to you because you are not in established houses of religion in Catholic lands. Consider the exemplary life that I have put before your eyes. Nor should living in great poverty, completely cast into the arms of divine providence, [seem harsh either]. If you truly love God, who became poor for love of you, and lowered Himself to the most wretched degree of need and disdain, you will follow industriously in his footsteps sooner, and the spirit and gallantry of those who have gone before you will condemn any reticence of yours and will make it unbearable, for fear of falling into that severe reprehension that Moses gave to the people of Israel: "*Generatio perversa et infideles filii.*"[7] You will take the advice of the apostle St. Peter: "*Christo igitur passo in carne, et vos eadem cogitatione armamini.*"[8] Arm yourselves with this thought against all disloyalty for God. And you will keep watch for this with one hundred attentive eyes, so as not to consent that anything of such quality either enter or leave your heart, though it cost you happiness and life, since for God nothing is lost, but rather is exchanged for the better.

10. You will take all possible care to walk ever in the presence of Our Lord, for it is a fount of great benefits. And believe that, to the extent that you take advantage of this, your spiritual riches will grow. You will greatly love and esteem those moments of retirement in prayer, seeking them beyond the indicated hours, but not such that you depart the slightest from obedience of or charity toward your sisters, nor anything else that must be done around the house in which you can help and which are your responsibility. You will employ your time in prayer well, although it may cost you work and a difficult battle against vague thoughts which, like leeches, suck all the substance and power which is due the soul from this most holy exercise, and noticeably debilitate it and dry it out .

11. Do not be conceited about tenderness and delights that lack force and solidity, but when you feel that devotion is abandoning you,

---

[7] "Froward generation and children in whom there is no faith" (Deut. 32:20).

[8] "Forasmuch as Christ hath suffered for us in the flesh, arm yourselves likewise with the same mind" (I Peter 4:1).

la fe y perseverancia. Poned delante de vuestros ojos el ejemplar de Cristo en un pesebre, y muerto en una cruz, y representad a este médico celestial las llagas que más os impiden y parecen incurables, pidiéndole humilde y confiadamente las sane, y os dé luz y amor eficaz para obrar lo más perfecto, y transformaros del todo en Él. No os olvidéis ningún día, en su soberano acatamiento, de las necesidades de la santa Iglesia, instando por su acrecentamiento y conversión de las almas que están fuera de ella en todo el universo mundo. Rogaréis por los fieles difuntos que padecen en el purgatorio, por la salvación de vuestros deudos y amigos, y por los que, con espirituales o temporales beneficios o con sus oraciones, os tienen obligadas, porque Dios no ama a los ingratos y fríos en la fraterna caridad, y esto se puede hacer con gran fruto.

12. Procuraréis corto discurso y encendido afecto. Os guardaréis de ilusiones en la oración y fuera de ella. Daréis cuenta muy menuda de todo lo que sintiereis en estas materias a vuestro confesor y superiora; esto os librará de muchos peligros y engaños del demonio, y os causará gran consuelo y dilatación, si procediereis en ello con verdad, sinceridad de ánimo y humildad.

13. Seréis muy exactas en guardar silencio, trocando conversación de modo que, cuando la lengua callare con las hermanas, hable el corazón con Dios, o escuche con los amigos, que dice la Santa Esposa. Pedidle os haga oír su voz y eterno Verbo que en todas las cosas por Él criadas nos está hablando y en sí mismo con suma alteza y primor. No os derraméis en pensamientos vanos y llenos de imperfección, porque este tal silencio sería para Dios fruta aceda y sin sazón.

14. Huid con todo cuidado la ociosidad, a quien llama San Jerónimo madre de todos los vicios, con gran propiedad. Ponderaréis que, con ser tal cual es la liberalidad de Dios, quiso dejar (generalmente hablando) librada la conservación de la natural vida humana en la comida y ésta, en el sudor del rostro, como Su Majestad dijo a Adán, y en ocupación y trabajo y más trabajo, misericordiosa traza para librar al mundo de tan peligrosa bestia. Porque si, siendo tan malos

let faith and perseverance make up for it. Put before your eyes the example of Christ in the manger, and dead on a cross, and represent to this heavenly doctor the wounds that most impede you and seem incurable to you, asking Him humbly and confidently to heal them and give you light and efficient love to act in the most perfect fashion and transform yourselves completely into Him. Do not forget a single day, in His divine veneration, the needs of the Holy Church, urging its growth and the conversion of the souls that do not pertain to it around the world. You will pray for the faithful dead that suffer in purgatory, for the salvation of your kin and friends and for those who, by means of spiritual or temporal benefits or with their prayers, oblige you to do so, for God does not love those who are ungrateful and cold in fraternal charity, and this can be carried out with great fruit.

12. You will strive to short conversations and burning affection. You will protect yourselves from illusions in prayer and out of it. You will account for all you have felt in these matters to your confessor and superior in much detail; this will free you from many dangers and deceits of the devil and will bring you great consolations and serenity, if you proceed through it with truth, candor of soul, and humility.

13. You will be very exacting in keeping silent, exchanging conversations such that when your tongue falls silent with your sisters, your heart speaks with God, or listens with the companions, as the Holy Spouse says.[9] Ask Him to make you hear His voice and the eternal Verb which is speaking to us in all the things created by Him and in Himself in the most sublime and exquisite fashion. Do not allow yourselves to overflow into thoughts that are vain and full of imperfection, because this type of silence would be sour and unfitting fruit in God's eyes.

14. Flee with all care from idleness, which St. Jerome called the mother of all vice, and quite rightly.[10] You shall ponder on the fact that, God's liberality being what it is, He chose to deliver (generally speaking) the conservation of natural human life unto food, and [obtaining] food, in the sweat of our brow, as His Majesty said to Adam,[11] and in being occupied, and in work and more work, a merciful scheme to free the world from such a dangerous beast. Because, evil people

---

[9] "Thou that dwellest in the gardens, the companions hearken to thy voice: cause me to hear it" (Cant. 8:13).

[10] Cf. *In Ezech.* lib. V, Cap. XVI, ML 25, 155 (Abad, ed. EA 324).

[11] "In the sweat of thy face shalt thou eat bread, till thou return unto the ground" (Gen. 3:19).

los que en él están ocupados por sólo conservar su vida, no se hallaran con necesidad de comer y vestir, fácilmente se puede considerar dónde llegaría la soberbia y la maldad.

15. Encárgoos mucho que, todo el tiempo señalado para el trabajo de manos, lo gastéis aprovechadamente. No penséis que os excusáis de ociosidad por hacer labor y ocuparos en cualquier otra obra y trabajo de manos, si lo hacéis con flojedad y grande remisión, que poco o nada aprovechéis a la necesidad de la casa, ni al alivio de la carga que la superiora tiene de su provisión y sustento. A las tales bien se les puede aplicar la calidad de la mosca, como San Francisco llama a los frailes ociosos y de poco provecho, que huelgan de sustentarse del trabajo de sus hermanos. "Tantos somos, mis hermanas, en verdad, cuantos somos delante de los ojos de Dios y no más." Bien podremos engañar a los hombres y a nosotras mismas, mas a Dios Nuestro Señor no es posible.

16. Muy buena y provechosa es la virtud que se ejercita en diversas religiones y monasterios que se han fundado en otros reinos, mas yo os aseguro que será muy aceptable a la majestad divina si tratareis de veras de toda la perfección posible aquí en Inglaterra, para que el olor suavísimo de vuestros fervorosos deseos y santas obras suban al cielo y pidan misericordia contra tanta abominación de herejías y otras maldades que se cometen cada día e incitan a su divina majestad para tomar venganza.

being those in it who are occupied only in the conservation of their lives, if they should have no need to eat and clothe themselves, one can easily imagine to what far extremes pride and arrogance would reach.

15. I put you completely in charge of spending all time allotted to work with your hands in an opportune fashion. Do not think that you free yourselves from idleness by simply working and by occupying yourselves in any task at all and handwork, if you do it carelessly and in abatement, for you will thus meet the needs of the house little if at all, nor will you alleviate the burden that the Mother Superior has for its provision and sustenance. Such women as these may be called flies, as St. Francis calls those idle friars of little benefit to anyone, who delight in living off their brothers' work.[12] "We are as many in truth, my sisters, as we are before the eyes of God and no more."[13] We may well deceive human beings and ourselves, but it is impossible to deceive God Our Lord.

16. The virtue exercised in various types of religious practice and in monasteries that have been founded in other kingdoms is very good and beneficial, but I assure you that it will be quite acceptable to the Divine Majesty if you attempt truly, and in all possible perfection here in England, to make the sweet fragrance of our fervent desires and holy works rise to heaven and seek mercy for as many heretical abominations and other evils as are committed daily and incite His Divine Majesty to vengeance.[14]

---

[12] Reports of St. Francis of Assisi associating idle friars with flies appear in his several *vitae* and in the twelfth-century *Mirror of Perfection*, a collection of legends about him.

[13] This unidentified citation probably comes from the works of Teresa of Ávila, from a collection of sayings attributed to her, or a similar collection attributed to St. Claire.

[14] The idea that by virtue of their prayers nuns could mitigate divine wrath against sinners was widely propagated during this period, not only in support of the positive effects of prayer but also to justify the enclosure of women, whose prayer on behalf of others was their most important task; see Rhodes, "Y yo dije."

## Distribución del tiempo

17. En despertando a la mañana, lo primero que se haga será levantar el corazón a Dios Nuestro Señor con el más tierno afecto de reconocimiento y amor que se pueda. Puestas en pie, ya con vestido, se postrarán luego en la tierra en la soberana presencia, y envuelto el corazón en los mismo afectos, se le ofrezcan con sumo deseo de que cada vez quede más seguramente por suyo. Y junten algún hacimiento de gracias por haber pasado aquella noche sin pecado. En esta devoción, y en aderezar y componer sus camas, se gaste tan poco tiempo que no pase de media hora. La de levantar, sea en verano desde la Resurrección hasta San Miguel de septiembre, a las cinco. Y desde San Miguel a la Resurrección, a las seis.

18. Recogidas todas en el oratorio, tengan una hora de oración mental, ayudándose de alguna lección que lo facilite, si así fuere menester. Los lunes y tres siguientes días de la semana, se ejercitarán en la consideración de las postrimerías: muerte, juicio, infierno y gloria, ahondando siempre en el conocimiento de sí mismas. Los viernes y sábados, de la sagrada Pasión, muerte y sepultura de Cristo, y los domingos, de la Resurrección. Y cuando se hubiere de hacer mudanza en esta dirección, sea con aprobación.

19. Tengan en su meditación atento y vigilante el corazón, procurando sacar de las diversas flores el rocío del divino amor en grado muy puro, aborrecimiento de sí, cansancio y mortal tedio con todo cuanto no es Dios. No sufran en sí flojedad ni descuido alguno en resistir ni desechar pensamientos bajos o desconvenientes a tal ocupación. La abominación de los más nocivos y viciosos, clara se está. Si conviniere que alguna tenga su oración a solas, cuando le pareciere así a la superiora podrá dar licencia para ello.

## *Schedule*[15]

17. Upon waking in the morning, the first thing to be done is to raise one's heart to God Our Lord with the most tender affection possible of gratitude and love. Having gotten up and dressed, they will then prostrate themselves on the floor in the sovereign presence, and with their hearts wrapped in the same feelings, let them offer themselves unto Him along with the greatest desire to be every more securely His. And let them join to this some act of thanksgiving for having passed the night without sinning. In this act of devotion, and in arranging and making their beds, they will let no more than half an hour pass. Let the time for rising in summer, from the Resurrection until St. Michael's in September, be five o'clock. And from St. Michael's until the Resurrection, at six.[16]

18. Gathered together in the oratory, they should spend an hour in mental prayer, helping themselves along with some reading to facilitate it, if necessary. On Mondays and the three subsequent days of the week, they will exercise themselves in consideration of life's end: death, judgment, hell, and glory, ever deepening their knowledge of themselves. On Fridays and Saturdays, [they will meditate on] the sacred Passion, death and burial of Christ, and on Sundays, on the Resurrection, and whenever any change is made in these instructions, let it be with approval [of the Mother Superior].

19. Let them keep their hearts attentive and vigilant in their meditation, seeking to pluck from diverse flowers a very pure degree of the dew of divine love: self-abhorrence, weariness, and mortal tedium for all which is not God. They must not tolerate in themselves any weakness or carelessness in resisting or rejecting base thoughts or those unbecoming to said occupation. The abomination of the most harmful and vicious [thoughts] is obviously necessary. Should it be appropriate for anyone to take her prayer alone, permission may be granted to do so whenever the Mother Superior finds it fitting.

---

[15] This section of the document is written in imperatives. In her *Constitutions*, Teresa of Ávila instructs her nuns in the same style, and Carvajal seems to have had her model in mind.

[16] St. Michael, Archangel, whose feast day was Sept. 29. The Resurrection was celebrated on Easter Sunday.

20. Acabada la oración, digan Prima, y en el invierno, tercia y sexta. En el recitar de los salmos y oficio divino, cuiden mucho dar una acordada música al Rey celestial de sus almas. Guárdense no haga disonancia en los divinos oídos la tibieza de afectos, falta de humildad y de profunda reverencia con que deben estar, ni aun pequeñas distracciones de ánimo que se adviertan.

21. Salidas de las horas, acudirán a sus labores y manuales ejercicios, y en ellos se ocupen cuidadosamente, pero no les sea impuesta tarea, y no piensen les excusa de ociosidad el estar en su labor o en cualquiera otra obra o trabajo. El trabajar todas juntas o apartadas queda a disposición de la superiora, la cual, conforme a la diversidad de los tiempos y de los espíritus, ordenará lo que juzgare ser de mayor aprovechamiento y de consuelo. Procuren con suavidad conservarse en la devoción y recogimiento con que salieron de la oración. Si la salud corporal lo pidiere así, se podrá, en este tiempo de labor, hacer algún ejercicio en la huerta de casa u otros solitarios y desembarazados lugares de ella, con devoción y recogimiento.

22. Guardarán silencio desde que se levantan hasta la misa, la cual, cuando se levantan a las cinco, se dirá a las ocho en su oratorio; y cuando a las seis, se dirá a las nueve. Cuando hubiere sermón, siempre sea después de la misa, si se puede, y si no, la superiora señale la hora más conveniente en mañana o tarde.

23. Acabada la misa y el sermón, si le hubiere, se diga nona en el invierno, y en el verano tercia y sexta, y la nona a las diez. En la cuaresma se digan vísperas a las diez. Hasta nona, y desde ella al examen, cuando no impidiere el oratorio, se ocupen en la labor, y podrán hablar cosas espirituales y de edificación, cuidando de no mezclar palabras vanas, y mucho más, las que desayudan al espíritu.

24. Pasados los tres cuartos de las diez, harán el examen de la conciencia y después de él, si sobrare tiempo, se podrá cada una divertir religiosamente a lo que quisiere hasta las once. Cuando se hiciere

20. Once prayer is finished, let them say prime, and in winter terce and sext.[17] In the recitation of the psalms and the Divine Office, let them be very careful to offer harmonious music to the celestial King of their souls. Let them keep lukewarm feelings, lack of humility and profound reverence which they should have, or even small distractions of the soul which they might notice, from providing dissonance to the divine ears.[18]

21. Having completed the Office, they will attend to their handwork and manual labor; and let them busy themselves carefully therein, but let them not go about it as if it were imposed upon them, and neither should they think that doing their work or any other labor lazily frees them from idleness. Whether they work all together or separate is up to the Mother Superior, who, in accordance with the changing of the seasons and their spirits, will order whatever she might determine to be of greatest benefit and consolation. Let them gently seek to maintain in themselves the devotion and recollection with which they emerged from prayer. Should their bodily health so require, they may take some exercise during this work period, in the garden of the house or other solitary and removed places therein, with devotion and seclusion.

22. Let them keep silent from the time they rise until mass, which, when they rise at five, will be at eight in their oratory, and when [they rise] at six, will be at nine. Whenever there is a sermon it will always be after mass, if possible, and if not, the Mother Superior will indicate the most suitable hour of the morning or afternoon.

23. After mass (and the sermon, should there be one), none will be said in the winter, and in summer terce and sext and none, at ten o'clock. During Lent, vespers will be said at ten. Until none, and thereafter until the examination [of conscience], whenever the exercise of prayer does not impede it, let them busy themselves with handwork, and they may speak of spiritual things that are edifying, taking care not to mix idle words therein, and more so, to avoid those which are not helpful for the spirit.

24. After 10:45, they will make their examination of conscience, and after that, should time remain, each one may entertain herself religiously with whatever she pleases until eleven. Whenever a signal

---

[17] As most monastic communities, Carvajal's Society prayed the Divine Office, which divides the day into seven periods separated by specific prayers: matins (with lauds), prime, terce, sext, none, vespers, and complin.

[18] The music of the celestial spheres, God's own perfect harmony, was believed to be set out of tune by human error.

señal o se llamare a cosa en que hayan de concurrir todas juntas, cada una acudirá a la cámara más cercana a aquel lugar, y junta y ordenadamente entrarán a él.

25. A las once irán a comer en todo tiempo. Y entrarán a la mesa con algún salmo breve, según el tiempo y fiestas, y delante de ella en pie, con los corazones levantados al cielo, la bendecirá la superiora brevemente. Asentaránse de la manera que fueren entrando. No se hablará sin precisa necesidad y con voz baja. La semanera de la lección leerá todo el tiempo de la comida, si la superiora no hiciere señal que lo deje. No se gaste más tiempo en la mesa de lo que pide su religiosa profesión. Después de la comida, la relojera volverá el reloj de arena y tendrán una hora de recreación, y templando las pláticas de entretenimiento con muy religiosa modestia.

26. Pasada esta hora, acudirán a sus labores o a otras ocupaciones que estén a su cargo, y las necesarias, a fregar por semanas, empezando desde la superiora, que, en cuanto fuera posible, debe darles ejemplo de humildad, siguiendo el de la profunda humildad de Cristo, explicada en aquella palabra, *"Ego autem in medio vestri sum, sicut qui ministrat."* Acabando allí, irán a su labor con las demás. Guardarán silencio muy preciso hasta las dos, y de dos a tres, excepto en lo que se dirá.

27. En la segunda hora de silencio, los días que le pareciere a la superiora — por lo menos uno en cada semana forzosamente —, les hará una exhortación a las virtudes a todas juntas en la cámara de la labor; o, retirándose, llamará a sí, de una en una, [a] las que tuvieren necesidad de algún aviso o corrección. En esta misma hora, todos los viernes, juntas en el oratorio, saludarán de rodillas a la Santísima Virgen Nuestra Señora con el *Ave, Regina caelorum*. Y asentadas ya en sus lugares, empezando de la menos antigua, cada una se levantará, y postrándose delante de la superiora, aguardará que la mande levantar. Y puesta en pie, dirá con modestia y discreción las faltas que reconoce en sí, guardándose de tocar en cosa que desedifique o tenga alguna indecencia. Y acabando, la celadora,

be given or a call to something which all must attend, each one will approach the closest room and enter therein together in an orderly fashion.

25. At eleven o'clock, lunch will be served throughout the year. And they will approach the table with some short psalm, depending on the season and holidays, and standing before it, with their hearts raised to heaven, the Mother Superior will bless it briefly. They will sit in the same order in which they entered the room. They will not speak without a specific need to do so, and in a low voice. The reader for the week will read during the entire meal, unless the Mother Superior should indicate that she stop. No more time will be spent at meals than that which their religious profession dictates. After the meal, the keeper of the clock will turn the hour glass and they will have an hour of recreation, and tempering their conversational entertainment with very religious modesty.

26. After said hour, they will take up their handwork or other tasks for which they are responsible, including the latrines, to be cleaned weekly, working down from the Mother Superior who, as much as possible, should provide an example of Christ's humility, set forth in that verse, "*Ego autem in medio vestri sum, sicut qui ministrat.*"[19] That job having been finished, they will take up their handwork with the others. They will maintain strict silence until two o'clock, and from two to three, except in that which follows.

27. During the second hour of silence, on whatever days that the Mother Superior might so determine — at least once a week without fail —, she will exhort to virtue everyone gathered together in the workroom; or, removing herself elsewhere, she will call in, one at a time, those who might need some warning or correction. During this same hour, every Friday, together in the oratory, they will greet the Most Holy Virgin Our Lady, on their knees, with the *Ave, Regina caelorum*. And then, seated in their places, beginning with the newest member of the community, each will stand and, prostrating herself before the Mother Superior, await her order to rise. And on her feet, she will modestly and discretely announce the faults she recognizes in herself, avoiding the announcement of anything that sets a bad example or is indecent in any way.[20]  And having finished, the

[19] "I am among you as he that serveth" (Luke 22:27).

[20] The avoidance of confessional specifics that might inspire "impure" thoughts in the listener was a common recommendation in early modern confessor's manuals. The community-wide confessional ritual described here was standard in convent practice, and complemented the women's regular confession with a religious man.

si tuviere orden para ello o suficiente causa, haciendo una muy baja venia a la superiora, dirá, "Con vuestra licencia, diré lo que se le olvida o no conoce de sí." La superiora dirá, "Decidlo." Y harálo sin alguna exageración en breves razones, demostradoras de un ánimo piadoso y caritativo. Y habiendo acabado, la superiora les encargará el cuidado de sus almas brevemente, en el grado que lo profesan, y se acabará todo con el *miserere* y oración. Los días que esta hora estuviere vacía de las dichas ocupaciones, se gaste en lecciones que todas oigan, de historias y ejemplos de santos u otras cosas que sirven de doctrina y recreación, todo junto.

28. A las tres dirán vísperas, oyéndolas aquellas a quien no tocare decirlas, si no fueron impedidas de la superiora, o de ocupaciones que estén a su cargo.

29. Acabadas vísperas, se diga la Letanía de la vida y muerte de Cristo Nuestro Señor, en la cual hallarán muchas dulces estaciones de su amor y un almacén real do[nde] podrán seguir aqueste consejo: "*Vos eadem cogitatione armamini.*" Tras esto dirán el Rosario de Nuestra Señora de Cinco Misterios. En la cuaresma se diga esta letanía y rosario a la misma hora de las tres.

30. Consiguientemente guardarán silencio hasta las cinco, y en cuaresma hasta las seis, ocupadas en sus labores. Y quedando algún tiempo vacío hasta completas, seguirán la instrucción de los intervalos de antes de nona, y después de ella hasta el examen. Este tiempo de silencio parece más de propósito para hablar con los que vinieren de fuera a ver a alguna, si para ello le fuere dada licencia; en lo cual, no habiendo negocio o respectos que obliguen, a juicio de la superiora, se gastará sólo una hora, y con los de poco cumplimiento media o un cuarto. Y ninguna ha de estar con los de fuera sola, aunque sean mujeres y deudas suyas.

31. Las Completas se dirán en verano, a las cinco y media, y en invierno a las seis y media, y acabadas tendrán media hora de oración por el reloj de arena, y se rematará con la Letanía de Nuestra Señora que se canta en Loreto, y *Sub tuum praesidium*. Si sobrare tiempo hasta la cena, seguirán la instrucción del cuarto antes de las once.

sister warden, if she as been so commanded or should have reason to do so, bowing deeply to the Mother Superior, will say, "With your leave, I shall say what she has forgotten or does not know about herself." The Mother Superior will say, "Say it." And she will do so briefly without any exaggeration, in the manner of a pious and charitable spirit. And having finished, the Mother Superior will briefly entrust all the sisters with the care of their souls, to the degree that they each profess, and the act will conclude with the *Miserere*[21] and prayer. Whatever days this hour is free from said occupations, let it be spent in readings, which all should hear, from the lives and examples of saints, or other things that serve as both doctrine and recreation.

28. At three o'clock, vespers will be said, while those who are not saying it listen, unless the Mother Superior, or other occupations for which they are responsible, should impede them from so doing.

29. After vespers, let the Litany of the Life and Death of Christ Our Lord be recited, in which will be found many sweet stations of His love and a royal storehouse wherein they may follow this counsel: "*Vos eadem cogitatione armamini.*"[22] After this they will say the Rosary of Our Lady of the Five Mysteries. During Lent, this litany and rosary should both be said at three o'clock.

30. Thereafter they will keep silent until five o'clock, and during Lent until six, busy at their work. And since some time remains before complin, they will follow the instructions for the periods before none, and thereafter until the time for examination. This time of silence seems the most propitious for speaking with those who may come to see one of them, if she were given permission to join them, on which period, provided the Mother Superior determines that there is no pending business or obligation, only one hour will be spent, and on those [visits] of mere formality, half an hour or fifteen minutes. And no sister will be alone with anyone from outside the house, even though they be women and her family members.

31. Complin will be said in summer at 5:30, and in winter at 6:30, and once finished they will have half an hour of prayer set by the hour glass, and it will be concluded with the Litany of Our Lady which is sung in Loreto,[23] and *Sub tuum praesidium*. Should any time remain before dinner, they will follow the instructions for the fifteen minutes before eleven a.m.

---

[21] The penitential Psalm 51, "Have mercy upon me, oh God, according to thy loving-kindness."

[22] "Arm yourselves likewise with the same mind" (1 Peter 4:1).

[23] Loreto, Italy, a popular pilgrimage site.

32. La cena sea en verano a las siete, y en invierno a las ocho, procediendo con la misma orden que se declaró a la comida, hasta el fin de la recreación. Entrarán a maitines en verano a las ocho y media, y en invierno a las nueve y media. Acabados maitines, se hará un breve examen de conciencia, y se tendrá disciplina lunes, miércoles y viernes, y en la cuaresma cada noche; excepto, en todo tiempo, los domingos y fiestas solemnes, retirándose cada una a hacerla a sus solas. Los días que no la hubiere, se lee una breve lección de la meditación del día siguiente.

33. Acabada, se irán a reposar en el Señor. Si a la superiora le pareciese, se podrá tener la disciplina por la mañana antes de empezar prima; pondrán silicio un día en la semana, y dos o tres en la Cuaresma.

32. Dinner in the summer will be at seven, and in winter at eight, following the same order as indicated for the midday meal, until the end of the recreation period. They will enter into matins in summer at 8:30 and in winter at 9:30. After matins, they will examine their consciences briefly, and on Mondays, Wednesdays and Fridays will take a discipline, and in Lent every night (excepting, in all seasons, Sundays and solemn feast days), with each one retiring to do it alone.[24] The days on which there is no discipline, a short lesson from the next day's meditation will be read.

33. Having finished, they will go to rest in the Lord. If the Mother Superior should find it appropriate, the discipline may be taken in the morning before prime; they will wear a hair shirt once a week, and two or three during Lent.[25]

[24] "To take a discipline," meaning to carry out some physical penitential act, usually self-flagellation; see LS "Introduction."

[25] The penitential exercises that Carvajal describes here, presumably representing her own prescription, are very mild in comparison with the ones she describes being obliged to carry out under her uncle's supervision during her adolescence (LS ¶¶77-85). The contrast suggests that Carvajal intended to make clear just how excessive her uncle's regime was by providing her own example of religious propriety. However, in early modern Spanish religious texts of an autobiographical nature, holy individuals always describe their youthful mortification of the flesh as unreasonably severe, and later describe their mitigation of that severity as a consequence of attaining religious maturity.

## *Introduction: Letters*

> "If I had a companion who would write to me it would be
> a great help, when I am not well or I am tired,
> which is most of the time."
> (to Lorenzo Da Ponte, 14 March 1607)

*T*he 178 letters now extant by Luisa de Carvajal surely comprise but a small portion of those she wrote. Reading them in the absence of those to which she is usually responding is a bit like listening to someone else talk on the phone; the lively dialogue that Carvajal kept running with some of her correspondents, sometimes bridging delivery delays of over a year, often frustrates for its irresolvable mysteries. Also, there are crucial letters missing from the collection, most notably those she wrote to Michael Walpole, SJ (1570-1624), her confessor from the time she was in Madrid until her death in London. In 1610, Walpole was arrested and imprisoned because of his association with Carvajal, then freed thanks to the intervention of the Spanish ambassador, on the condition that he leave England. Carvajal and Walpole surely corresponded during the three-year separation that ensued. However, Walpole was again in Carvajal's house when she was arrested the second time, in 1613, and while the sheriff's officers were searching her house, she managed to burn a good number of her papers, in part to protect Walpole specifically. Therefore, it is likely that their entire correspondence went up in flames. Walpole was also at her deathbed at the Spanish embassy in 1614, when she handed over her papers to him, at which time he may have destroyed whatever referred to himself, moved by modesty and an interest in protecting the privacy of some facets of their relationship.

Written correspondence, perilous as it was for its potential interception by English spies, was the only means Carvajal had of maintaining contact with her friends on the continent and her superior in Madrid, Lorenzo Da Ponte, and she regularly availed herself of the Spanish Ambassador's diplomatic immunity to send mail out with his courier. She also secreted letters via a Catholic merchant in Brussels to people at the Flemish court, where her childhood companion,

Isabel Clara Eugenia, was Archduchess, and a close friend and nun, Magdalena de San Jerónimo, was one of the Archduchess's confidants.

Since it is obvious that a large portion of Carvajal's correspondence has been lost, it is unwise to make concrete conclusions about its nature and development over the years. She claimed to maintain an iron discipline that prohibited her from writing to anyone for human consolation (see Letter 94 ¶20). Still one trend in the extant letters bears pointing out: Carvajal initially compensated for her acute loneliness and isolation in London by writing to female friends, and women are the addressees of almost all her correspondence until after her first arrest. After 1609, as her mobility and comfort in London increased, she began writing to men, notably powerful men such as her cousin's husband Rodrigo de Calderón (a scandalous favorite of King Philip III). Had some of those letters been intercepted, such as the one she wrote in late 1613 to Calderón about urging Philip III to arm Ireland, she could have been tried for treason against the English state. Indeed, the interception of such letters as that one may have been what provoked the Archbishop of Canterbury's fury over Carvajal's continued presence in London.

According to testimony by Inés de la Asunción, upon "abandoning the world," as Carvajal's rejection of her life as a secular noblewoman was then called, Luisa vowed to address everyone with utmost formality (Test. 278r). This linguistic register, which she employed when speaking and writing, theoretically signaled an egalitarian respect for her fellow human beings and also marked her distance from everyone. Thus Carvajal writes to individuals from the Duke of Lerma down to her former serving women as "Vuestra Merced," 'Your Grace,' and "Vuestra Reverencia," 'Your Reverence.' These were standard forms of address in Carvajal's time, when they had a less stilted and false ring than they do now.

Carvajal's epistolary style, like that of many of her spiritual writings, displays features of informal discourse, most notably an overabundance of the conjunction "and," used to sustain the flow of the prose and compensate for the physical separation between addresser and addressee. I have broken unbearably long sentences into smaller ones when the subject matter can accommodate such a pause. Each letter is numbered following the chronological enumeration used by Abad in his 1965 edition. Individuals and events are identified only the first time Carvajal refers to them.

Two factors complicate the dates used by Carvajal, who presumably used the Spanish calendar to date her letters rather than the

English. As did other nations, the English began the year on March 25, the feast day of the Incarnation, rather than Dec. 25, that of the Nativity, which provokes discrepancies in years on occasion. Also, Pope Gregory XIII instituted his calendar reform on 24 Feb. 1572, a reform not adopted by Protestants, for obvious reasons. The Gregorian Calendar required the immediate suppression of ten days from the year 1582, among other alterations, and was initially accepted only by Spain, Portugal, and Italy. Living in England, Carvajal was acutely aware of the conflict between her dates (which she calls "new style") and those of the English. Her response to these distinctions illuminate little of the Christian charity and humility to which she so often laid claim: "The English don't want anybody to visit the prisons to celebrate Easter in them. And so they begin it [Easter] when all the rest of the world is finishing it. And I tell you that you can see how they are in this, since the business of the ten days has been so reasonably received around the world, and they won't swallow it just because it was the Pope's idea" (22 March 1606).

## 40

### *A Magdalena de San Jerónimo*
#### *Londres, 2 de marzo de 1606*

### Jhs

1. He recibido la de 14 de febrero de vuestra merced, y vuestra merced habrá tenido otra última carta mía bien larga, de los trabajos de los católicos, aunque quedaron hartos por decir. Y puedo decir con verdad a vuestra merced que me consuelan cada día más sus cartas, y me hace compañía acordarme que está vuestra merced en Flandes; y adonde quiera que fuese gloria de Nuestro Señor, le deseo la salud y la vida muy de veras. Y holgaría harto saber los designios que vuestra merced no quiere fiar de las cartas, pero yo creo que vuestra merced puede hacerlo seguramente por la vía que vienen, y estar cierta del secreto de esta su sierva en todo cuanto me lo mandare tener. Y aunque no sé lo que se le ofrece a vuestra merced que podrá hacer de más fruto en otros cabos, pienso que ahí no hace poco ni tiene pequeñas ocasiones de él. Y creo de su ánimo de vuestra merced cualquier cosa, y que no le embarazará el mar océano y peligro de holandeses, ni dificultades de Inglaterra, si entendiese que la llamaba Dios por aquí, ante cuya grandeza suplico a vuestra merced cuanto puedo me ayude instantemente, para que yo pueda acertar con su mayor gloria, que es la cifra y blanco de todos mis deseos y afectos. Y en la vivienda aquí, como cosa a mí tan importante y grave, principalmente deseo esa ayuda.

2. Y crea vuestra merced que me ha traído su benigna y soberana misericordia por un camino y en un modo que no es fácil desbaratarle y volver las espaldas al negocio. Y conociendo que su dulce mano lo guía, no procuro averiguar mucho para qué

**40**

*To Magdalena de San Jerónimo*[1]
*London, 2 of March, 1606*

**Jhs**

1. I have received Your Grace's letter of 14 February, and Your Grace has probably received another long one from me, about the trials of the Catholics, although many were left unspoken. And I can say truly to Your Grace that your letters console me more every day, and recalling the fact that Your Grace is in Flanders keeps me company; and wherever it would be to the glory of Our Lord, I most truly wish you health and life. And I would much like to know what are the intentions that Your Grace chooses not to entrust to letters, but I believe that Your Grace can do so safely by the route they now travel, and be assured of the secrecy of this your servant, in all that you should ask me to keep secret. And although I do not know what has come up that would allow you to reap greater fruit in other places, I think that there [Brussels] you attain not a little nor have few occasions to do so. And I believe anything is possible in Your Grace's soul and that the sea and the dangers posed by the Dutch will not get in your way, nor the difficulties posed by England, if you should come to believe that God were calling you here, before whose greatness I insistently beg Your Grace to help me so that I might ascertain His greater glory, which is the key and target of all my desires and affection. And I desire that assistance mainly in the business of living here, as something so important and serious for me.

2. And believe that His compassionate and sovereign mercy has brought me along a path and in a way that makes it hard to discard and turn my back on the whole business. And knowing that His sweet hand guides my way, I do not attempt to ascertain the reason

---

[1] The letter to which Carvajal is responding here clearly contained an accusation that she addresses many times in her correspondence: her activities in London were jeopardizing the Catholic cause, and her motivation for remaining there smacked of self-aggrandizement. Magdalena de San Jerónimo, probably a bit jealous of Luisa, was rightly concerned about the prudence of her friend's actions, given the delicate political situation at hand. Carvajal's failure to respond to Magdalena's repeated suggestions to come to Brussels may be why Magdalena broke off ties with her. Carvajal's last letter to Madre Magdalena, after an intense correspondence lasting all of 1606, is dated 17 July 1607.

fin, o en qué han de parar mis trabajos y resoluciones, gustando de que esto esté en su dulce gusto y voluntad envuelto y encubierto. Y sobre este presupuesto, será cualquier efecto y remate dichoso, aunque sea deslucido a los humanos ojos. Al punto que yo entienda que se inclina a mi partida, partiré, señora, que acá no hay cosa que tire, y en España y Flandes, muchas de consuelo, de cuerpo y espíritu.

3. Ahora han puesto en la capilla el Santísimo Sacramento, con que me hallo enriquecidísima. Cae muy cerca de mi escalera y es fácil, sin verlo nadie, ir allí muchas veces. En lo demás se puede hacer cuenta que se está en un yermo, estando en esta tierra, y bien semejante en los peligros y dificultades al de los santos del otro tiempo, pues es más lleno de animales no menos fieros, y, por lo que tienen de discurso, cautelosos e intrincados.

4. Hame hecho Nuestro Señor merced de darme dos compañeras muy a mi contento, doncellas muy religiosas y devotas, las cuales procuro conservar en todo género de servicio con humildad y satisfacción mía. Y así, si salen a lo que es necesario, lo hacen bien y con alegría, y si están solas y encerradas, las hallo con la misma, y parece tendrán perseverancia.

5. Estoy siempre con ellas sola, cerrada mi puerta con llave y hablando en su lengua, porque no saben otra ninguna. Y como no sea contar historias, puedo hacerlo razonablemente en cosas ordinarias, y aunque con cortedad de razones, puedo hablarlas en Nuestro Señor muchas veces, y me entienden, que es lo que vuestra merced dice que no acaba de entender, y tiene razón. Y ninguna, de pedirme perdón por lo escrito, de que me encojo o confundo, que la dureza de algunas palabras, saliendo de tronco tan dulce como el de la caridad, las debía y debo estimar en mucho. Y siempre que veo que vuestra merced se acuerda de escribirme, me maravillo y reconozco en eso lo mismo. Y digo, señora, que, en saliendo de aquí, será bien cierto el dar en Bruselas.

behind many things, or what end my trials and resolutions will have, enjoying the fact that all this is enwrapped and hidden in His sweet pleasure and will. And based on this supposition, any effect and ending will be happy, although it may be dull to human eyes. The instant that I understand that God is inclined toward my departure, I shall depart, Madame, for there is not a thing here that attracts me, and in Spain and Flanders there are many, of consolation to body and soul.

3. The Holy Sacrament has just been placed in the chapel, with which I find myself most enriched. It happens to be very close to my stairway and it is easy, without anyone seeing, to go there many times.[2] As far as the rest, it is like living in a desert on earth and quite similar to the dangers and difficulties of the saints of days gone by, since it is full of animals that are no less fierce, and, with that talk of theirs, guarded and complicated.

4. Our Lord has shown me the mercy of granting me two companions much to my liking, very religious and devout maidens, whom I attempt to maintain in all type of service in a humble and satisfactory fashion. And thus, if they go out for what is necessary, they do so well and happily; and if they are alone and enclosed, I find them the same, and it seems that they will persevere.

5. I am always alone with them, with my door locked and speaking their language, for they know no other.[3] And as long as I don't have to tell a story, I can get along reasonably in ordinary things, and although with a shortness of concepts, I can speak to them often about Our Lord and they understand me, which is what Your Grace says you do not understand, and you are right. And you are wrong in begging pardon for asking forgiveness for what you write, which trips me up and confounds me, for I should and do esteem greatly the harshness of some [of your] words, emerging from a source as sweet as that of charity. And whenever I see that Your Grace remembers to write to me, I marvel and recognize the same [act of charity] therein. And I repeat, Madame, that upon leaving here, I will surely wind up in Brussels.

---

[2] At the Spanish Embassy in London, Carvajal occupied the quarters of the Ambassador's confessor, who generously turned them over to her upon her arrival there. She enjoyed not only all of his apartments, but also their private entrance, accessed by the stairs she describes here.

[3] Although living in the Embassy and therefore presumably safe from arrest, Carvajal nonetheless locked her door, doing so not only for extra security but also to protect her virtue and that of her companions. One wonders whether Inés de la Asunción's testimony on the topic of her lady's modesty is apocryphal: she swore that Carvajal always carried a lock and screws with her, to attach to the door of whatever room she was assigned and so safeguard her physical integrity (Test. 273ᵛ).

6. Pésame de que los ojos estén tan malos, pero la letra se me ha hecho a mí muy buena.

7. Ya habrá sabido vuestra merced cómo está preso el padre Garneto, superior de la Compañía en este reino, de que ha redundado mucha edificación en católicos y herejes, de los cuales le han hablado muchos, y con eso descubierto las grandes partes que en él se encierran de santidad y prudencia, con una apacibilidad muy rara, que lleva a todos tras sí. Hanle tratado hasta ahora con toda blandura y cortesía, y fuera de la Torre, y sin atarle, como suelen. Pero ya está en la Torre, donde, aunque dicen tiene cama y lo demás necesario, creemos le darán tormentos, y ya debe de empezarse eso.

8. Otros muchos amigos están presos, de ellos apretados y de ellos en cárcel donde pueden ser visitados y sin hierros. Yo fui la semana pasada a una do[nde] hay seis, y luego, sin dificultad, dando un golpe a la puerta de la calle, vino el carcelero, que lo oye desde su casa, que es allí junto. Y con un real que le da cada uno, abre la puerta con gran gusto, y luego torna a cerrar y se va, hasta que se da otro golpe para salir. Yo fui derecha, sin ruido ni ver gente, a la sala donde los seis tenían su estancia, y otros católicos que yo conocía, y estuve una hora o más, y me volví con harto consuelo con mis dos inglesas que fueron conmigo, y yo con mascarilla sin quitarla nunca.

9. Y antes de acabar ésta quiero suplicar a vuestra merced me haga merced de hacerme buscar un relojillo, que pueda yo llevar conmigo donde quiera, porque aquí no se pueden tener cosas más embarazosas que eso. Y que sea fiel, y de provecho, que aquí no se halla apenas uno que lo sea. Y como soy tan pobre, procuro no gastar en balde los dineros. Y compro reloj porque no puedo pasar sin él, ni tener orden ni concierto donde no se oyen los del lugar. Y díceme una señora que tiene uno muy bueno y no caro, que se

6. I am sorry your eyes are so bad, but your handwriting has become quite easy for me to read.

7. Your Grace has surely heard how Father Garnett, superior of the Jesuits in this kingdom, has been arrested, which has served to edify many Catholics and heretics, many of whom have spoken with him, and in so doing his great hidden sanctity and prudence have come to light, as well as his rare gentleness, for he has them all following along behind him. Until now they have treated him gently and courteously, out of the Tower, without tying him up as they usually do. But now he is in the Tower where, although it is said that he has a bed and other necessary things, we believe they will torture him, and that has probably already begun.[4]

8. Many other friends have been arrested, among them those who are being pressured and those in jail where they can be visited and are unchained. I went to one last week where there are six, and immediately, without difficulty, knocking at the street door, the jailer came, who hears the knock from inside his house, which is right there. And with a *real* from each of us, he opens the door with great pleasure and then locks it up again and leaves, until he hears us knock again to get out.[5] Without making any noise or seeing anyone, I want straight to the room where the six were, along with other Catholics that I knew, and spent an hour or more, and returned mightily consoled with my two English ladies who went with me, and I never took my mask off.

9. And before closing this letter I want to beseech Your Grace to have someone look for a little clock for me that I can carry around with me wherever I want, because here you can't find anything more awkward than carrying around a clock. And it should keep good time and be a good one, for here you can scarcely find one that is. And since I'm so poor, I try not to spend money unnecessarily. And I buy a clock because I can't get along without one, nor establish any order or schedule in my life anywhere that the public bells can't be heard. And a lady tells me she has a very good one that was not

---

[4] Henry Garnett (1555-1606) was, as Carvajal indicates, the superior of the English Jesuit province. He was tried for complicity in the Gunpowder Plot and found guilty of treason. His dramatic arrest (25 Jan. 1606), trial (28 March 1606), and execution (6 May 1606) are briefly related in DNB VII: 881-84. Carvajal describes his death in Letter 47.

[5] The *real* was a silver coin, so named because it bore the royal arms. There were 34 *maravedís* in a *real*; 10 *reales* and 25 *maravedís* in one *florín*. In Letter 78 (¶3), Carvajal states that a whole chicken cost between two and three *reales*, so the jailer's income from these bribes was respectable, since each person entering paid him.

lo compraron en Bruselas. Y luego como vuestra merced me avise del precio, enviaré los dineros con el correo, o los daré a quien vuestra merced ordenare, o enviaré en una u otra manera, que me hace grande falta, cierto, y vuestra merced hará una obra de caridad no pequeña. Y, aunque no querría me costase demasiado, porque tengo limitados dineros, sobre todo deseo sea cierto y de dura, con el que haré remate a compras a la medida de mi pobreza, que no llega, aunque es mucha, a ser tan grande que iguale al contento que me causa verme en ella, donde lo más que he tenido que romper ha sido la dificultad y delicadeza extraordinaria que toda mi vida he tenido en no querer cama que no fuese hecha para mí misma, y acá he dormido en las que las señoras, de limosna, me han querido prestar. Y es lo bueno que se les hacía a veces muy de mal darme sábanas, y yo sonreíame y decía en mi pensamiento, "Si me conociésedes el humor, veríades cuánto más hago en tomarlo que vosotras en dármelas." En esto he sentido interior resistencia extraordinaria y terrible, y también en cosas de la comida.

10. A Su Alteza beso los pies, y no sabría decir el amor y cuidado que me debe; tengo gran confianza en Nuestro Señor de las cosas de sus estados. Guárdela Dios, amén, y enriquezca su real corazón con un divino amor tal como yo siempre le suplico. Y a la señora doña Juana, beso las manos muchas veces. Y mándenos vuestra merced en qué puedo servirla, y de su sobrina, que no he sabido nada. Y

expensive that was bought for her in Brussels. And as soon as Your Grace tells me how much it was, I will send the money with the mail, or give it to whomever you tell me to, or I will send it in one way or another, for I really need it, surely, and Your Grace will perform a considerable act of charity. And although I would not want it to cost too much, for I have limited money,[6] above all it should keep exact time and be long-lasting, with which I will adjust my purchases in measure with my poverty, which, although great, is not so great that it equals the happiness I have in seeing myself in it, in which my greatest challenge has been to cure myself of the difficulty and extreme scrupulousness I have had all my life in not wanting a bed that was not made for me alone, and here I have slept in those that ladies, as alms, have been willing to loan me.[7] And the great thing is that they were very reluctant to give me sheets, and I smiled and said to myself, "If you knew my inclination, you would see how much more I do in taking them than you in giving them." In this business I have felt an extraordinary and terrible inner resistance, and also in questions of food.

10. I humbly greet Her Majesty, and cannot tell the debt of loving care she owes me.[8] I have great confidence in Our Lord regarding the business of her States. May God keep her, amen, and enrich her royal heart with a divine love such as I desire. And I humbly greet doña Juana [Jacincourt] many times.[9] And do tell us how we can serve you; and news of your niece, of whom I have heard nothing.

[6] Carvajal's poverty, upon which she insists so much, was far from absolute, as her Vow indicates. Her insistence here that the clock be of high quality indicates that she was able to spend whatever money necessary when her conscience so dictated.

[7] "Bed" here refers to the mattress, which she wanted for herself alone to avoid the vermin that might reside in anyone else's. Mattresses, pillows, and bed linens were an important, expensive part of a woman's dowry. Although in her Vow of Poverty Carvajal specified funds for a bed (¶4), she probably felt that her unstable situation at this point of her mission did not justify the expense.

[8] The first clause says literally, "I kiss Her Majesty's feet." She refers to Princess Isabel Clara Eugenia (1566-1633), her childhood companion, married to Archduke Albert of Austria, ruler of the Netherlands. The last clause means that the loving care that Carvajal felt for Isabel was so great it could never be repaid. There is no record of Carvajal ever writing to Isabel Clara Eugenia, although she sent many and sometimes complicated messages to her in every letter she wrote to Magdalena de San Jerónimo.

[9] Juana Jacincourt had been a highly esteemed lady in the court of Isabel Valois (Philip II's first wife). She was Isabel Clara Eugenia's first lady-in-waiting in Brussels. Carvajal probably met her at the Madrid court during her childhood (Abad, ed. *Epist.*, 67).

no olvide a lo de Lovaina, le suplico humildemente. Y guarde Dios vuestra merced y abrásela en su amor, amén.

11. De marzo 2, estilo nuevo, 1606

12. Sierva de vuestra merced, Luisa.

13. Desgracia tengo en no poder escribir al señor Octaviano, pero para él no lo es, pues se excusa de trabajo. Si es vuelto, le beso las manos y le suplico no se pierdan las cartas de España que van o vienen.

[sobrescrito] A mi madre y señora Madalena de San Jerónimo, que Dios guarde muchos años.

Bruselas.

And do not forget that Louvain business, I humbly beseech you. And may God keep Your Grace and enflame you in His love, amen.

11. 2 March, new style, 1606.

12. Servant of Your Grace, Luisa.

13. I am most unfortunate in not having been able to write to Mr. Octaviano, but for him it there is no misfortune, since it saves him work.[10] If he has returned, I humbly greet him and beseech him not to lose any letters from Spain that come or go [through Flanders].

[address] To my mother and lady Magdalena de San Jéronimo, whom I pray that God safeguard for many years.

Brussels.

---

[10] Octaviano, probably Carvajal's financial administrator, was a merchant in Brussels who delivered her letters (*Epist.* 473). In Letter 5, she describes him as someone known by the Jesuits (*Epist.* 151).

47

## A Magdalena de San Jerónimo

*Londres, 12 de abril de 1606*

Jhs.

1. El jueves pasado escribí a vuestra merced harto largo, y así en ésta seré más breve. Deseo saber bien de cierto si es verdad lo que allí dije a vuestra merced que se decía acá del rey de Francia en materia de amistad con nuestros amos y en casamientos con España, y no querer ayudar los holandeses, que la culpa de estos malos hechos cargan aquí al padre Cotón, y dicen es famoso traidor y mal hombre porque embauca al rey. Ahora tienen condenados, entre otros, a seis o siete ministros de Escocia por traidores por una rebelión que allá intentaron, que aquí es plática que corre ordinariamente ésta de traiciones.

2. El padre Garneto fue el viernes sacado en público. Hubo mucha curiosidad sobre el oírle, y así mucha gente pagó con tiempo lugares cercanos a él, y creo que no pocos ministros. Lleváronle en un coche, cosa desusadísima, y hablándole con cortesía los jueces, que pienso fueron seis, y Cecilio el uno, y el almirante y camarero mayor, y Northampton, tío del conde de Arundel, hermano de su abuelo y no sé qué otro. Y en fin, le condenaron a muerte, habiendo tardado en el juicio desde las ocho de la mañana hasta las seis de la tarde. Y la causa no pudo ser otra sino porque no descubrió lo de la pólvora, habiendo sabídolo en confesión no más, y no de ningún cómplice de la traición, sino de otro padre que lo había oído también en confesión.

47

## *To Magdalena de San Jerónimo*
### *London, 12 April 1606*

**Jhs.**

1. Last Thursday I wrote at length to Your Grace and so will be briefer here. I wish to know for certain if what I told Your Grace therein is true, about what people were saying there [Brussels] about the King of France's friendship with our master and mistress and about the marriages with Spain, and about the Dutch not wanting to help, for Father Cotton bears the blame for those evil deeds, and they say he is a famous traitor and evil man because he is tricking the King.[1] Now they have condemned six or seven Scottish ministers, among others, as traitors, due to a rebellion that they attempted there, for such talk about treason is frequent here.

2. Father Garnett was brought out in public last Friday. People were very curious to hear him, and so many paid to reserve places close to where he was, and I believe not a few were ministers [of state]. They brought him in a carriage, which is extremely unusual, and [with] the judges, whom I believe were six, speaking courteously to him, and Cecil one of them, and the Admiral and the royal steward and Northampton, the Count of Arundel's uncle, his grandfather's brother, and I don't know who else. And in the end they condemned him to death, with the trial having lasted from eight in the morning until six in the evening.[2] And the reason couldn't be any other but that he didn't reveal the business of the Gunpowder Plot, having known of it only in confession, and not through any traitorous conspiracy, but rather from another Father who had also heard it in confession.

---

[1] Abad suggests the reference is to Peter Cotton, preacher and confessor of Henry IV of France (ed. *Epist.* 167). Henry IV converted from Protestantism to Catholicism in 1593, to the great disappointment of the English. Loomie describes some of the Scottish rebellions, mentioned in the next sentence, in *Guy Fawkes.*

[2] Everything Carvajal describes is borne out by official records, with minor variants (i.e., the trial lasted until seven rather than six). Until his death, Garnett maintained that, although he did indeed know of the plan of some English nobles to blow up Parliament (the Gunpowder Plot, discovered on 5 Nov. 1605), he had learned of it in confession and was thus unable to reveal his knowledge to anyone. The prosecution insisted on his approval of the plan based on his continued association with the conspirators.

Y demás de esto, sería por ser sacerdote y jesuita, que sus leyes le hacen dos veces traidor por esas dos profesiones.

3. El dijo tenía cuatro puntos en que hablar. Y el primero, de la verdad de su católica religión, y en él empezó a hablar muy bien y doctamente. E interrumpiéronle los jueces diciendo, "¿Venís aquí a persuadir al pueblo, señor Garneto?" Él prosiguió todavía en cuanto le fue posible. Volviéronle a la Torre, donde está. Y unos dicen que morirá porque el Rey lo jura, y otros han esperado su vida, por estar tan blando con él el Consejo. Dijéronle allí los jueces que, porque se decía que había sido muy atormentado y maltratado y sin sueño y comida, dijese si era verdad, y él respondió que había sido tratado con toda cortesía. Han dicho de él mil bellaquerías y maldades, pero la verdad es que él se ha portado con el Consejo y ministros artificiosísimamente, por ir deshaciendo con maña y gran cristiandad la furiosa indignación que tenían contra la Compañía, queriendo no parar un punto hasta consumirlos a todos. Y hálos ablandado grandemente. Preguntáronle, entre otras cosas: la primera, si era la Iglesia de Inglaterra herética, teniendo los dos credos, cuatro concilios y escritura sagrada. Dijo que sí, que era herética, porque no estaba a las definiciones del Pontífice Romano. Segunda, y si se podía adorar a Dios en el diablo. Respondió que era cuestión muy metafísica y que no se debía proponer al pueblo y que no quería cansarse en tratar de ella. Tercera, si había ahora en la Iglesia cosas de fe que no lo hubiesen sido en tiempo de los apóstoles. Dijo que todo lo que ahora hay de fe lo tuvieron por de fe los apóstoles y la Iglesia entonces, aunque, con el tiempo y sucesos varios de cosas del mundo, se habían muchas olvidado e ido perdiendo de la noticia de los hombres. Cuarta, si se podía dar noticia de una traición contra el rey y el Estado, sabiéndose sólo por confesión. Dijo que no, de ninguna manera.

4. Mistress Ana Vas ha estado graciosa con ellos cuando le tomaron la confesión. (Tienen por costumbre decir que todas las señoras

And aside from this, it was probably because he was a priest and a Jesuit, for their laws make him twice traitorous for those two professions.

3. He said he had four points to address. And the first, regarding the truth of his Catholic religion, and upon that he began to speak very well and in a most learned fashion. And the judges interrupted him saying, "Have you come here to persuade the public, Mr. Garnett?" He proceeded as long as he could. They returned him to the Tower, where he is now. And some say that he will die because the King swears it, and others have hoped for his life, since the Council is so soft on him. There the judges asked him, because it was said that he had been greatly tortured and mistreated, and had been denied sleep and food, whether that was true, and he responded that he had been treated with all courtesy. They have said a thousand rogueries and evils against him, but the truth is that he has behaved most art-fully with the Council and ministers, by undoing the furious indig-nation that they feel for the Society [of Jesus] with cunning and great Christianity, intending not to let up one bit until he had overcome them all. And he has greatly softened them. They asked him, among other things: first, if the English Church was heretical, having two credos, four Councils and a Sacred Scripture. He said yes, that it was heretical, because it did not fall within the definitions of the Roman Pontificate. Second, whether God could be worshipped in the devil. He responded that that was a very metaphysical question and that one should not deal with it before the public and that he did not want to tire himself by treating it. Third, if there were now in the Church items of faith that did not exist in times of the apostles. He said that all that is now an article of faith was held by the faith of the apostles, although, with time and various worldly happenings, many had been forgotten and had been lost to the awareness of humanity. Fourth, if one could reveal news of treason against the State, if the information were known only by means of confession. He said no, by no means.

4. Mistress Anne Vaux was quite entertaining with them when they took her confession.[3] (They have the habit of saying that all Catholic

---

[3] Anne Vaux (fl. 1605-1635), member of a prominent noble English Catholic family, adopted the pseudonym "Mrs. Perkins" to avoid the suspicion that her real name generated. A staunch supporter of Henry Garnett, she was among the group of Catholics who ran his house at White Webbs while it was used as a rendezvous for the conspirators of the Gunpowder Plot. Remarkable for her nerves of steel, Vaux was the one who hid Henry Garnett in the Habbington house where he was arrested after a search lasting twelve days. While hidden in a secret compartment in which he almost died of suffocation, Garnett was sustained by broth passed to him

católicas, según he oído, son ruines mujeres, porque tienen sacerdotes y padres en su casa, porque, demás de su malicia y odio contra la religión, por sí pueden juzgar poco bien de otros en esa materia.) Y dicen que Mistress Ana ha vivido mal con Master Farmer, que es el padre Garneto, y dijéronselo a ella, y ella aunque presa y en la Torre, dio dos o tres risadas muy grandes (que tiene buena gracia y es muy despejada), y dijo, "¿Con estas niñerías e impertinencias me venís? Señal que no tenéis nada de importancia que achacarme." Y rióse bravamente de ellos, haciendo gran burla de su proceder en aquella materia. Dijéronle si había sabido lo de la pólvora. Dijo que claro estaba que lo había de saber, que, si era ella mujer, ¿que había de pasar nada en Inglaterra sin que [se] lo dijesen? Preguntáronla si lo supo Master Farmer. Dijo que, siendo él el mayor traidor del mundo, que no habría dejado tampoco de entrar en aquella traición. Y que ella les debía mucho, porque no hallando en todo Londres donde meterse, ni aun con dineros, ellos le habían dado posada de balde. A otras preguntas de más peso respondió ella también muy cuerdamente, y no hace ningún caso de ellos, y así los tiene espantados y dicen, "¡Cierto que no sabemos qué hacernos con esta mujer!" Ella no los tiene en cosa chica ni grande, y está sola, sin criado, y sin poderla nadie hablar sino allá los carceleros y jueces.

women are ladies of ill repute, so I have heard, because they have priests and Fathers living in their homes, because, aside from their malice and hate against [the Catholic] religion, they are ill able to judge others in this matter.) And they said that Mistress Anne has lived in sin with Master Farmer, who is Father Garnett, and they said as much to her, and she, even though she was imprisoned there in the Tower, laughed loudly two or three times (for she is really quite funny and very lively), and she said, "You come to me with this child's play and impertinence? A sign that you have nothing of importance with which to charge me." And she laughed bravely at them, making a great joke of their behavior in that business. They asked her whether she had known about the Gunpowder Plot. She said of course she had known, for, since she was a woman, how could anything possibly happen in England without her being told of it? They asked her if Master Farmer knew about it. She said that since he was the biggest traitor in the world, he hadn't missed getting involved in that treason. And that she was in great debt to them, because she hadn't been able to find a single place in all of London to stay, even with money, and they had given her room and board for nothing.[4] To more weighty questions she responded very sensibly, and she pays no attention whatsoever to them, and so she has them amazed and they are saying, "We absolutely do not know what to do with that woman!" She doesn't let them get away with anything and she is alone, without a servant, and no one is allowed to speak with her there except the jailers and judge.

by Vaux through a reed that she ran down the wall from her private quarters, through the floor, and into his hiding place under the house. It is likely that she provoked her own arrest so as to be put in the Tower while Garnett was there, to provide items of need to him which she brought in with her. Carvajal tells of Vaux's imprisonment in a letter of 21 March 1606; on 12 Sept. of the same year, she reports in another that Vaux had been freed (*Epist.* 165; 190; she was actually freed before September). After some years in obscurity, Vaux emerged again running a school for the children of the Catholic gentry at Stanley Grange, which was dispersed in 1635 by warrant of the privy council. The date of her death is not known. (see DNB XX: 190 and DNB VII: 882).

[4] The joke derives from the fact that, as the persecution of Catholics intensified, it became ever harder for them to find places to reside because anyone associated with them ran the risk of arrest.

5. Al padre Al y a Mister Abington han llevado a su provincia, para hacer allí juicio de ellos, y a un criado suyo, o de Al. Vuestra merced dará parte de esto a las señoras religiosas inglesas y mil humildes encomiendas mías, y a todas pido sus oraciones muy de veras, y a los padres, por intercesión de vuestra merced.

6. A Su Alteza beso los pies. Guárdenosla Nuestro Señor, amen. ¡Si se sirviese Su Majestad de darle una hija muy linda, que se casase con nuestro príncipe, si no le toma primero Francia, como se dice, y se tornasen a juntar los Estados a España!  Que creo le importa tener escudo delante, y más por los pasos de las Indias. En fin, es[as cosas], aunque sean grandes, mayores son las del alma, y si ellas tienen alg[una im]portancia, es sólo por lo que toca al bien de las almas y gloria de Nuestro Señor, y [la prin]cipal que deseo es ver una gran santa a Su Alteza, y crecidísima en un muy encendido amor de Nuestro Señor, que es cosa gloriosa ver un corazón real en[cendido] con el divino amor, cuyo fuerte y eficaz ejemplo tira rayos de luz has[ta el] mundo, y, como piedra imán, atrae a otros bravamante.

7. Este pliego se dé a recaudo a Octaviano. Y deseo entrañablemente que allá se pr[oceda] de suerte que acá no se engrían tanto, y la gloria de Nuestro Señor vaya adelante en [todo], que esto dará buenos sucesos sin duda.

8. El señor don Pedro tiene fama con los católicos y con todos de muy cuerdo y virtuoso, que no podrá creer vuestra merced cuánto lo está, y la merced que Nuestro Señor le ha hecho en darle luz para que vea cuán necesario es dar aquí buen ejemplo el embajador de España. Nuestro Señor, en fin, tomó este medio de traerle aquí para bien de su alma y toda su casa. Vive con grande orden y cuidado de los sacramentos, y acudir a hacer oración a la capilla cada día un rato, y a su misa por la mañana. Y el señor don Pedro ningún día deja,

5. They have taken Father Hall and Mister Abbington to his province, to try them there, as well as a servant of his, or Hall's.[5] Give some of this news to the English ladies [in the Flemish court] and a thousand humble greetings from me, and I most sincerely beg for their prayers through your intercession.

6. I humbly greet Her Majesty. May Our Lord keep her, amen. If only His Majesty saw fit to give her a lovely daughter who could marry our Prince, if they don't take him first in France, as people say will happen, and if the two kingdoms were to return to Spanish domain![6] For I think it behooves the nation [the Low Countries] to show a coat of arms abroad, and more so through the passages to the Indies.[7] In any case, those things, important though they may be, are inferior to concerns of the soul, and if they are important at all it is only to the extent that they touch upon the soul's good and the glory of Our Lord, for it is a glorious thing to see a royal heart ignited with divine love, whose strong and efficient example emits rays of light throughout the world, and, like a magnet, valiantly attracts others to the same.

7. Give this sheet to Octaviano for safekeeping. And I dearly wish that things would progress there such that those [people] here not be so vain, and that the glory of Our Lord be advanced in everything, for this will produce good things without a doubt.

8. Lord Don Pedro[8] is famous among the Catholics and in general as a sensible and virtuous man, such that Your Grace would not believe how much so, and the favor Our Lord has shown him by enlightening him about how necessary it is that the Spanish ambassador provide a good example here. Our Lord, indeed, took the measure of bringing him here for the good of his soul and that of his entire household. He lives a very orderly life, mindful of the sacraments, and goes to pray in the chapel every day for awhile, and to his mass in the morning. And Lord Don Pedro does not fail a single day,

---

[5] Hall was the pseudonym of Edward Oldcorne, SJ (1561-1606), a companion of Garnett's who was arrested with him. Sent to Worcester for trial, Oldcorne was convicted of treason on 21 March 1606, hanged, disemboweled, and quartered on 7 April. The man who had denounced him as a conspirator subsequently admitted to having wrongfully accused him.

[6] Isabel Clara Eugenia's fervent desire to have children at this time evidently provided the nobility with gossip. She died childless.

[7] She refers here to Flemish mercantile and exploratory expeditions to the Americas.

[8] Pedro de Zúñiga, who had arrived in London as the Spanish Ambassador on 14 July 1605.

o a la tarde o a la noche, de entrar a estar un rato delante el Santísimo Sacramento, según me afirma el padre Maestro, y entrambos padres son muy cuerdos y muy siervos de Nuestro Señor, como lo he escrito a vuestra merced, a quien guarde Nuestro Señor, como esta su sierva de vuestra merced lo desea.

9. De abril, estilo nuevo, 12, 1606 — Luisa

10. Dícenme que no hay en otro ningún cabo el Santísimo Sacramento, sino en esta casa y que ha mucha cantidad de años que no le ha habido así de asiento en toda Inglaterra. Yo he tenido gran dicha en esto, que, después que estoy en esta casa, se ha puesto Su Majestad en ella. Sea glorificado para siempre. Y el señor Vies estima la memoria que vuestra merced hace de él. En cuanto a lo demás, no trate vuestra merced nunca del nombre de Miguel, acá ni allá; no diga vuestra merced jamás padres en las cartas.

[sobreescrito] A la madre Magdalena de San Jerónimo, que Nuestro Señor guarde muchos años, etcétera

Bruselas

in the afternoon or at night, to go in and spend awhile before the blessed Host, as his chaplain has informed me, and both Fathers are very judicious and good servants of Our Lord, as I have written to Your Grace, whom Our Lord safeguard, as this Your Grace's servant desires.

9. On April, by the new style, 12, 1606 — Luisa

10. I am told that the blessed Host is not kept anywhere else except in this house and that, for many years, it was not kept anywhere at all in all of England. I have been very fortunate in this, for since I have been in this house, His Majesty has been put in it.[9] May He be glorified forever. And Mr. Vies[10] holds your remembrance of him dear. As for the rest, never ever use the name of Michael [Walpole], here or there; never name Fathers in your letters.

[address] To Mother Magdalena de San Jerónimo, whom Our Lord safeguard for many years, etc.

Brussels

[9] Carvajal is boasting about her success at installing the Eucharist in the Ambassador's chapel; the Italian and Venetian embassies followed her example shortly thereafter (Abad, ed. *Epist.* 37). She considered it one of her dearest triumphs, since the Eucharist, holiest of holy material, was usually kept only in churches. In England this prohibited Catholics from taking communion, and Carvajal moved authorities to allow for temporary mitigation of this norm. Her passionate devotion to the Eucharist acquired a political significance in England, where the host symbolized not only Christ's presence, but the Catholics' as well. Although the Anglican Church celebrated communion, the political differences between the two groups made such symbolic gestures important.

[10] The complete name is illegible on the manuscript.

69

## *A Madgalena de San Jerónimo*
*Londres, 5 de diciembre de 1606*

Jhs

1. De la última que escribí a vuestra merced no he tenido respuesta. Ahora suplico a vuestra merced mande dar ese pliego en su mano al señor Octaviano y enviarme su respuesta.

2. Y lo que puedo decir de acá a vuestra merced es que, después que el padre benito, superior, que vino de Italia y estaba preso en Newgat, fue remitido a destierro por petición del hermano del de Lorena, la gente toda común y de menos confianza, que no puede alcanzar nunca a los padres o sacerdotes escondidos, estaba sin confesor. Y ya la alta providencia de Nuestro Señor les ha proveído de otro sacerdote, que fue preso quince o veinte días ha y puesto en Newgat, con el hombre y su mujer dueños de la casa do[nde] le cogieron, y todos tres están en la misma prisión. Quitáronles cuanto tenían de muebles, y echaron los hijos fuera, y cerraron la casa por de fuera. Ellos están alegres como una pascua; y con razón, por cierto. El otro día fui yo a verlos, y hallé también alegre al carcelero, que, después que faltaba sacerdote, estaba con desconsuelo. Mire vuestra merced las grandezas de Dios, que, de la condición de este hereje, hace eficaz medio para tanto provecho de almas, que por lo que cada uno le da a la entrada, que es muy buena renta al año, gusta tanto de que vengan muchos y de que no se impida, que lo procura cuán astutamente puede. Y cuando no tiene sacerdote, que le pongan el primero que se prende con los justicias sus conocidos. Y dice el padre misa cada día y suelen oírlas cien personas y más.

3. No hay ahora otro preso sino ése y Tomás Strang en la Torre. A ése nadie puede hablar; está con muy poca salud.

4. No sé si ha oído allá vuestra merced lo de la figurita del padre Garneto. Por si no lo han escrito, lo diré yo aquí, como

69

## *To Magdalena de San Jerónimo*

*London, 5 Dec. 1606*

Jhs

1. I have had no answer to the last letter I wrote Your Grace. I now entreat Your Grace to have that sheet of paper given into the hands of Mr. Octaviano and the response sent to me.

2. And from here, what I can tell Your Grace is that, after the Benedictine Father, a Superior, who came from Italy and was imprisoned in Newgate, was sent into exile by petition of the man from Lorena's brother (people totally common and worthy of least confidence, who can never find the Fathers or priests in hiding), I was without a confessor. And already the mighty providence of Our Lord has provided them with another priest, who was imprisoned fifteen or twenty days ago and put into Newgate with the owner of the house where they captured him and his wife, and all three are in the same prison. What furniture they had was taken away, and the children thrown out, and the house locked from outside. They are as happy as larks, and certainly with good reason. The other day I went to see them and I found the jailer happy as well, who, once the priest was gone, was disconsolate. Observe, Your Grace, the greatness of God who, from the condition of this heretic, derives an efficient means to benefit souls so much, for as much as each one gives him upon entering, which is a very good annual income, that much is he pleased to have many [visitors] arrive and that the process not be impeded, which he procures as astutely as he can. And when he has no priest, [he arranges it so] that they assign to him the first [Catholic] taken by the justices his friends, and the Father says mass every day and usually one hundred or more people hear it.

3. There is no other prisoner now except that one and Thomas Strange in the Tower. To the latter no one can speak; he is in very poor health.

4. I don't know if Your Grace has heard there about the little figure of Father Garnett. In case no one has written of it to you, I shall do so

quien la ha visto muy bien. Cuando el padre fue hecho cuartos, los católicos presentes tomaron disimuladamente cuantas menudencias pudieron, y uno de ellos, una espiga de la paja do[nde] quemaron su corazón, porque tenía una gotilla de sangre en una pequeña pajita, más angosta que la uña de mi pequeño dedo, que lo es harto, y hecha una como guirnaldilla, la puso en un cerco de ébano con un viril y guardóla en su baúl. Y ahora, sacándola, halló en lugar de la gota un rostrico muy bien proporcionado, con su frente, cejas, narices y boca, y barba un poquito larga y rubia, y su cuello, y en medio de la frente, una señalita colorada y la color blancuzca, que afirman le vieron la señal en la frente al padre, porque se la hizo cuando le arrojaron de la horca abajo. Mirando de repente, no se ve tan bien; pero, haciendo cualquier reflexión, clara y distintamente, y con vela mejor, a mi parecer, aunque siempre muy suficientemente, como si estuviera pintada por algún pintor, y los ojos no abiertos, como figurita muerta. El señor don Pedro la ha tenido algunos días, y hecho que la vean algunos del Consejo, y creo milord Cecilio. El gran chamarlengo dijo que era maravilla, y su mujer, pero que no se parecía al padre. Pero a mí me parece que, después de muerto, sí debe parecérsele, porque sin duda es verdad lo que dicen algunos que, si buscan a quién se parece, no hallarán otro a quien se parezca tanto como al padre entre mil.

5. Buenas nuevas vienen acá de Flandes, por otras vías de Bruselas, Nuestro Señor las aumente por su misericordia.

6. El reloj que pedí, pues no está comprado, no me lo compre vuestra merced, que no tengo ya más dinero de doscientos reales, poco más o menos; y esos voy gastando en lo necesario que se ofrece; que no se puede pedir todo en casa del señor don Pedro, aunque la caridad que ha tenido él y los dos padres conmigo ha

here, as one who saw it very well.[1] When the Father was quartered, the Catholics who were present discreetly picked up as many bits as they could, and one of them [took] a spike of the straw on which they burnt his heart, because it had a drop of blood on a little spike, narrower than the nail of my little finger, which is quite narrow, and it formed something like a little garland. And he put it in an ebony ring in a monstrance and put it away in his trunk. And then, removing it, he found in place of the drop a well-proportioned small face, with its forehead, eyebrows, nose and mouth, and longish blond beard, and a neck, and in the middle of the forehead, a small colored mark of a whitish tinge, and it is affirmed that the same mark was seen on the Father's forehead, because it was made when they threw him down from the scaffold. Looking quickly, one does not see it well, but reflecting at all upon it, it becomes clear and distinct, and by candlelight even better, it seems to me, although one can always see it sufficiently, as if it had been painted by some painter, and the eyes not open, like a little dead figure. Don Pedro has had it for a few days and has arranged for some members of the Council to see it, including, I believe, Lord Cecil. That great charlatan said it was a wonder, and so did his wife, but that it did not look like the Father. But it seems to me that, once he was dead, it did look like him because, without a doubt what some say is true, that if you look for the person whom it looks like, you will not find another in a thousand whom it resembles as much as the Father.[2]

5. Good news is arriving here from Flanders, from routes other than Brussels.[3] May Our Lord augment them through His mercy.

6. Since you have not bought the clock that I requested, do not buy it for me, for I have no more money than two hundred *reales*, more or less, and I am spending those on what necessities present themselves, for everything cannot be requested from Don Pedro's house, although the charity that he and the two Fathers have shown

---

[1] What follows is Carvajal's rendition of one of the miracles associated with Garnett's execution, "Garnett's straw," rumored to have converted hundreds of people. The DNB adds, "Archbishop Bancroft was commissioned by the privy council to call before him such persons as had been most active in propagating the story, and if possible to detect and punish the impostors" (VII: 883). Carvajal obviously participated in precisely that activity.

[2] In a 1608 letter to Joseph Creswell, Carvajal told him that the straw figure that he had sent her as a relic was a fake: "The one Your Grace sent is one the heretics have made up as a joke here" (*Epist.* 239).

[3] Regarding the victory of the Marqués de Espínola (Abad, ed. *Epist.* 194).

sido muy extraordinaria, sin conocerme. Consuélome con que por buen Señor lo ha hecho, que no se le pasa nada por alto.

7. Acá dicen se quieren los holandeses dar al rey de Inglaterra. No lo creo de ellos en buena razón de Estado y prudencia, pues con eso perderán otros amigos de más importancia; que acá no hay dineros, sino pícaros y hombres presos que sueltan para que vayan a ser soldados de Mauricio, y no sé yo si el rey trocará su quietud y caza por tan trabajosa soldadesca.

8. A Sus Altezas nos guarde Dios y a sus hermanos y sobrinos, y a vuestra merced aumente en el amor suyo que yo deseo.

9. Mande vuestra merced quemar las cartas mías, que esa malaventura de embajadores ingleses, de por allí, escriben luego lo que alcanzan a saber y los autores, y una hormiga es un elefante y una grande traición.

10. Un calendario para rezar el oficio divino, este nueve año que entra, suplico a vuestra merced me mande enviar de limosna, que la letanía de la Vida y Pasión de Cristo jamás lo entendieron. Y envióme el señor Octaviano unos libros muy buenos de ellas, pero para mí no servían de nada, que no venía allí aquélla, pero han servido para sus amigos.

11. Ahora todo es hacer *serches* y dar tras las haciendas, con que muchas almas caen, de gente importante y popular, y muchos también en entrambas suertes están con gran fortaleza.

12. Uno bien principal y muy rico, me decía ayer un amigo, que fue a la iglesia, y otro día o dos después, perdió el juicio. Y otra también muy grave murió súbito la mañana después de ir a la iglesia.

13. Mucho me he alargado, por creer gustará de saber vuestra merced estas cosas.

De diciembre 5, 1606 — † Luisa

me has been most extraordinary, since they do not know me.[4]   I console myself with the fact that he has done so as a good lord, for nothing escapes him.

7. Here it is said that the Dutch want to hand themselves over to the King of England. I don't believe it makes sense for them, for reasons of state and prudence, since should they do so they will lose other, more important friends, for here there is no money but rather picaros and imprisoned men whom they release so they can go serve Mauricio as soldiers.[5]   And I don't know if the King would trade his tranquillity and hunting for such unruly troops.

8. May God keep Their Majesties and their siblings and nephews and nieces, and may He augment His love for Your Reverence as I desire.

9. Order that my letters be burnt, for those disgraceful English ambassadors around there write immediately of whatever they manage to find out and who wrote it, and an ant is made into an elephant and a huge betrayal.

10. I beg that Your Grace send me as alms a calendar to pray the Divine Office this new year, for they never understood [here in England] the Litany of the Life and Passion of Christ. And Mr. Octaviano sent me some very fine books about that, but for me they weren't worth anything since the Passion wasn't in them, but they have served his friends.

11. Now everything is searches and chasing after estates, such that many souls fall among the important and the popular people, and many as well, of both types, are showing great strength.[6]

12. Someone of a most high position and very wealthy, a friend told me yesterday, went to the [Anglican] church and the next day or the day after lost his mind. And another very important person died suddenly the morning after going to [an Anglican] church.

13. I have gone on at length, believing that Your Grace would like to know these things.

On December 5, 1606 — † Luisa

---

[4] The annual salary of a Spanish chaplain during this period was approximately 360 *reales*, so Carvajal had a small sum of money.

[5] Maurice Nassau, William of Orange's son and general of the Protestant Dutch troops (Abad, ed. *Epist.* 194).

[6] The fact that Carvajal writes "serches," using the English word rather than simply translating it into Spanish, underscores how foreign the process was to her, because the Spanish Inquisition performed relatively few searches of the type Carvajal had already experienced. English individuals convicted of heresy lost their estates to the crown, just as convicted heretics in Spain lost theirs to the Inquisition. The contrast of "important" with "popular" people is between the nobles and everyone else.

14. En otra he suplicado a vuestra merced por milady Lovel, señora viuda inglesa muy principal y constantísima en la fe católica, sin haber hecho nunca cosa contraria a todo valor en eso. Y ahora le suplico de nuevo la allegue y haga toda amistad, pues será tanto servicio de Nuestro Señor. Y dígale vuestra merced que su pariente, si es verdad lo que dicen de haberse vuelto loco, no ha sido tan fuerte ni dichoso como ella, aunque lo parecía como el que más.

15. A las señoras monjas beso las manos.

[sobrescrito] † A la madre Magdalena de San Jerónimo, que Dios guarde, Bruselas

14. [on the outer page] In another [letter] I have entreated Your Grace on behalf of Milady Lovell, a very noble English widow most constant in the Catholic faith, who has never done anything lacking valor in that regard. And now I implore you again to take her in and show her all friendship, for it will be such a great service to Our Lord. And tell her that her relative, if what they say about his having gone crazy is true, was not as strong or as fortunate has she, although he seemed to be the stronger.[7]

15. I humbly greet the nuns.

[address] † To Mother Magdalena de San Jerónimo, may God preserve her.

Brussels

---

[7] The reference appears to be to the anonymous individual mentioned in ¶12.

78

### *A Inés de la Asunción*

*Londres, 21 de abril de 1607*

Jhs

1. Más persuadida de amor que de temor de su queja, aunque la siento, tomo la pluma en la mano con malísima disposición, por que no se vaya Rivas sin carta. Habrá recibido ya dos o tres mías, y con las suyas huelgo tanto como tengo dicho. Y con esto y la caridad que siempre le he debido, pienso dejarla obligada a que me escriba y dé de sí mil buenas nuevas.

2. Llegando aquí recibo una suya, fecha de un año y siete meses, y héme alegrado y leídola con tanto gusto como si fuera muy fresca. Sin duda se han perdido suyas y mías muchas, sólo por no querer tener un poco de cuidado aquellos a quien se encomiendan, que, por lo demás, es facilísimo, puestas en manos del padre Cresvelo venir a las del padre Baulduino a Bruselas y de las suyas a las mías o de don Pedro.

3. Dame en ésta suya una gran enhorabuena de la pobreza. Y sepa que, aunque la llego a ver cuy cerca, anda Nuestro dulcísimo Señor luego remediándolo de manera que no me deja abrazar estrechamente con ella. Primero tomó por medio unos dineros de Mistriss Margarita, que por suyos me los hicieron tomar. Y después fue necesario pagárselos y volver ella lo demás al noviciado porque no tuvo salud, según dicen, para perseverar en el monasterio. Y después, don Pedro ha sido tan liberal cuanto me ha sido necesario, y pienso

78

*To Inés de la Asunción*[1]

*London, 21 April 1607*

Jhs

1. More persuaded by love than by your complaint, although I heard it, I take pen in hand with no desire to do so, in order than Rivas not leave without a letter.[2] You have probably received two or three from me, and I am as pleased with yours as I have said before. And with this and the debt of charity I have always owed you, I plan to oblige you to write to me and tell me a thousand bits of good news about yourself.

2. Upon arriving here I received a letter from you, dated a year and seven months ago, and I have delighted in it and read it as if it were fresh. Doubtless many of yours as well as mine have been lost, due only to a lack of desire to exercise diligence on the part of those to whom they are entrusted, since, as for the rest, it is extremely easy, having placed the letters in the hands of Father Creswell,[3] to have them arrive in those of Father Baldwin to Brussels and from his to mine or don Pedro's.

3. In this letter of yours, you congratulate me much for my poverty. And you should know that, although sometimes I see it quite close, our most sweet Lord keeps resolving things in such a way that He does not let me embrace it tightly. First He took some money from Mistress Margaret as a measure against it, which they made me take because it came from her. And then I had to pay it back and she had to return the rest to the novitiate because she didn't have the health, so they said, to endure life in the monastery.[4] And then, don Pedro has been as generous as I have needed, and I think he will

---

[1] In this letter Carvajal waxes nostalgic for her homeland and reveals some delightful, if clearly prejudiced, impressions of life in London. Her letters to Inés, her living companion of thirteen years, are the only ones in which she treats domestic issues and they provide important information about private life during this period.

[2] Rivas was probably the Spanish Ambassador's courier, and Carvajal was able to send letters only when he was making a trip for other reasons. This meant writing even when she was not so inclined, as she says, although she warms to the enterprise immediately.

[3] Creswell was the director of the English Jesuits in Spain; Letter 94 is to him.

[4] The ambiguous third-person pronouns here make it impossible to specify who was paying whom or why. How Carvajal gained funds from this exchange is unclear.

que lo será hasta que se vaya, que él imagina será este verano por una carta que ha recibido, con que está lleno de gozo. Y no me espanto porque, a mi opinión, sólo por el gusto de Dios se puede tolerar la vivienda de acá. Y sobre todo, es muy cara y no se puede uno sustentar con menos dineros que en la corte de España, y esto es, sin duda, verdad en Londres, y el haber siempre asentada peste sin remedio. ¿Podrá creer que para sola una forzosa y ordinario comida de cuatro personas que somos, y casa no mayor de lo que basta para caber en ella estrechísimamente y sin lugar de añadir una sola cama más en toda ella, y vestidos muy pobres, son necesarios cuatro mil reales? Y así la gente pobre pasa gran necesidad. Y para remediarla hay costumbre de tomarse unos en casa de otros, y aunque sean señores, pagarles un tanto por la comida, y unos con otros pasan mejor. Y no ha de haber más que dos mesas en cada casa, aunque sea de duques: una para los señores y gente que viene de fuera y criados de alguna estofa, y para los criados y mozos y mozas de servicios y de cámara, otra. Y todos comen en el plato grande y todos beben en un jarro, y en esta manera toda la llaneza posible y falta de aseo. Comen pan negro, de ordinario, generalmente todos, y los hijos y los criados de los señores, y vaca asada y cocida, a cuartos enteros, y carnero y corderos, y guardado frío de tres o cuatro días y de una semana entera, y caliente y frío se sirve de ordinario. Y con esto se crían los niños más delicados, y de manjares mejores toman tres o cuatro bocados a la postre. Andan todos muy galanos, y en esto gastan muchísimo. Las cosas son todas más baladíes, generalmente, que en España: los mantenimientos, de buena vista, pero sin olor y casi sin sabor, y de poca fuerza, y sin poderse guardar, ni en invierno, cuatro días enteros sin algún mal sabor. Y como venden a pedazos y no hay libras en eso, hase de tomar por fuerza más de lo necesario en casa pequeña. Y eso remedian ellos con asarlo y guardarlo fiambre o empanado. Las gallinas son a dos reales y medio o tres, lo más ordinario, pero tan sin sustancia y dejativas que, a solas, no bastan ni se pueden comer, y son muy

continue to be so until he leaves, which he imagines will be this summer, judging by a letter he has received, which has made him delighted. And I'm not surprised because, in my opinion, only to please God can one tolerate living here . And above all, it is very expensive and you can't maintain yourself with less money than at the Spanish court, and this is, without a doubt, the case in London, and the plague is ever in the area and nothing can be done about it. Can you believe that for just an essential and ordinary meal for the four of us, and a house no larger than what suffices to fit us tightly within it and with no space to add a single bed more in the whole place, and our very poor clothing, it costs four thousand *reales*?[5] And thus poor folk endure great need. And to remedy it, there is the custom of taking up house with someone else, although they be lords and ladies, paying a stipend for board, and getting by easier by being together. And there may not be more than two tables in each house, even though it be a duke's: one for the gentlefolk and people who visit and servants of a certain category, and the other for the servants and serving men and women and the chamber servants. And they all eat from the serving plate and all drink from one pitcher, and in this manner there is all possible lack of formality and of cleanliness. Everyone usually eats dark bread,[6] including the children and servants of gentlefolk, and roasted and stewed beef in entire quarters, and mutton and lamb, and they keep it cold for three or four days and even an entire week, and it is usually served hot and cold. And with this even the most sickly children are raised, and they have three or four bites of better foodstuffs at the end of the meal. They all dress quite impressively and spend a lot of money on that. Things are generally of cheaper quality than in Spain: the food, which looks good but has no aroma and is almost completely lacking in flavor, stays fresh only for the shortest time, and cannot be stored even in winter for four days without some foul taste. And since items are sold by the piece rather than by the pound, one must take more than is necessary for a small household. And this they remedy by roasting and stuffing it or wrapping it in bread. Chickens usually cost two and a half or three *reales*, but have such little substance and taste that, served alone, they are insufficient and cannot even be eaten, and they are very

---

[5] The four in Carvajal's house were herself, her two English companions, and her French manservant Lemeteliel. Four thousand *reales* was an extravagant sum, given that Carvajal claimed to have only two hundred *reales* to her name in Letter 69 (¶6).

[6] Dark, or "black" bread means any whole grain bread; i.e., one made without white flour, which was the most costly at that time.

chiquitas. Y así, en lugar de ellas sirven capones, que son como gallinas buenas de allá, aunque no en el sabor, y esos cuestan cinco reales o seis, y pocas veces veo que cuesten cuatro solamente.

4. Yo estoy con la misma necesidad de ese mantenimiento que allá, y de lo demás que pide mi caída salud, sin querer Nuestro Señor dispensar en eso. Y así, dice una de mis compañeras, que es menester, en faltando las limosnas gruesas, pedir gallina y mazapán por cada puerta. El considerar esto y cuál es esta tierra para pobres aviva mi esperanza y gusto de ver cómo están enlazando las dulces manos de Dios tan grandes dificultades y humanas disconveniencias en corazón tan pobrecito y flaco. No se me puede descubrir qué quiera Su Majestad de mí en Inglaterra, aunque parece querer la perseverancia en ella, hasta ahora a lo menos. Y esa fuerza poderosa de su gusto me tiene aferrada aquí con la misma fuerza que me sacó y arrancó de España, y deseo seguir aquel consejo, *"Bonum est praestolari cum silentio salutare Dei,"* esto es, el cumplimiento de su dulcísima voluntad, *"sicut in caelo et in terra,"* que entiendo puramente y sin mezcla de permisión, en que consiste la verdadera satisfacción del alma a tanta gloria de Dios y estrecha unión del dulcísimo Amado, Cristo Nuestro Señor. Mi indignidad y faltas han crecido, porque no se han desaugmentado, y para flojos es terrible vivienda porque la multitud de varios descontentos y penosos objetos de alma y cuerpo en quien desea llegarse a Dios, naturalmente desaguan y dejan caídos los brazos y el corazón. Y con poca salud, es un género de padecer, si se esfuerza el alma, que allá no se calará muy presto. Hágame merced de hacer instancia con Nuestro Señor para el remedio de mis males, que yo suelo decir a Su Majestad que, cómo siendo tan sumamente benigno, dulce y bueno, y ellos tales, no llegan a lastimarle hasta el total remedio, porque mis esfuerzos no bastan, aunque algunas veces llego a esperar mucho y a tomar grande aliento con los ojos y corazón puesto en Él, llegándome a comulgar, y pidiendo se sirva de que sea aquel día el postrero de su suma paciencia y de mi mal.

5. Esta Cuaresma tuvimos un mártir de una dichosa muerte: envié ya la relación al padre Lorenzo, y creo que habrá llegado también

small. And so instead of them they serve capons, which are like the good chickens there, although not the same in taste, and those cost five or six *reales*, and a few times I have seen them for only four.

4. I continue here with the same need for that sustenance as I had there, and for the other things that my fallen health requires, without Our Lord caring to dispense with that. And so, as one of my companions says, [when we are] lacking large donations it is necessary to beg for chicken and sweetbread from door to door. Considering that and how this land is for poor people sparks my hope and pleasure in seeing how God's sweet hands are joining such great difficulties and human inconveniences in such a poor and weak little heart. I cannot seem to figure out what His Majesty might want of me in England, although He seems to wish that I persevere here, at least for the moment. And the powerful force of His pleasure has me soldered here with the same power that removed and pulled me out of Spain, and I wish to follow that counsel, "*Bonum est praestolari cum silentio salutare Dei*," which is to say, the fulfillment of his most sweet will, "*sicut in caelo et in terra*,"[7] which I understand as meaning purely and without the mixture of any compromise, in which the soul's true satisfaction consists to such glory of God and intimate union of the most sweet Beloved, Christ Our Lord. My unworthiness and flaws have increased, because they have not decreased, and for weak people this is a terrible way of life due to the multitude of various discontents and objects painful to soul and body for the one who desires to get close to God, which naturally dilute and leave one's arms and heart fallen. And with little health, it is a type of suffering, if one forces one's soul, that won't catch on very quickly there. Show me the mercy of petitioning Our Lord for the remedy of my flaws, for I usually ask His Majesty how it is, since He is so very merciful, sweet, and good, and those flaws are such as they are, that they don't pain Him to extremes, because my efforts are insufficient, although sometimes I wind up hoping for much and taking great courage with my eyes and heart set on Him as I come to communion, and asking that on that final day He avail Himself of his greatest patience and of my wickedness.

5. This Lent we had a martyr who died a fortunate death: I already sent an account of it to Father Lorenzo [Da Ponte], and I think another one has probably arrived among those

---

[7] "For it is good to await the wellbeing of God in silence" (Lam. 3:26); from the Lord's Prayer, "as it is in heaven" (Matt. 6:10).

otra a las del padre Ricardo, en una que le escribí. Había estado en Valladolid cinco años al principio del Colegio, y acá trece. Era de treinta y nueve o cuarenta años, pero en el aspecto muy más mozo y de gentil talle y disposición. Estaría como un mes preso, y, habiendo otros, tenían una gana de matarle a él extraña, aunque no era de los que ellos más aborrecían, pero queríale Dios para no menos alto estado. ¡Oh juicios suyos inmensos! Habíase proveído de sotana y bonete, y abierto la corona para este efecto, y así fue llevado en el carro por toda la ciudad, que creo es casi una legua o más. Yo no lo supe, ni otros muchos amigos suyos lo pudieron saber, hasta que era ya muerto, porque haciendo eficaces y encubiertas diligencias don Pedro, se tuvo grande esperanza de su vida y de la de otros que no murieron, aunque había sido con él condenado uno de ellos. La tarde antes gasté gran rato hablando con él, que lo hacía en español muy bien, y mostrábame gran amor y más que a nadie de cuantos le venían a ver. Y yo procuré dilatarle y confirmarle tan fuertemente cuanto me fue posible en que no se dejase vencer de las bravas persuasiones que le hacían, para que siquiera hiciese el último juramento que ahora un año hicieron en el Parlamento, en que otros se han dejado vencer. Y el obispo de Londres, ante quien fue presentado, habrá ya visto su dicha y podido decir, *"Hi sunt quos aliquando habuimus in derisum: quomodo computati sunt inter filios Dei,"* porque se fue a tener la pascua al infierno su infelice alma. Espero que ha de querer Nuestro Señor hacer merced

[accounts] of Father Ricardo, in one I wrote to him.[8]  He had spent five years in Valladolid just after the College was founded and spent thirteen here.[9]  He was 39 or 40 years old, but much younger in appearance and of a genteel breed and disposition. He must have spent about a month in prison and, since there were others, they had a remarkable desire to kill him, although he was not among those they most abhorred, but God wanted him for no less a noble station. Oh His tremendous judgments!  He had been provided with a cassock and biretta and had a tonsure cut in his hair for this purpose, and thus he was carried in a carriage through the entire city, which I believe is a league or more. And I did not find out about it, nor were his many other friends able to know about it, until he was already dead, because, due to don Pedro's efficacious and secret efforts, we held great hopes that he would live as well as the others who did not die, although one of them had been condemned with him. The previous afternoon I spent a long time speaking with him, for he spoke very good Spanish, and he showed great love to me, and more to me than to anyone else among those who came to see him. And I managed to get him to open up and to convince him as much as I could that he not let himself be overcome by the fierce arguments they were using on him that he take the last oath that was passed a year ago in Parliament, by which others have let themselves be overcome. And the Bishop of London, before whom he was presented, will have seen his [the martyr's] good fortune by now and will have been able to say, "*Hi sunt quos aliquando habuimus in derisum [ . . . Ecce] quomodo computati sunt inter filios Dei,*"[10] because his [the Bishop's] unfortunate soul really got things backwards. I hope that Our Lord will want

---

[8] The "martyr" was Robert Drury, SJ (b. 1567), an English-born priest who had been working in the London area since 1593. In 1606 he was arrested for being a priest and remaining in the country. He refused to take the Oath of Fidelity and was hung and quartered on 26 Feb. 1606/1607 (DNB VI: 58). According to Abad, English ministers of state put particular pressure on Drury to take the Oath of Fidelity to the English monarch, which implied accepting the king as head of the English Church, because Drury exercised considerable influence over the English Catholics (Intro. *Epist.*, 49). The Oath was required of men in May 1606, of women in 1611. After Drury's execution, Carvajal took responsibility for the care of his aged mother.

[9] The Jesuit College of San Alban's in Valladolid was founded in 1589; see Loomie, *Spanish* 187-92.

[10] "These are the ones whom we held in contempt. . . . Behold how they are counted among the sons of God" (Wisdom 5: 3; 5).

a su Iglesia santa con buenos sucesos, entre tanta aflicción como ha padecido en nuestro tiempo. Y por esto deberíamos clamar de noche y día en su divino acatamiento, sin acordarnos de particulares trabajos.

6. Mi Inés, y cierto muy entrañablemente mía, mire que me diga muy particularmente cómo se va hallando y siente su espíritu, y tirando la cortina del silencio, muestre y descubra sus aprovechamientos y misericordias divinas para mi consuelo, que le tengo en eso cuanto no sabría decir. Y de nuestra madre y señora me diga también mil cosas. Isabel no me ha escrito ni una sola vez, pero ya he dicho que se lo perdonaré con que se acuerde de mí muy de veras con Nuestro Señor y con saber en sus cartas de ella. ¡Cuál imagino a mi amada y bonísima hermana con su hábito y velo, y qué contento me fuera verla! Y eso se ofrece con lo demás. Los conocidos están buenos, aunque esto no se puede asegurar de una hora a otra, a lo menos de que no estarán presos. Al padre Antonio casi nunca veo: no sé qué es la causa de no acordarse de mí más si no estuviera en Inglaterra. El padre M[iguel] huelga siempre de saber de ella.

7. A la capilla de don Pedro voy cada mañana a misa, porque estoy muy cerca de su casa. Y por estar y ser juntamente necesaria casa no más cara de lo que se puede y recogida suficientemente, tenemos una que casi no tiene aire, y el que tiene es muy poco sano porque pasa por otras muchas casas pobres primero, y para la peste es esto lo que más se teme. Pero eso es ser pobre.

8. Hablo ya algo mejor inglés y no bien, por falta de medio que, como he dicho en otras, no hay esperar que persona alguna quiera cansarse un solo día en eso, ni de las mismas que tengo en casa, ni en enmendarme si yerro. Y si les pregunto, es menester de ordinario hacerlo dos o tres veces, y al cabo, como quien despierta de un sueño, responden, "No, es muy bueno."

9. Inés mía, que me llega ahora otra carta suya de febrero, y viene una de Isabel y otra de doña María Ponce, a quien nunca he escrito, y con todo eso no se queja. Graciosísimos fueron los

to show mercy to His Church with happy events amidst such affliction as it has suffered in our times. And for this we ought to clamor day and night in his divine worship, without thinking about our individual trials.

6. My Inés, and surely most profoundly mine, take care to tell me in great detail how you find yourself and feel your spirit to be, and drawing aside the curtain of silence, show and reveal your progress and divine mercies that I might be consoled, for it does console me more than I know how to say. And tell me a thousand things as well about our mother and lady.[11] Isabel has not written to me even once, but I have said that I will forgive her as long as she remembers me most truly to Our Lord and provided that there is news of her in your letters.[12] How I imagine my beloved and dearest sister with her habit and veil and how happy I would be to see her! And this is offered [as a sacrifice to God] with the rest. Our acquaintances are well, although you can never be sure from one hour to the next, at least about whether or not they will be imprisoned. I hardly ever see Father Antonio; I don't know why he doesn't remember me any more than if he weren't in England. Father M[ichael Walpole] is always happy to have news of her.[13]

7. I go every morning to mass in don Pedro's chapel. And because I live in and need a sufficiently private house that is no more expensive than I can pay for, we have one that has almost no air, and the air in it is most unhealthy because it passes through many poor houses first, and for the plague this is what one fears the most. But such is being poor.

8. I speak English a little better already and not well, due to lack of means for, as I have said in other letters, there is no hoping that a single person would want to wear herself out for even one day doing that, not even the women I have in the house, not even correcting me if I make a mistake. And if I ask them something, I usually have to do so two or three times, and in the end, like someone waking from a dream, they respond, "No, it's very good."

9. My Inés, another one of your letters from February has arrived, and one from Isabel and another from doña María Ponce, to whom I have never written, and even so she does not com-

---

[11] Mariana de San José, Inés's superior, Carvajal's friend, and foundress of the convent where her documents and remains are kept.

[12] Isabel de la Cruz, one of Carvajal's living companions in Madrid, was Inés's cousin. She had professed as a Recollect Augustinian in Medina del Campo.

[13] "Her" refers to Isabel de la Cruz, whom Walpole would have met in Madrid.

ringloncillos de nuestra Madre en esta materia, en la margen de la suya, y lo que yo gusté de ellos: ¡qué buena y dulce señora! Y sola su memoria me alegra. Nunca puedo leer el nombre del padre que dice me hace merced y se digna de hablar con ella de mí, porque están casi borradas las letras. Ya veo estoy de todo punto inútil para ofrecerle algún servicio o consuelo, pero si en algo pudiere, estaré muy pronta a hacerlo con el amor que le debo.

10. Escríbenme se iban pagando ya muy aprisa mis deudas. De la suya dejé claridad suficiente, demás de su escritura, y de los seiscientos ducados de ajuar y año de noviciado, e imagen, que fuera de eso le han de dar del precio que se señaló en la memoria de mis deudas.

11. Mil cosas me dice en las suyas de que huelgo saber. En lo que dice el padre Luis [de la Puente] y el padre Antonio [Padilla] y doña Marina [de Escobar] no sé qué le diga, sino que es grande el contrapeso que hay en favor de la perseverancia, hasta ahora a lo menos, y me hallo muy destetada de cualquier delgada cosa que me pueda dar humano alivio o contento, y de la vuelta, mucho más, por el demasiado que habría en ella. Y yo no pienso sino morir de esta manera, y pretendo sea tan asida de Dios como desasida de todo lo que hay fuera de Él.

12. Díceme que le diré yo de curandajas. Basta, y creo me lo podrá mejor decir ella, que escribo con prisas de correos por la mayor parte, y no se aliña con ellas tan presto cosa que puede ser de mucho consuelo. Y ahora me dicen se cierra el pliego.

Guárdemela Dios, hermana mía, como deseo, en continuos crecimientos de su amor santísimo.

De Londres y abril, 29, 1607

Su más verdadera hermana, Luisa.

[sobrescrito] A Inés de la Asunción, mi muy amada hermana, que Dios guarde, etc., Valladolid

plain. Our Mother's remarks about this business in the margins of your letter were quite entertaining, and I enjoyed them immensely: what a good and sweet lady! And just the memory of her cheers me. I can never read the name of the Father she says is doing me a favor and deigns to speak with her about me because all the letters have been erased. I can see that I am completely worthless to be of any service to her, but if I could in any way, I will be quick to get to it with the debt of love I owe her.

10. I have received word that my debts are being quickly paid. I left things clear enough about your portion, besides your deed and the six hundred ducats for your dowry and novitiate year, and the image, for aside from that they are to give you the amount indicated in the declaration of my debts.[14]

11. Your letters say a thousand things that I would like to know about. As far as what Father Luis [de la Puente] and Father Antonio [de Padilla] and doña Marina [de Escobar] are saying, I don't know what to say, except that the weight for the opposite side of the argument is great, at least so far, and I find myself quite weaned from any slim thing that might provide me with human comfort or contentment, and for my return [to Spain], much more [comfort or contentment], due to the excess of the same that I would find in that act. And I pretend to nothing except to die in this fashion, and I seek to be as attached to God as unattached to all that is not God.[15]

12. You tell me that I will tell her about *curandajas*.[16] That's enough about that, and I think she could tell me better, for I usually write in haste to make the post, and with that rush one cannot season [one's letters with] something that could provide much consolation so quickly. And now they are telling me to seal this sheet.

May God keep you, my sister, as I desire, in continual growth in His most holy love.

From London on April 29, 1607

Your truest sister, Luisa

[address] To Inés de la Asunción, my very beloved sister, whom God keep, etc. Valladolid

---

[14] In her will, Carvajal left money to Inés for her novitiate and convent dowry, as well as a marble crucifix (EA 250). Funds to cover these expenses were charged against Carvajal's estate before her death, since Inés made her religious profession immediately after Carvajal left for England.

[15] The three individuals named in the first sentence all put pressure on Carvajal to return to Spain.

[16] Neither Abad or I can identify this word. It seems to refer jokingly to healing women (*curanderas*).

94

*Al Padre José Cresvelo, S. I.*
*Londres (Haigat), 29 de junio de 1608*

Jhs.

1. Mucha merced y consuelo recibo con las de vuestra merced, y espero que vuestra merced habrá recibido consuelo con las últimas mías, viendo la gran constancia de los santos mártires Garves y Fludder. Y de mí, puedo decir a vuestra merced que he andado entre la cruz y el agua bendita, como allá dicen, porque he estado presa, y como ha sido en cárcel pública, no me bastará callarlo.

2. La causa fue, porque llegando un día a una tienda de Chepsaid, desde afuera, como suelo, de pechos sobre el tablón, se ofreció preguntar a uno de los mancebos si era católico, y él respondió, "No, God forbid!" Y yo repliqué, "No permita Dios que no lo seáis, que es lo que os importa." Con esto acudieron la señora y el señor de la tienda y otro mancebo y mercaderes vecinos, y trabóse grande plática de religión católica. Preguntaron mucho de la misa, de los sacerdotes, de la confesión, pero lo principal en que se gastó en tiempo (de más de dos horas) fue en si la romana religión es la sola verdadera, y si el Papa es cabeza de la Iglesia, y si sucesivamente en ellos [los Papas] han quedado las llaves de San Pedro para siempre.

## 94

### *To Father Joseph Creswell, S. J.*[1]
*London (Highgate), 29 June of 1608*

Jhs.

1. I receive great mercy and consolation from Your Grace's letters, and I hope that Your Grace has received consolation with my last correspondence, seeing the great constancy of the holy martyrs Garves and Fludder.[2]  And of me, I can tell Your Grace that I have walked between the cross and holy water, as they say there, because I have been in prison, and since it was in the public jail, it would be useless for me to keep silent about it.[3]

2. The reason was because, arriving one day at a store in Cheapside, leaning on the door sill from outside, as is my custom, the occasion offered to ask one of the young attendants if he was Catholic presented itself, and he responded, "No, God forbid!" And I replied, "May God not permit that you not be, which is what matters for you." At this the mistress and master of the shop came over, and another youth and neighboring merchants, and a great chat about religion ensued. They asked a lot about the mass, about priests, about confession, but what we spent the most time on (over two hours) was whether the Roman religion was the only true one, and whether the Pope is the head of the Church, and whether St. Peter's keys have been left to them [the Popes] forever in succession.

---

[1] Joseph Creswell (1566-1623) was the director of the English Jesuits in Spain and Portugal (see Loomie, "'A Seminarie'"). Carvajal probably met him in Madrid during the late 1580s. Five letters are extant that Carvajal wrote immediately after release from her first prison term. Four are dated 29 June: to Creswell (#94, which follows here), to her spiritual advisor in Madrid, the Franciscan Lorenzo da Ponte (#96), to Mariana de San José (#97), and to Inés de la Asunción (#98). The fifth (#95) is undated and lacks addressee. Later, on 28 Aug. 1608, she again related the event to her cousin, the Marqués de Caracena, then Viceroy of Valencia (#99). In this last one, she specifies the week of her prison term as being that of the feast of the Eucharist, which would have been early June (*Epist.* 251).

[2] In Letter 93, also to Creswell, Carvajal describes two executions, one of a man named "Fludde" or "Fennel" in York, and that of George Garves in London, who, left dying but not dead by his first hanging, cried out "Let me alone!" to the man about to quarter his body (*Epist.* 241).

[3] Her several letters recalling the experience indicate how delighted Carvajal was to tell this story, in spite of her protestations to the contrary.

3. Algunos oían con gusto, otros con rabia, y tanta que advertí algún peligro, por lo menos de ser presa. Pero no lo estimé en nada, a trueco de ponerles aquella luz delante de los ojos en la mejor manera que pude. Y en estas cosas llanas de fe hay razones sabidas muy convenientes a quienquiera, y con que se puede hacer guerra al error. Y aunque no lo tomen bien de presente, en fin les quedan aquellas verdades en la memoria, con motivo para discurrir y puerta abierta a las santas inspiraciones, y justifícase mucho la causa de Dios para su salvación o condenación de ellos. Y hay muchísimos que jamás llegan ni aun a saber dó[nde] están los sacerdotes, y de los católicos legos, no muchos quieren aventurarse tanto sin conocido fruto. Y los mercaderes de Chepsaid exceden en malicia, error, y odio del Papa y de nuestra santa fe al resto de la ciudad, como también en gente y dinero. Y puédese algo de esto conocer en que, habiendo yo diversas veces hablado en ocasiones con otros de la misma manera sin diferencia, siempre lo tomaron apaciblemente.

4. La señora de la tienda procuraba levantar la cólera a todos, y otro infernal mancebo que estaba allí, menor en edad y mayor en malicia. La mujer decía que era lástima que me sufriesen y que, sin duda, yo era algún sacerdote romano en hábito de mujer, para poder persuadir mejor mi religión. Sirvióse Nuestro Señor que pudiese hablar mejor en inglés que después que he estado en Inglaterra, y pensaban era escocesa por la lengua y mostrar afición al rey, porque, llegando uno de los más ancianos a mí, dijo que si él no era harto sabio para no hacer seguir error en su reino. Respondí que no tratasen del rey, que había quedado niño sin su santa madre católica, en poder de puritanos, y que ellos tenían más verdadero y legítimo rey que lo fue la reina Isabel.

5. Pretendí con esto no disimular la verdad y hacerles olvidar la maliciosa pregunta del rey, sobre que levantaran

3. Some listened with pleasure, others with fury, and so much that I sensed some danger, at least of being arrested. But I thought nothing of it, in exchange for setting that light before their eyes in the best way I could. And in these simple matters of faith there are known methods [of convincing] which are very handy for anyone, and with which one can wage war on error. And although they might not take it very well at first, in the end those truths remain in their memories, to be meditated upon and open to holy inspirations, and God's cause for their salvation or condemnation is greatly justified. And there are very many who never manage to find out even where the priests are, and among the lay Catholics, not many want to run that risk [of contact with priests] without a guaranteed benefit. And the merchants of Cheapside exceed the rest of the city in malice, error, and hatred for the Pope, as well as in the quantity of its residents and money. And some of this can be observed in the fact that, when I have spoken on several occasions with others about exactly the same things, they have always taken it affably.

4. The mistress of the shop tried to stir everyone to anger, as did another infernal young man who was there, younger in age but with greater malice. The woman said it was a shame that they were tolerating me and that, without a doubt, I was some Roman [Catholic] priest dressed like a woman so as to better persuade people of my religion. Our Lord saw fit that I speak the best English I've spoken since I've been in England, and they thought I was Scottish because of the way I spoke and because I showed affection for the King, because one of the eldest men came over to me and asked whether he [James] wasn't quite wise for not making his entire kingdom continue in error.[4]  I responded that it wasn't a question of the King, who had been left as a child, without his saintly Catholic mother, in the power of the Puritans, and that they had a truer and more legitimate King now than they had had in Queen Elizabeth.

5. Thus I tried not to evade the truth and make them forget the malicious question about the King, about which they are extremely

---

[4] James I (1566-1625; king of England in 1603), the son of Mary Queen of Scots (1542-1587).

caramillos. Y así ellos preguntaron luego por qué era éste más verdadero. Y dije que, por ser bisnieto de la hija mayor de Enrique VIII, e Isabel, su hija, nacida en vida de la reina Catalina, madre de María. Y de esto infirieron que la hacía yo bastarda, pero, como pasó ya y no dejó hijos, no era cosa de importancia. Y en breves palabras se pasó y volvimos a la santa religión otra vez.

6. Y oyendo yo que a mis espaldas uno llamaba traidor a Mr. Jarves, y mi Ana, mártir, sobre que litigaban, la impedí, temiendo que diría algo que no conviniese. Y díjele a él que me dijese por qué había muerto el Jarves. Dijo que por sólo ser católico romano. "¿Y no por otra ninguna cosa?" repliqué. Dijo que no. "Pues luego," le dije yo, "no os espantéis que sea llamado mártir." Y parece lo tomaba bien.

7. Con esto me volví a casa y quedaron como leones contra mí. Y pasados quince días, acertáronme a ver, que fue necesario salir, lo cual hago pocas veces sin muy particular causa de comprar lo necesario o ir a ver [a] los dichosos confesores de Cristo a las cárceles, o cosa semejante, y jamás a visitas de nadie (que mi natural condición me inclina a ello y

touchy.[5] And so then they asked why it was that the King was truer. And I said that because he was the great-grandson of the eldest daughter of Henry VIII and Elizabeth, his daughter, was born during the life of Queen Catherine, Mary's mother. And from that they inferred that I was calling her a bastard but, since it had already happened and she left no sons, it wasn't a matter of importance. And we got through that with few words and returned to questions about the true religion once more.

6. And hearing behind me that someone calling Mr. Garves a traitor, and my Ann, [insisting he was] a martyr, were disputing, I prohibited her from continuing, fearing that she might say something impolitic.[6] And I asked him to tell me why Garves had died. He said only because he was a Roman Catholic. "And for no other reason?" I replied. He said yes. "Well then," I said to him, "don't be shocked that he is called a martyr." And he seemed to take it well.

7. With this I returned to my house and I left them like lions against me. And two weeks later they managed to spot me, for it was necessary for me to go out, which I do but few times without a very specific need to buy necessary things or to go see the felicitous confessors of Christ in the prisons, or something similar, and never to visit anyone (for my natural condition so inclines me and my

[5] The English would not arrest Carvajal for being a Catholic, but they would arrest her if she contested or subverted the sovereignty of the English king in any way. Thus she was trying to evade topics that were more political than theological. Catherine of Aragon (1485-1536), Mary Tudor's mother, was Henry VIII's first wife. He had their 18-year marriage annulled so as to wed Anne Bolyn, mother of Queen Elizabeth I (1533-1603), an act that forced him to name himself as Head of the English Church, for which the Pope excommunicated him. Henry had Anne beheaded in 1536.

[6] Ann Garnett was Henry Garnett's cousin, Carvajal's companion since Jan. 1606 (*Epist.* 227; 271). In Letter 98 , she describes Ann saying, "She is young and good for everything; she does nice needlework and makes lovely hosts and waxen candles and knows a lot about sewing, although this is not always what we need most, and in anything she is handy. She wishes to see herself in Spain with me, but, since I'm living here, she in no way wishes to leave me, according to what she makes evident. And she is a little lion in religion, when she gets her feathers up. One day, I was coming out of mass at don Pedro's house, months ago, with my rosary in my hand, and someone passing in the street, a heretic, managed to take it away from me, she immediately took off after him and started punching him saying, 'Evil man! What do you want with a rosary?'" (*Epist.* 267).

mi poca salud y fuerzas lo piden). Y en fin, me cercaron, mirándome como basiliscos, y con un alguacil que trujeron, decían era necesario ir a sir Tomás Benet, juez de la paz, no lejos de allí. Y aunque no tenía mandamiento, no resistí, porque no me asiesen del brazo o voceasen en medio aquella calle. Y al alma tampoco no le era mala ocasión. Y afablemente nos fuimos todas tres presas, digo Ana y Fe, mis compañeras, y yo  (que las otras dos quedaron en casa). Y nuestro criado, que es un virtuoso viejo muy honrado y antiguo católica, fue con nosotras.

8. Hallamos al juez sentado debajo de un tejadillo en su patio do[nde] debe despachar sus negocios, y allí nos tuvo, examinando testigos y haciendo preguntas, desde las seis de la tarde o poco más, hasta las nueve o más, que empezó a anochecer. Los testigos juraron sobre su Biblia verdades, entre algunas mentiras, pero todo ello dentro del compás de los puntos que he tocado, sin inventar cosa nueva fuera de ellos. Y desbarataban a veces, de modo que me hicieron acordar de aquello, *"Et testimonia convenientia non erant."* Y habían dos o tres de ellos concitando el pueblo de aquellas calles contra mí, diciendo que era un sacerdote en hábito de mujer que andaba persuadiendo mi fe. Y como cosa tan nueva, creo que en media hora había ya más de doscientas personas, según decían, a la puerta del juez, llena la calle de un grande y confuso ruido. Y entre ellos, ya se decía que eran tres los sacerdotes, con ropas largas negras, que es nuestro traje. Levantóse algunas veces a

poor health and strength require it).[7] And in the end they surrounded me, looking at me like basilisks,[8] and with a sheriff they brought, they said I had to go to Sir Thomas Bennet's house, the justice of the peace, not far from there. And although they had no warrant, I didn't resist, so they wouldn't grab me by the arm or raise a ruckus right in the middle of the street. And it wasn't a bad moment for my soul either. And all three of us went along agreeably, I mean Ann and Faith, my companions,[9] and myself (for the other two [companions] had stayed at home). And our servant, who is an old and virtuous man of honor and long-standing Catholic faith, went with us.

8. We found the judge seated beneath a little roof on his patio, where he probably conducts his business, and he had us there, examining witnesses and questioning people from six in the evening or a bit later until around nine, when it started to get dark. The witnesses swore on their Bible what truths they said, with a few lies, but more or less within the limits of what I've already touched upon, without inventing anything else. And they talked so much nonsense sometimes that they made me recall that line, "*Et testimonia convenientia non erant.*"[10] And there were two or three of them stirring up the people of the nearby streets against me, saying I was a priest in a woman's clothes who was walking around persuading people of my faith, and since it was something so unheard of, I believe in half an hour there were more than two hundred people, so they were saying, at the judge's door, with the street full of a great, confusing noise. And among them they were already saying that there were three priests, with their long black gowns, which is our garb.[11] The judge got up

[7] References to illness were standard features of Catholic women's spiritual writings of the time and do not necessarily refer to a woman's actual health. Carvajal led a very active life in London. However, in this letter she takes care to underplay her activity so as to represent herself conservatively, which during this period meant describing herself as enclosed and ill.

[8] Basilisks, small, snake-like creatures mentioned in Pliny's *Natural History*, were believed to kill with their sight and their breath.

[9] Carvajal describes Faith in Letter 98 as "a little dove, who had joined me the day before I was arrested" (*Epist.* 268).

[10] The passage describes the Jewish priests' accusations against Christ before Caiphas; the Vulgate reads "Et convenientia testimonia non erant" ("but their witness agreed not together"). The picture Carvajal paints of her examination, down to the image of the Justice seated under a canopy, is meant to recall paintings of Christ before Caiphas.

[11] This sentence continues Carvajal's indirect quotation of what her enemies were saying, that the three women arrested were really priests, because they wore black gowns.

apaciguarlos el juez, porque hacían gran fuerza por entrar. Y díjome que, si él me enviaba a la cárcel entonces, que el pueblo me daría buena mano. Yo le dije que más caridad creía que tenía que aquélla.

9. Preguntó mi patria, nombre, vivienda y venida a Inglaterra, y con la verdad atajé mucho, diciéndole me llamaba Luisa de Carvajal, y era española, y vivía cerca del señor don Pedro, donde iba a oír misa, y que había venido por seguir el ejemplo de mucho santos de la santa iglesia que se desterraron voluntariamente de su patria, deudos, y amigos por amor de Nuestro Señor, y vivieron en tierra extrañas con desamparo y pobreza. Y aunque era algarabía para el mísero viejo, ésta era la mejor respuesta, sin duda.

10. Él se rió como de locura, y díjome si era así que afirmaba ser el Papa cabeza de la Iglesia y su religión la sola verdadera. Dije que sí. Dijo que si quería siempre permanecer en tales opiniones. Y respondí que sí quería, y estaba aparejada a morir por ellas. Entonces blasfemó mucho del Papa, y díjome que si había yo dicho que no se podían salvar en la religión de Inglaterra. Dije que no había dicho esas palabras, pero lo mismo en otros términos, porque yo había afirmado que en sola la verdadera fe de la Iglesia romana se podían salvar, y que todas las demás religiones de todo el mundo eran errores y que en esta generalidad se incluía Inglaterra suficientemente. Díjome si sabía que en España ponían a la muerte a los ingleses que no querían tener su religión y que si no era justo hacer acá lo mismo con los españoles. Y tras esto pasó a preguntarme por qué decía yo que era Mr. Jarves mártir, no lo siendo. Yo dije que lo que yo había dicho era que, habiendo muerto por sola causa de nuestra santa religión, lo era, sin duda. Dijo él, *if he did*, si fue así, bien, pero no murió por religión. Díjele yo, "¿Pues por qué?" Y dijo que porque era un loco. Y vino a lo de la reina, y dijo que por qué creía yo que era menos legítima que el Rey. Y dije lo que he referido de la reina Catalina. Y él dijo que eso era no saber las historias, porque Catalina no había sido legítima mujer de Enrique.

to calm them down a few times, because they were trying hard to get in. And he told me that if he were to send me to the jail then, the people would go at me. I told him I thought he had more charity than that.

9. He asked my homeland, name, address, and the reason I was in England, and by telling the truth I cut it short, saying my name was Luisa de Carvajal, and I was Spanish, and I lived close to don Pedro's house, where I went to hear mass, and that I had come to follow the example of many saints of the holy church who voluntarily exiled themselves into foreign lands, being unprotected and poor. And although it was all gibberish to the pitiful old man, that was the best answer, without a doubt.

10. He laughed as if he were crazy and asked me if it was the case that I affirmed the Pope to be the head of the Church and his religion the only true one. I said yes.[12]  He asked me if I wanted to remain in said opinions. And I responded that yes I did, and that I was prepared to die for them. Then he blasphemed a great deal against the Pope and asked me if I had said that one could not be saved in the English religion. I said that I had not said those words, but had said the same thing in other terms, because I had affirmed that all the other religions of the world were erroneous, and that under this generalization England was sufficiently included. He asked me if I knew that in Spain they put English people to death who didn't want to take their [Spaniards'] religion and didn't I think it was fair that the same be done with Spaniards. And after this he went on to ask me why I had said that Mr. Garves was a martyr, since he was not one. I told him that what I had said was that, since he died solely for the cause of our holy religion, he was, without a doubt. He said, "If he did," if it had been that way, then yes, but that he hadn't died for reasons of religion. Then I said to him, "Well then why?"  And he said it was because he was a crazy man. And then he came to the business about the Queen, and he asked why I believed that she [Elizabeth] was less legitimate than the King [James]. And I told him what I have said about Queen Catherine. And he said the reason I said that was because I didn't know what had happened, because Catherine had not been Henry's legitimate wife.[13]

---

[12] Carvajal's syntax, usually lengthy and ornate, takes on the succinct quality of her interrogation during this passage.

[13] Henry VIII claimed that Catherine of Aragon was not his legitimate wife because she had been married to his brother, Arthur, before him; God, then, was punishing him for this sin by not providing him with an heir by Catherine.

11. A las dos doncellas trató más cortesmente que a mí, y quizá por ser inglesas, aunque le ponían en más cuidado que yo, porque les pareció lo mejor disimular. Yo dije que ellas eran, sin duda, sinceras y sin malicia alguna. A mí [me] llamó su secretario hipócrita, y por lo menos lo parecía. (¡Qué desgraciada cara tiene, señor, el padecer, a los ojos del mundo, y qué hermosa es a los de Dios, cuando cae sobre inocencia!) Y era lo bueno que sobre el brazo en que daba toda la luz, tenía yo un gran remiendo o dos, y sobre la cabeza un tafetán negro roto, y con esto y el ser española y tan católica como ellos echaban de ver, no fue mucho que me menospreciasen tanto como lo hicieron de palabras. Y con todo eso, me tomó por muy verdadera el juez, y me dijo una vez, hablando con las doncellas, que le respondiese yo, porque él pensaba que no querría yo mentir. Y apretó algo en saber quién me las había dado, y si ellas oían misa y cosas semejantes. Pero díjele que en las que tocasen en daño de otros, yo no respondería palabra, y con eso al punto calló.

12. Hízonos Dios merced de que no interviniesen "pursivantes," que son alguaciles de los obispos, en aquel caso, porque son la gente más descompuesta de Inglaterra en mirar por agnus-deyes y reliquias y rosarios en las mangas o faldriqueras. Y nuestro juez era muy reposado. Y todos los demás, desde el primer punto hasta el postrero, se hubieron con toda la posible modestia, y nuestro recato y decencia se conservó como yo lo podía desear, y suelo ser bien delicada en esta materia. ¡Glorificada sea la dulcísima providencia de Dios, que en esto nos has asistido sobre todo lo demás, y en ninguna cosa ha faltado. *"Descenditque cum illo in foveam et in vinculis non dereliquit illum."* Y esto me deleita incomparablemente el corazón y me da ánimo.

13. Sus hijas del juez andaban yendo y viniendo, y su mujer; debía de ser por vernos. Al cabo nos llevaron a la cárcel, habiendo estado desde que anocheció en una sala baja junto al mismo patio, a

11. He treated my two maidens more courteously than me, and perhaps because they are English, although they gave him more trouble than I because they thought it best to cover up [their relationship with me]. And I said that they were, without doubt, truthful and without any malice. His secretary called me a hypocrite and indeed I did seem like one. (What a disgraceful face suffering has, Sir, to the eyes of the world, and how beautiful it is to those of God, when it falls upon innocence!)[14]  And the best thing was that my sleeve, on which all the light was falling, had a mended spot or two showing, and on my head was a ragged black taffeta, and with this and being Spanish and as Catholic as they could see, it wasn't surprising that they disdained me as much as they did with words. And in spite of all that, the judge took me to be a very truthful person, and he addressed me once, when speaking with my maidens, asking me to answer that time because he believed I didn't want to lie. And he pressured me a bit in trying to find out who had given them [Ann and Faith] to me, and whether they went to mass and similar things. But I said to him that in things that might bring harm to others I would not answer a single word, and with that he stopped immediately.

12. God showed us mercy in that the pursuivantes, who are the bishop's constables, did not intervene in our case, because they are the most insolent people in England in looking for Agnus Deis[15] and relics and rosaries in people's sleeves or pockets. And our judge was very calm. And all the others, from the first instant to the last, behaved with all possible modesty, and our virtue and decency were preserved as well as I could have desired, and I tend to be very fussy about that. May God's sweet providence be glorified, which has attended us in this as in all else, and has failed us in nothing! *"Descenditque cum illo in foveam et in vinculis non dereliquit illum."*[16] And this delights my heart beyond measure and gives me courage.

13. The judge's daughters kept coming in and out, as well as his wife; it must have been so they could see us. In the end they took us to the jail, after we had been in a lower room adjoining the same patio

---

[14] Interestingly, this pious aside is inserted exactly where Carvajal says she lied to the judge about her relationship with Ann and Faith.

[15] An Agnus Dei is a little wax disk with a lamb impressed on it, blessed by the Pope. According to Covarrubias, "it serves against storms, fire, lightning, plague and against the incursions of the devil, and thus should be treated with much respect and reverence" (25).

[16] "She [wisdom] descended into the pit with him [the just man] and in prison did not abandon him" (Wisdom 10:13).

veces paseándonos, y yo, a veces, hincando las rodillas en uno de sus rincones para suplicar a Nuestro Señor nos asistiese. Y no pudimos ir antes de las once y media, por poder ir sin gente, y con todo, de la vecindad nos siguieron como veinte personas. Iba allí el secretario del juez, que es primo hermano del buen Tomás, que está ahora preso, haciendo falta a todos los amigos. Éste dijo al carcelero que nos tratase bien, pero aquella noche no debió de poderse, y así nos pusieron en un pedacillo de desván estrecho en lo más alto y con vela encendida, y la puerta cerrada con llave que se llevó el carcelero, sin poder alcanzar de él una gota de agua ni cerveza, ni un solo bocado de pan. Y con esto y no estar muy buena, y sin acostarnos, dormí harto poco, pero con muy notable consuelo, y éste se disminuía viendo cuán poco llegaba todo aquello a ser.

14. Habíales yo rogado que, por dinero, me pusiesen cerca de la mujer y mozas del carcelero, aunque fuese de peor comodidad que era aquel alojamiento. Ymu a la mañana nos pusieron en uno de los aposentos de ella, a hora de las diez, y aunque lóbrego y sin aire, razonable, y ellas, todas gente comedida y afable. Entraban en él a cada paso, por tener allí sus arcas y algunos mantenimientos en alacenas, y con todo y costarnos a razón de 40 (cuarenta) reales cada semana, sólo estar dentro de él, y una sola cama, lo tuvimos por gran regalo. Y no dudaba yo de que nuestro dulce Señor proveería para todo, como Su Majestad lo hizo por medio del señor don Pedro, que conmigo ha tenido notable caridad siempre.

15. Estuvimos allí cuatro días, desde sábado hasta miércoles a las diez de la noche, que envió orden el Consejo para que me sacasen libre, habiendo el juez enviádoles mis papeles, y no a los obispos, en lo que nos hizo honra, por lo que tocaba a Ana y a Fe, que luego quisieran ofrecerles el juramento. El señor don Pedro, con su prudencia, que la tiene grande en los negocios, no se había metido a hablar ni una palabra por mí, como me lo hizo decir, y eso parece fue lo más conveniente.

since nightfall, sometimes walking about, and sometimes with my kneeling in one of its corners to pray that God help us. And we could not leave until after eleven thirty, so as to depart without there being a lot of people, and even so about twenty from the neighborhood followed us. The judge's secretary was among them, one of good Thomas's cousins, who is now imprisoned,[17] much needed by all our friends. He told the jailer to treat us well, but that must not have been able to happen that night, and so they put us in the highest part of a narrow little attic, with a lit candle and the door locked with a key the jailer took with him, without our being able to get so much as a drop of water or beer or even a bite of bread. And what with this and not being very well, and without being able to get into a bed, I slept little indeed, but with notable consolation, and this diminished when I considered what little the whole business amounted to.

14. I had asked them if, for money, they would put me close to the jailer's wife and female servants, even though it were less comfortable than that lodging. And in the morning they put us in one of her rooms, around ten o'clock, and although dingy and without air, it was reasonable, and the women were all courteous and affable. They entered into the room every time we turned around, since their chests and some storage cupboards were in there, and all in all, and although at a price of 40 (forty) *reales* per week, just to be in it, and only one bed, we took it as great luxury. And I never doubted but that our sweet Lord would provide for everything, as His Majesty did by means of Lord don Pedro, who has always shown remarkable charity to me.

15. We were in there for four days, from Saturday until Wednesday at ten at night, when the Council sent orders for them to set me free, with the judge having sent them my papers, and not the bishops, actions in which he did us honor, as far as Ann and Faith are concerned, for [had we been sent to the bishops] they would have wanted to ask them to take the Oath. Lord don Pedro, in his prudence, and he is very prudent in business matters, had not said even a word on my behalf, as he let me know, and this seemed to be the most appropriate course of action.[18]

---

[17] At the end of letter 95 Carvajal identifies this Thomas as a man in the Tower, brother of a Carmelite in Louvain (*Epist.* 255).

[18] The Spanish ambassador was quite taken aback by Carvajal's extreme lack of prudence. It is likely that Carvajal's first prison term increased her notoriety, which raised the ante on her second arrest.

16. En la cárcel hablé de religión mucho más que fuera de ella lo había hecho, con todos los carceleros y oficiales y deudos y amigos suyos que, con mi licencia, trujeron para hablarme. Y tomáronlo muy suavemente. Y no quise excusarlo, acordándome del Santo Apóstol, que dice que la palabra de Dios no estaba atada.

17. Éste ha sido mi primer encuentro con los herejes, y porque es llano que se sabrá luego, he querido que vuestra merced sepa puntualmente lo que ha pasado. Y en caso que otros no hablen en ello con incierta y no conveniente relación, suplico a vuestra merced sea esto para sí solo y para el padre Hernando de Espinosa. Con esa carta que va aquí al hermano Tomás, me encomiendo, y muy humildemente, a todos los padres y hermanos de ese Colegio, que no sé cuáles de los conocidos están en él.

18. Acá todo es temor de Irlanda, y dicen están todavía fuertes en ella los católicos. Y háblase mucho de la venida de Don Pedro de Toledo a Francia. ¡Ojalá se uniese en hora dichosa con España, y que las paces de Holanda sean gloriosas a ella y a la Iglesia! Con esto y un nuevo rey de romanos muy bueno, y guardarnos al nuestro, la herejía espero irá cuesta abajo a su centro, por más hondas raíces que tiene. Por estas cosas clamo y por la Iglesia santa de día y de noche. Y por esto muchas veces me olvido de mí misma e insto y voceo porque la divina grandeza bendiga a España y a su monarquía, rey y reina e hijos nacidos y por nacer, con dobladas y felicísimas bendiciones.

19. Todos sus amigos de vuestra merced tienen salud; sólo Mr. Strange está sin ella en la Torre. Y en Gathouse están Mr. Tomás Garnett y Mr.

16. While in jail I spoke about religion much more than I had out of it, with all the jailers and officials and their families and friends whom, with my permission, they brought to speak with me. And they listened nicely. And I didn't want to let the chance slip by, remembering the Holy Apostle who says that the word of God is not tied down.[19]

17. This has been my first encounter with heretics, and since it is clear that people will know about it later, I wanted Your Grace to know right away what has happened. And to avoid others speaking about it based on uncertain and improper information, I beseech Your Grace to keep this to yourself and Father Hernando de Espinosa.[20] With that letter to Brother Thomas[21] here enclosed, I commend myself to all the Fathers and Brothers of that College, as I do not know which of the ones I know are there.

18. Here everyone is afraid about Ireland, and it is said that the Catholics are still strong there. And Don Pedro's arrival in France is much talked about.[22] I do hope for that happy hour when France is united with Spain, and that the peace with Holland be glorious for Holland and for the Church! With this and a very good new Roman king and our own being kept safe, I hope that heresy will lose ground down to its roots, regardless of how deep they are.[23] I cry out day and night for these things and for the holy Church. And for this reason I forget myself many times and clamor and cry out so that divine greatness bless Spain and her monarchy, king and queen and children born and yet to be born, with doubled and most happy blessings.[24]

19. All of Your Grace's friends are in good health; only Mr. Strange, in the Tower, is not. And Mr. Thomas Garnett and Mr.

[19] (2 Tim. 2:9). No one was allowed in to see Carvajal the second time she was imprisoned, probably because of what she describes here.

[20] Espinosa had been Carvajal's confessor in Madrid and, in his testimony for her beatification, describes her illness in Valladolid as an eye witness (*Proceso* 211[r-v]).

[21] The coadjutor who was with Creswell (Abad, *Epist.* 248).

[22] Don Pedro de Toledo arrived in France from the governorship in Milan (Abad, *Epist.* 249).

[23] Rudolph II (1552-1612) was Holy Roman Emperor from 1576 until his death. He was notably inept at resolving the religious crises that shook his kingdoms. His mental and emotional instability compelled the Hapsburg archdukes to entrust the conduct of Hungarian affairs to his brother Matthias in 1605. Rudolph was likewise forced to cede control of other countries in subsequent years; Carvajal probably refers to the 1606 official recognition of Matthias as the archdukes' candidate for Rudolph's succession.

[24] This passage exemplifies the increasing political, specifically nationalist flavor that Carvajal's ideas acquired as she spent more time in England, ideas which are virtually invisible in her early writings and which doubtless helped provoke her second arrest.

Joan Roberts, el uno jesuita y el otro monje benito, constantísimos y muy unidos en amor y en religión y esperando cada día cuando los llamarán a las sesiones.

20. A mi prima y al señor don Rodrigo beso las manos y huelgo en extremo de los lindos niños que dice vuestra merced les ha dado Nuestro Señor, y deseo que eso, ni la demás prosperidad humana, les lleve el corazón tras sí, ni empape el amor que se ha de poner en sólo Dios. No los escribo porque en esta peregrinación tuve por muy necesario al espíritu no meterme en tomar más consuelo de deudos ni amigos que el que me forzase la devoción de los que con ella me provocasen o con otro espirituales fundamentos. Y por sólo deudo, amistad o humanos respectos, yo no sé que haya escrito hasta ahora a ninguno de los que bien quiero. A los católicos pido los encomienden a Dios, como vuestra merced manda. Y yo, por mi particular obligación (que la tengo cierto, a la merced que el señor don Rodrigo me hizo siempre), los encomiendo a entrambos a Nuestro Señor, con gran deseo que Su Majestad los asista con muy especial gracia.

21. Y suplico a vuestra merced se acuerde de la necesidad con que estamos yo y mis cuatro compañeras de tener en qué trabajar, para que es necesario tijeras de bordar oro e hilarlo, y acá no se hallan. Y háme escrito mi monja Sor Inés, que ha enviado una caja a vuestra merced con unas muy escogidas, y husos, y otras cosas necesarias. Y si no han venido aún a manos de vuestra merced, vuestra merced me haga merced de escribirla que lo envíe, antes que Rivas vuelva a Inglaterra, que él me ha prometido traerlo todo, que es muy piadoso y caritativo conmigo. Y el señor don Pedro dice se las mandará traer también. Y no hay hallar labor que hacer de provecho, porque de tiendas; siendo nosotras católicas, con dificultad la alcanzaremos,

John Roberts are in Gate House, one a Jesuit and the other a Benedictine, most constant and very united in love and in religion and waiting daily to be called to the sessions.

20. I send humble regards to my cousin and Lord don Rodrigo [de Calderón] and rejoice greatly in the lovely children whom Your Grace tells me Our Lord has given them, and I wish that this succession, or other human prosperity, not carry their hearts away nor drench the love that one must put only in God. I am not writing to them because on this pilgrimage I decided it was very necessary for my spirit not to meddle in taking more consolation from relations or friends than that which is necessitated by devotion for those who provoke devotion in me, or for other spiritual reasons. And for only familiar, friendly, or human reasons, I'm not aware that I have written to date to any of those people whom I love well. I ask the Catholics to commend them to God, as Your Grace orders. And I, for my special obligation (and I do have one, for the favors that don Rodrigo always showed me), commend them both to Our Lord, with great desire that His Majesty attend them with special grace.[25]

21. I beseech Your Grace to recall the need that my four companions and I have to find some work to do, for which we need some embroidery scissors for working with gold and spinning it, and here there are none.[26] And my nun Sor Inés has written to me that she has sent a box to Your Grace with some selected items, and spindles, and other necessary items. And if they have not yet reached Your Grace's hands, do me the favor of writing to her that she send it before Rivas returns to England, for he has promised to bring it all, since he is very pious and charitable with me. And Lord don Pedro says he will order that they be sent as well. And there is no way to find needlework that we can do for profit because of the stores; since we are Catholics we will only to find it [the work we need] with difficulty

[25] In spite of all these claims of self-denial, Carvajal did indeed begin writing to Rodrigo de Calderón when she wanted him to represent her interventionist politics to the Duke of Lerma. Her first extant letter to him is from July of 1609 and in it she claimed not to have written sooner because he was so busy and her letters of little worth (*Epist.* 287).

[26] Carvajal did not share St. Teresa's poverty-pursuing scruples with regard to what sort of needlework was done under her supervision, and her enthusiasm for meeting this consumer demand in London betrays her noble upbringing, for only wealthy women worked with precious threads. Teresa specified for her nuns, "Their earnings must not come from work requiring careful attention to fine details but from spinning and sewing or other unrefined labor that does not so occupy the mind as to keep it from the Lord. Nor should they do work with gold or silver" (*Constitutions* 9).

y no conveniente. El oro dicen no se hila aquí, y así será lo mejor que podremos hacer. Y está todo cada día más caro: el pan creo llega ya a real, y el moreno lleno de salvado, a 20 maravedises, y a ese paso va lo más. Si Rivas puede traer algún libro de los que he suplicado a vuestra merced, recibiré gran merced.

22. Dice vuestra merced habrá allá algún bueno para embajador. No sé yo cierto quién. Holgara saber el nombre que, de oídas, conozco a muchos, y no pienso es fácil enviar otro que acierte a hacerlo como el señor don Pedro, que el Rey y Consejo le han cobrado respeto y le muestran amor, y los católicos le quieren mucho. Él desea irse, y no me espanto, que es vida de perros la de esta tierra. En el estado en que está, sólo parece será gustosa para quien ama libertad y ocasiones de pecar.

23. Si cuando Rivas se vuelva no se han podido traer las tijeras de Inés, suplico a vuestra merced que, por medio de la señora doña Juana de Bobadilla o de la señora doña Ana María de Vergara, nos busque unas, que en esa Corte hay mujeres que hilan oro, y en las tiendas do lo venden sabrán dónde viven.

24. Y deseo mucho que no tenga noticia de mí el ministro que se convirtió allí, ni me dirija cartas en ninguna vía para su mujer, ni dineros, porque trae grandes inconvenientes para mí, y es muy fácil hacer esas cosas por vía de los padres, como se ha hecho ahora con los 200 ducados, sin haberme yo metido en ello. Y ella no está aquí, sino en la tierra adentro, y el ministro con quien se ha de tratar no conviene me conozca.

25. Con el padre fray Juan, que se va a España, creo irá un mancebo *gentilman* llamado Brigman, hijo mayor de un cismático, que pienso tiene buena hacienda, y el mozo tiene fama de muy buen estudiante aquí en Londres, y eslo en el temple y con muy buena comodidad. Hále tocado Nuestro Señor, a lo que se puede juzgar, para dejarla e irse a un seminario: tiene agudeza de ingenio y muestra harta devoción. Va con esperanza que le ha de valer mi intercesión para ser recibido en Valladolid: suplícolo así a vuestra merced de rodillas, que lo estimaré como [si] se hiciera conmigo misma.

26. Dígame vuestra merced si podríamos alcanzar del piadosísimo pecho del Rey Nuestro Señor, por medio del duque, y del duque por el señor don Rodrigo, que Su Majestad se hiciese patrón del noviciado de Lovaina, pues tiene la mitad o más de la renta de patronazgos de la Casa de Austria, por lo cual no se le pudo dar el obispo sin aprobación

and lack of decorum. They say that no one spins gold here, and so it will be the best thing we can do [to make money]. And everything grows more expensive by the day: bread is up to a *real* already, and dark bread, full of bran, costs twenty *maravedís*, and at this pace we spend most of what we have. If Rivas can bring one of the books I have asked Your Grace for, it would be a great favor.

22. Your Grace says that someone good will be appointed as ambassador. I really don't know who. I would really like to know the person's name for, by word of mouth, I know many, and I don't think it is easy to send someone who could manage to do the job as has Lord don Pedro, for the King and Council have come to respect him and they show him love, and the Catholics are very fond of him. He wants to leave, and I'm not amazed, for it is a dog's life in this country. With the state it is in, it seems it would only be pleasing to someone who loves the loose life and opportunities to sin.

23. If when Rivas has returned it has not been possible to bring Inés's scissors, I beg Your Grace to find some for us by means of Lady doña Juana de Bobadilla or Lady doña Ana María de Vergara, for at that court there are women who spin gold, and in the stores where it it sold they will know where they [the specified ladies] live.

24. And I greatly desire that the minister who was converted there have no notice of me, nor send me letters for his wife, nor money, because that forces me to do things that are inappropriate, and it is very easy to do those things by way of the Fathers, as has been done with the two hundred ducats, without getting me involved. And she isn't here, but rather inland, and the minister with whom I would have to deal should not know who I am.

25. With Father Fray Juan, who is going to Spain, I believe a young gentleman named Brigman will go, the eldest son of a schismatic, who I believe has a good estate, and the youth has a reputation as a very good student here in London, and he is so in temperament and is very beneficial. Our Lord has touched him, as far as one can tell, to abandon it [his estate] and go into a seminary; he has a fine wit and displays appreciable devotion. He is going with hopes that my intercession will help him be well received in Valladolid. I beseech it of Your Grace on my knees, for I shall esteem your help as if it were given to myself.

26. Tell me if we could reach the most pious heart of the King our Lord, through the Duke [of Lerma], and the Duke through Lord don Rodrigo [de Calderón], so that His Majesty would become the patron of the novitiate in Louvain, for it has half its income or more from House of Austria's patronage, because of which the Bishop could

del archiduque, a lo que he entendido. Y sin dar Su Majestad nada, será gran lustre para aquella santa y devota casa, y espero crecería a su gran consuelo y gloria de Nuestro Señor, delante cuyo acatamiento no le cabría al duque pequeño galardón. Y su excelencia debe hacerme el favor, por la afición que yo le he tenido y tengo en todos tiempos. Y a mi buena prima pongo por intercesora con su marido. Y hagan grandes obras del servicio de Dios, que eso les durará, y todo lo demás se acaba con la brevedad que la vida.

27. Esas cartas me haga vuestra merced que se den a recaudo y que me traiga Rivas respuesta, si la dieren. Y si algún día llegase allá alguna en que diga que esta gente me ha enviado al cielo, dichoso remate sería de mi peregrinación, y entonces bien se podrían alegrar mis deudos y mis amigos. La voluntad de Dios se haga en todo, amén, que ésa me trujo puramente, y ésa espero guiará todas mis actuaciones hasta ponerme en el divino acatamiento.

28. No se olvide vuestra merced de avisarme en todas ocasiones de su salud, que se la deseo como veo es menester para tanto como cuelga de ella en esta grande y necesitada mies de innumerables almas. Si se conociese en España, ¡cuánto crecería la devoción en esta obra! Nuestro Señor le dé a vuestra merced vida y fuerzas y santo amor suyo, que yo le suplico.

De Haigat, a 29 de junio de 1608.

† Luisa

29. Al señor fiscal, Melchor de Molina y a la señora doña Juana beso las manos, y me he holgado de su temporal acrecentamiento, confiando no ha de disminuir el temor santo de Nuestro Señor en sus almas, y que el amor que le deben no será impedido, y por el que yo les tengo les suplico velen siempre sobre su corazón en este tan importante negocio.

[sobrescrito] Al padre José Cresvelo, que Nuestro Señor guarde, de la Compañía de Jesús, etcétera, etc.

Madrid

not give the balance without the Archduke's approval, as I understand it. And without His Majesty giving anything, it will be a great boon for that holy and devout house, and I hope it would grow, to the consolation and glory of Our Lord, with whose esteem the Duke would find no little reward. And His Excellence should do me the favor, for the affection I have held for him and hold at all times. And I propose my cousin as the one to intercede with her husband. And let them do great works in the service of God, for that will endure, and all the rest ends with the brevity of life.

27. Your Grace should do me the favor of securing those letters and having Rivas bring me answers, if they should be given. And if some day one should arrive saying that these people have sent me to heaven, it would be a fortunate end to my pilgrimage, and then my relations and friends could really be happy. May the will of God be done in everything, amen, for that alone brought me here, and that I hope will guide all my behavior until it puts me in divine obeisance.

28. Do not forget to notify me every time of how your health is, for I wish good health for you since I see it is necessary to accomplish all that depends on it in this great and destitute multitude of souls needful of conversion. And if this were known in Spain, how much devotion would grow for this task! May Our Lord give life and strength and His holy love to Your Grace, for so I beseech Him.

From Highgate, 29 June 1608.

†Luisa

29. To the fiscal lord, Melchor de Molia and Lady doña Juana I send most humble greetings and I have rejoiced much in their temporal gains, confident that it will not diminish the holy fear of Our Lord in their souls, and that the love they owe Him not be impeded, and for that which I feel for them, I beg them to always watch over their hearts in this very important matter.

[address] To Father Joseph Creswell, whom Our Lord keep, of the Society of Jesus, etc. etc.

Madrid

176

*A las carmelitas de Bruselas*

*Londres, 14 de noviembre de 1613*

Jhs

1. En fin, señora mía, el mísero hombre que me buscaba en rincones, pudiéndome tomar en las calles, me cogió lindamente, y estuve totalmente en sus manos y poder cuatro días no más, porque el señor don Diego, que es muy naturalmente esforzado, empleó su valer en sacarme de ellas. Y para mí esto no era lo mejor, a mi parecer, si no es que sea más gloria de Dios mi libertad que mi prisión. Por haber quedado nuestra casa sola, y en guarda de ella vecinos y extraños, y a uno y a otro, están desbaratadas y desparcidas cuantas cosas necesarias a la comodidad de ella había. Y así, apenas hallo con qué escribir, a do[nde] quedo en la casita de junto al señor don Diego, esperando cuándo Nuestro Señor se servirá de enviarme mis buenas doncellas, que me dicen será presto. No fue posible sacarlas conmigo, ni tampoco estábamos juntas en la prisión.

176

## *To the Carmelites in Brussels*[1]
### *London, 14 November 1613*

Jhs

1. In the end, my lady, the miserable man who searched for me in crannies,[2] although he could have found me in the streets, caught me nicely, and I was completely in his hands and power for no more than four days, for Lord don Diego, who is naturally very forceful, employed his merits to remove me from them [the Archbishop's hands].[3] And for me this wasn't the best of it, as I see it, unless my freedom be for the greater glory of God than my imprisonment. Since our house has been left empty, and with neighbors and strangers watching it and now one and then another in it, what necessary items there were for living in comfort are scattered and hidden, thus I can scarcely find anything to write with where I'm staying, in don Diego's little house, waiting for when Our Lord will see fit to send me my good maidens, which they tell me will be soon. It wasn't possible to get them out with me, and neither were we together in jail.[4]

---

[1] Carvajal was unstable when writing this letter, as her irregular syntax and her own admission indicate (¶3). At times, she is clearly addressing the foundress of the Discalced Carmelites in Paris and Brussels, Ana de Jesús (esteemed spiritual daughter of Teresa of Ávila), and at others, Mother Ana's community. When writing to her Carmelite friends, Carvajal had not received Ana de Jesús's letter to her of 13 Nov. 1613 from Brussels, which Ana opens with the following exclamation about Carvajal's second imprisonment: "Thanks be to God for, in 44 years and more that I have been a Discalced Carmelite, although unworthy, we have not merited the enjoyment of that which Your Grace has [enjoyed] in the nine that you have been in that kingdom, since you have already been twice imprisoned. Oh my lady!, I have shed many tears of envy!" Ana also offered to take in Carvajal's companions once they were released from prison (*Epist.* 462).

[2] George Abbott, Archbishop of Canterbury from 1610/11-1633. The enmity he felt toward Carvajal was so notorious that it merited mention in the *Dictionary of National Biography* (DNB I: 10).

[3] On this dramatic diplomatic incident, see the exchanges between the Spanish ambassador Diego de Sarmiento and Philip III (Loomie, *Spain* 15-25) and Senning.

[4] In his 16 Nov. report to Philip, Sarmiento recorded that Luisa was in his house, meaning the embassy itself or the small building next to it which Carvajal had previously rented, adding, "I will not agree to remove her from here unless it would be, as I said to the Council, that I should go with her" (Loomie, *Spain* 22; 23). Philip III later intervened personally to have Carvajal's companions freed from prison (Loomie, *Spain* 26).

2. Ha sido linda cosa lo que ha pasado, y todo tan de la mano de Dios que los que lo han hecho están afrentados como unas monas. Y con todo, procuran esforzar su parte contra la de Nuestro Señor, con que yo salga desterrada de este destierro áspero. ¿Puede ser esto, señora? Parece que no, si no se construye en aflicciones, porque de muchas se destierra quien de aquí sale.

3. El señor don Diego no traga esto de irme, si no le muestran por qué, y no tiene por suficiente la queja que le dan y se dio en el Consejo de Estado delante de él y más de veinte consejeros de ellos, que fue que si soy monja y he fundado algunos monasterios dentro de Inglaterra, y que persuado a muchísimos a que dejen su religión y tomen la mía, y así he pervertido gran número, trayéndolos a mi fe. Esto fue totalmente cuanto depusieron de mí. A nuestra madre y señora quería escribir algo más de lo que pasó y no puedo ahora, ni casi gobernar la pluma en ésta que, entre tanto, le suplico tenga por suya, y se acuerde de mí y de las presas.

4. Esa carta suplico a vuestra merced se dé muy a recaudo al que está ahí en lugar del señor don Antonio; es del señor Martín Varner, que ha llegado bueno, y dice desea escribir a vuestra merced, como lo hará por mostrar parte del gran reconocimiento que debe a las mercedes recibidas de vuestra merced.

5. A ese santo convento suplico me ayuden a glorificar a Nuestro Señor por estos notables favores y misericordias que a mí, indignísima, ha hecho en estos días, y al señor don Juan de Quintana Dueñas muy en especial, y a los padres carmelitos descalzos. Simón Estok se alegrará; dígale vuestra merced que nos llevaron desde el Spitile hasta Lambeth por calles cercadas de justicias y oficiales de ella, a pie y a caballo, con la admiración del pueblo que puede pensar, y allí iba la chiquita Francisca también. Y encomiende a Dios el alma de Michisan, que murió la mañana siguiente. Y estando (dice el doctor) sin calentura ni peligro alguno, de unas viruelas ya salidas afuera, el susto y dolor de verme llevar

2. What has happened has been a lovely thing, and all so much directed by the hand of God that those who did it are left chattering like a bunch of monkeys. And in spite of it all, they attempt to force their hand against Our Lord's, so that I will be exiled from this harsh exile. Can this possible be, Lady? It seems not, unless my departure be built with afflictions, because one who gets away from here is exiled from many [afflictions].

3. Lord don Diego [Sarmiento] isn't buying this business of my leaving, unless they can show him why it has to happen, and he doesn't think the complaint they gave him in the Council of State, while he was right there with more than twenty of their councilors, is sufficient, which was that I'm a nun and I have founded several monasteries within England, and that I am persuading a great number of people to give up their religion and take mine, and so I have perverted a great number, bringing them to my faith.[5] This was all they could present against me. I wanted to write more about what happened to our Mother and Lady and I can't now, nor can I control the pen in this letter which, in the meantime, I beseech her to read as if it were hers, and that she remember me and the women in prison.

4. I beseech Your Grace to give that letter carefully into the safe-keeping of the man taking the place of Lord don Antonio; he is Mr. Martin Warner, who has arrived in good health, and says he wishes to write to Your Grace, as he will do to provide part of the great acknowledgment he owes for the mercies he received from Your Grace.

5. I beseech that saintly convent to help me glorify Our Lord for those notable favors and mercies He has shown to me, the most unworthy, during those days, and Lord don Juan de Quintana Dueñas[6] in particular, and the Discalced Carmelite Fathers. Simon Stock will be happy: tell him that they took us from Spitalfields to Lambeth[7] through streets closed off by justices and officers of the peace, on foot and horseback, to the astonishment of the people, as one might imagine, and there as well went little Francisca. And commend Michisan's soul to God, for she died the next morning, and being without fever or in danger at all (according to the doctor), of pockmarks which had erupted before, the shock and pain of seeing me

---

[5] Sarmiento resisted Carvajal's banishment because it would have dishonored her (and him).

[6] Primary patron of the Carmelite mission in France (Abad, *Epist.* 414).

[7] Carvajal's second house, the one she rented for reasons of health, was in Spitalfields, on the outskirts of London; Lambeth was the Archbishop's palace.

así fue tal que luego se puso mortal, y se vieron señales de muerte en ella; mostraba haberse persuadido que me harían aún mayor mal. Bien vendrá ahora aquel verso con que suelo desear convidar a los que saben glorificar a Dios: "*Magnificate Dominum meum, et exaltemus nomen eius in id ipsum*" (Ps. 33:4). Séalo para siempre, amen. Y guárdeme a vuestra merced como le suplico.

De Londres, a 14 de noviembre de 1613.

6. Mucho deseo tener respuesta de esta carta que escribo a la buena doña María de Quesada, que vive junto a Ruán. Suplico a vuestra merced que procure de veras que yo las tenga. A la infanta Nuestra Señora beso los pies, y también deseo que Su Alteza se alegre conmigo en la presencia de Nuestro Señor.

7. El auditor y su mujer me han hecho grande caridad en esta ocasión. El señor don Diego y la suya, no menor, y el padre maestro, que es honradísimo religioso, aunque, como he dicho, estas cosas no son para mí lo mejor; eslo para ellos, que creo lo hacen por amor de Dios. Al señor don Luis de Bracamonte beso las manos.

Humilde sierva de vuestra merced.

[sin firma]

carried away that way was such that the illness became mortal immediately, and signs of death were visible on her: she had convinced herself that they would do me even greater ill. That verse comes to mind with which I often wish to convene those who know how to glorify God: "*Magnificate Dominum mecum, et exaltemus nomen eius in id ipsum*" (Ps. 33:4).[8]  May it be so forever, amen. And may He keep Your Grace as I beseech Him.

From London, on 14 November 1613.

6. I greatly desire to have an answer to this letter that I'm writing to the good doña María de Quesada, who lives close to Rouen. I beseech Your Grace to be sure that I get [it].[9]  I humbly greet the Princess our lady, and I also desire that Her Majesty delight with me in the presence of Our Lord.

7. The auditor and his wife have behaved very charitably toward me on this occasion[10] ; no less Lord don Diego and his [wife]; and the Master Father, who is a most honorable religious man, although, as I have said, these things are not the best of it for me; they are for them, for I believe they do it out of love for God. I humbly greet Lord Luis de Bracamonte.

Your Grace's humble servant,

[unsigned][11]

[8] "Oh magnify the Lord with me and let us exalt His name together."

[9] The text says "that I get *them*."

[10] The Flemish ambassador, Ferdinand Boisschot, and his wife, Ana María de Zamudio. According to Sarmiento's report to the King, Boisschot arrived immediately at Carvajal's house when it was broken into by the Archbishop's men and saved Michael Wapole's life by pretending Walpole was his own servant and ordering him brusquely back to the Flemish embassy. Ana María joined the Spanish ambassador's wife Constanza at the jail where Carvajal was kept, and they both refused to leave until she was released, returning home only to sleep at night for propriety's sake (Loomie, *Spain* 21-22).

[11] Abad addends to this letter the testimony of the Carmelite Jerónimo Gracián de la Madre de Dios, stating that Carvajal was arrested because of her success in convincing members of several religious orders to come to England, and because she directed the traffic of many prohibited books in and out of the country (*Epist*. 414).

178

## Al Duque de Lerma

*Londres, 20 de noviembre de 1613*

Jhs

1. Vuestra excelencia vea cuán vana me hallo, con haber llegado ya a haber confesado dos veces el santísimo nombre de Cristo en las prisiones de sus enemigos en testimonio y ensalzamiento de la fe católica, pues me atrevo a escribir a vuestra excelencia; y cuánto fío de su piedad, pues no quiero dejar pasar esta ocasión sin suplicar a vuestra excelencia se alegre en ella conmigo, glorificando a Dios muchísimo por tan gran misericordia. Y deben aumentar el efecto de vuestra excelencia las particulares circunstancias de ser española y una sierva de vuestra excelencia que mucho le ama y estima.

2. Los bríos y valor de don Diego me han desbaratado una gloriosa corona que me parece llegué a ver desde muy cerca, y me deja en gran confianza de que ellos se buscarán modo y tiempo que don Diego ignore, si no es que Nuestro Señor quiera diferirlo más que el que él hubiere de estar aquí.

3. Puedo asegurar a vuestra excelencia de que la vocación de venir a Inglaterra que desde que era muchacha tuve, conforme a la doctrina de la Santa Iglesia, ha sido muy probable y clarísima vocación de Dios, y con los sucesos se ha confirmado de día en día. Y sin muy especial ayuda suya, no fuera posible haberme

178

## *To the Duke of Lerma*[1]
### *London, 20th of November, 1613*

Jhs

1. May Your Excellence see how vain I have become with already having twice confessed the most holy name of Christ in His enemies' prisons, in testimony and praise of the Catholic faith, since I dare write to Your Excellence, and [may you see] how much I trust in your mercy, for I do not want to let this opportunity pass without beseeching Your Excellence to delight in it with me, greatly glorifying God for such great mercy. And the particular circumstances, of my being a Spaniard and Your Excellency's servant who much loves and esteems you, should increase the effect on Your Excellence.

2. The spirit and valor of Don Diego [de Sarmiento] have spoiled for me a glorious crown that I believe I actually saw up close, and leave me in very great confidence that they [Anglicans] will seek out a means and time that Don Diego will not know of, unless Our Lord should choose to postpone it beyond the time that he [Sarmiento] will be here.[2]

3. I can assure Your Excellence that the vocation to come to England which I had since girlhood, in conformity with the doctrine of the Holy Church, can be proven to be a clear vocation from God, and with recent events has been confirmed day by day.[3] And without God's very special assistance, it would not have been possible for me

[1] Don Francisco de Sandoval y Rojas (?1553?-1623), Duke of Lerma, was the grandson of the Duke of Gandía (St. Francisco de Borja) and the favorite, or *valido*, of King Philip III (ruled 1598-1621). Eduardo Chamorro calls Lerma the master if not the lord of the kingdom, describing him as "the magnificent expression of the corruption into which the position of royal secretary had fallen through favoritism as a manifestation of regal indolence" (20). Carvajal wrote to the Duke, rather than to the King himself, as the surest avenue to the Council of Castile, in whose hands the future of her mission rested. There are pronouns in this letter, perhaps purposefully ambiguous, which could refer either to the Duke or to God ("su" and "sus").

[2] Diego de Sarmiento, the Spanish Ambassador in London, aggressively negotiated Carvajal's release from prison with King James; see Senning. The crown to which she refers is that of martyrdom.

[3] Carvajal here, as elsewhere, lays claim to a childhood vocation, a standard heroic motif. Since such a claim was an eminently useful way of convincing her superiors that God was long at work in her, it is difficult to know whether it pertains to her historical experience or to the larger narrative of hagiography. Abad believes her English vocation was formed by the time she left Pamplona; her will certainly indicates that by 1604 it was firm.

conservado tanto tiempo entre aquesta gente en la manera que ello ha sido. Y así, suplico a vuestra excelencia que jamás concurra con los que, por su medio, procuraren mi salida de este reino, dejándolos a ellos que, a sus solas, hagan por violencia o maña lo que Nuestro Señor les permitiere.

4. De dos delitos me ha acusado en la mesa del Consejo de Estado, delante de don Diego, el falso arzobispo de Cantorbery (que a la piedad llaman éstos impiedad): el uno, que he fundado monasterios de monjas, y el otro que he reducido con mi persuasión [a] muchos protestantes a mi religión. Y aunque tienen las lenguas de millares en sus manos, no han podido mostrar probanza alguna ni de la más mínima cosa que [a] aquesas dos toque, ni llegado a descubrir sus ciegos discursos las que mucho más los alterarían y sacarían de tino.

5. Si hubiese visto vuestra excelencia la providencia que Dios ha tenido en este mi suceso, mucho se admiraría, porque no han hecho ni dicho cosa sus enemigos (y míos en el mismo grado) que no sea como yo lo pudiese desear. Los que no son muy obstinados, sino gente moral y apacible, me muestran amor, y algunos han llorado de mi prisión y venídome a ver. Y multitud de estos protestantes de grande y mediana honra, concordando con la opinión de los católicos, han hablado mal de este hecho, teniéndole por locura y descrédito de los que lo han hecho. Pero a don Diego le ha estado muy bien, empezándose a acreditar mucho, con el valor y celo de religión y honra de España que ha mostrado, que ha sido, cierto, bien grande y dado una general satisfacción.

to have sustained myself so long among these people in the way that I have.  And thus, I beseech Your Excellence that you never mingle with those who, by means of your intervention, might procure my removal from this kingdom, leaving them on their own to do by violence and duplicity whatever Our Lord might permit them to do.

4. In the session at the Council of State, the false Archbishop of Canterbury has accused me of two crimes (for these men call piety impiety): one, that I have founded monasteries for nuns, and the other that I have brought many Protestants to my religion by means of persuasion.[4]  And although they have the testimony of thousands in their hands, they have not been able to provide any proof of even the smallest thing pertinent to these two accusations, nor has their blind reasoning managed to discover those [things] which would disturb and upset them even more.

5. If Your Excellence had seen the providence that God has exercised in this event of mine, you would marvel greatly, because His enemies (who are mine in like degree) have not done or said anything that is not how I would have it be.  Those who are not utterly obstinate, rather moral and peaceful folk, show me love, and some have wept over my imprisonment and have come to see me.  And a multitude of these Protestants of great and moderate honor, agreeing with Catholic opinion, have spoken out against this happening, believing it to be craziness and to the discredit of those who have done it.  But it has gone very well for Don Diego, who is beginning to prove himself well, and the valor and zealousness of Spanish honor and religion which he has displayed has certainly been a great good and provided general satisfaction.[5]

[4] In his report to Philip III of 16 Nov. 1613 about Carvajal's arrest, Diego de Sarmiento said, "What distresses me the most is that, in order to give colour to what has been done, they are charging her with a statement, as monstrous as it is baseless, that she wished to found a monastery for nuns in London, as if such a thing could be believed of a person who possesses such good judgment as this lady, and that it was to be bruited about without my being aware, as certainly no one had believed or heard such a thing until the Archbishop told me in the Council" (Loomie, *Spain* 18).  Denying these charges was pure posturing on Sarmiento's part and Carvajal's as well, because she indeed had founded her Society of the Sovereign Virgin, a convent in function if not in name, well before 1613.  In a Jan. 1621 report to the Spanish King, Sarmiento admitted that Carvajal had a house "where she founded in it a residence of nuns" (Loomie, *Spain* 23, n. 1).

[5] During her years as a holy woman in Spain, particularly in Madrid, Carvajal abjured honor as pernicious and publicly debased herself in an attempt to erase it from her personality.  As her political involvement in the Spanish-Catholic cause increased with the years she spent in London, she became increasingly enmeshed in the politics of opinion, or honor.

6.  Parece, señor, que me voy olvidando de que escribo a vuestra excelencia, pues me alargo tanto.  Vuestra excelencia me perdone.  Y al Rey nuestro señor suplico humildemente lo mismo que he suplicado a vuestra excelencia: que dejen a Dios hacer libremente lo que fuere más servido.

7. Guárdenos Dios a vuestra excelencia, como Su Majestad ve es menester y yo le suplico, amén.  Y Él bendiga a Vuestra Excelencia en todo y le enriquezca con grandes aumentos de su santísimo amor.

De Londres, a 20 de noviembre de 1613.  Sierva de vuestra excelencia.

†Luisa de Carvajal

6. It seems, Lord, that I forget to whom I am writing, since I go on at such length. May Your Excellency forgive me. And to the King Our Lord I humbly beg the same that I have entreated of you: that you all let God do freely whatever He pleases.

7. May God preserve Your Excellency for us, as His Majesty sees necessary and I beg of Him, amen. And may He bless Your Excellence in every way and enrich you with great abundance of His holy love.

From London, 20 November 1613. Your Excellency's servant,
† Luisa de Carvajal

❧

## *Postscript: for Luisa*

*Of immense Love this tight embrace
receive, Silva, from your sweet Beloved*
Poem 18

*I*n 1625, Carvajal's friend and admirer Mariana de San José, foundress and prioress of the Convento de la Encarnación, started the process of collecting information for the Cause of Carvajal's beatification, the first step toward canonization. There were clearly intentions afoot to clear a path for Carvajal's sainthood well before that, however, because Walpole had agreed to write her biography within less than a month after her death, and that biography has the format of a saint's life (for example, it concludes with miracles attributed to Carvajal's posthumous intervention). Testimonies were collected for the Cause between 1625 and 1627. In spite of these initial, zealous impulses, Carvajal's dossier was never presented to the Congregation of Rites, probably because of Pope Urban VIII's 1631 decree prohibiting the presentation of Causes until fifty years after their subjects' death. By the time those fifty years had passed, the individuals who had carried her case forward were dead, and Spain's Imperial Age, whose interests Carvajal represents so well, was well on the wane.

Subsequent efforts to stimulate a renewal of Carvajal's Cause, most notably Camilo Abad's burst of publicity on her behalf during the 1960's, have not sufficed to spark sufficient interest in her, in the Roman Catholic context. Now that Mariana de San José's Cause has been accepted in Rome, there is hope on the part of the community at the Encarnación that Carvajal's moment will eventually arrive, and the nuns welcome interest in her and study of her life and her works. Although visitors may review Carvajal's dossier with an appointment, requests to do so must begin at the Patrimonio Nacional at the Palacio Real in Madrid.

Real Monasterio de la Encarnación
Agustinas Recoletas
Plaza de la Encarnación 1
28013 Madrid

Patrimonio Nacional
Calle Bailén SN
Palacio Real
28071 Madrid

Abad, Camilo María (SJ). "Don Rodrigo Calderón, a la luz de una correspondencia inédita." *Boletín de la Real Academia de la Historia* 153 (1963): 247-93.

Abad, Camilo María (SJ). "Introducción." *Epistolario y poesías*. Ed. Camilo María Abad. Biblioteca de autores españoles, vol. 179. Madrid: Atlas, 1965. 15-94.

Abad, Camilo María (SJ). *Una misionera española en la Inglaterra del siglo XVII. Doña Luisa de Carvajal y Mendoza (1566-1614)*. Comillas, Santander: Universidad Pontificia, 1966.

Bataillon, Marcel. "Jeanne d'Autriche, Princesse de Portugal." *Études sur le Portugal au temps de l'humanisme*. Coimbra: Por ordem da Universidade, 1952. 262-83.

Berger, John. *Ways of Seeing*. London; New York: British Broadcasting; Penguin, 1972.

Bossy, John. *Christianity in the West. 1400-1700*. 1985; Oxford: Oxford Univ. Press, 1988.

Bynum, Caroline. *Holy Feast and Holy Fast. The Religious Significance of Food to Medieval Women*. Berkeley and Los Angeles: Univ. of California Press, 1987.

Carroll, Michael. *Madonnas that Maim. Popular Catholicism in Italy since the Fifteenth Century*. Baltimore: Johns Hopkins Univ. Press, 1992.

Carvajal y Mendoza, Luisa de. *Epistolario y poesías*. Ed. Camilo María Abad. Biblioteca de autores españoles, vol. 179. Madrid: Atlas, 1965.

Carvajal y Mendoza, Luisa de. *Escritos autobiográficos*. Ed. Camilo María Abad (SJ). Barcelona: Juan Flors, 1966.

Carvajal y Mendoza, Luisa de. Papers. Convento de la Encarnación. Madrid.

Carvajal y Mendoza, Luisa de. *Poesías completas*. Ed. María Luisa García-Nieto Onrubia. Badajoz: Diputación Provincial de Badajoz, 1990.

Chamorro, Eduardo. *La vida y la época de Felipe IV*. Barcelona: Planeta, 1998.

Christian, William A. *Local Religion in Sixteenth-Century Spain.* Princeton: Princeton Univ. Press, 1981.

Covarrubias, Sebastián de. *Tesoro de la lengua castellana o española [1611; 1617].* Ed. Martín de Riquer. Barcelona: Editorial Alta Fulla, 1987.

Cruz, Anne J. "Chains of Desire: Luisa de Carvajal y Mendoza's Poetics of Penance." *Estudios sobre escritoras hispánicas en honor de Georgina Sabat-Rivers.* Ed. Lou Charnon-Deutsch. Madrid: Editorial Castalia, 1992. 97-112.

Cruz, Anne J. "Luisa de Carvajal y Mendoza y su conexión jesuita." *La mujer y su representación en las literaturas hispánicas.* Ed. Juan Villegas. Irvine, CA: Asociación Internacional de Hispanistas, 1992. 97-104.

Daniel, E. Randolph. "The Desire for Martyrdom: A Leitmotiv of St. Bonaventure." *Franciscan Studies* 32 (1972): 74-87.

*The Dictionary of National Biography. From the Earliest Times to 1900.* Eds. Leslie Stephen and Sidney Lee. 1917; Oxford: Oxford Univ. Press, 1973.

*Donna Luisa of Carvajal, a Catholic Play by a Nun of Tyburn Convent.* London: Arthur H. Stockwell, [1922?].

Edwards, Francis (SJ). *The Jesuits in England. From 1580 to the Present Day.* Kent, England: Burns and Oates, 1985.

El Saffar, Ruth Anthony. *Rapture Encaged: The Suppression of the Feminine in Western Culture.* London; New York: Routledge, 1994.

Escobar, Marina de. *Copia de una carta que escribió la venerable Doña Marina de Escobar al Rmo. Padre R. Domingo Pimental, siendo Provincial de Santo Domingo. Y la tiene original el Conde de Benavente firmada de su mano.* [1634] BNM ms. 12.856, fol. 114.

Faber, Juan Nicolás de. *Floresta de rimas antiguas castellanas.* Hamburg, 1821.

Fernández del Hoyo, María Antonia. *Marina de Escobar.* Vol. Vallisoletanos 4.39: 113-140. Valladolid: Caja de Ahorros Popular, 1984.

Fullerton, Lady Georgiana. *The Life of Luisa de Carvajal.* London: Burns & Oates, 1904.

Gregory, Brad S. "The Violent Rending of Christendom: Martyrdom in the Early Modern Period." Paper presented at the Early Modern European and British Studies Workshop. Harvard Univ., April 30, 1996.

Holquist, Michael. "From Body-Talk to Biography: The Chronobiological Bases of Narrative." *Yale Journal of Criticism* 3.1 (1989): 1-35.

Huerga, Alvaro. *Fray Luis de Granada, una vida al servicio de la Iglesia.* Madrid: Editorial Católica, 1988.

Iparraguirre, Ignacio (SJ). *Práctica de los Ejercicios de San Ignacio de Loyola en vida de su autor.* Rome: Institutum Historicum Societatis Iesu, 1946.

Juan de Ávila, St. *Obras completas.* Ed. Luis Sala Balust, 6 vols. Madrid: Editorial Católica, 1970.

Juana Inés de la Cruz, Sor. *El sueño.* Ed. Alfonso Méndez Plancarte. Toluca: Instituto Mexiquense de Cultura, 1995.

Jütte, Robert. *Poverty and Deviance in Early Modern Europe.* Oxford and Cambridge, MA: Cambridge Univ. Press, 1994.

"Libro de la vida y virtudes de la venerable virgen doña Luisa de Carvajal y Mendoza." Biblioteca Nacional de Madrid, Ms. 1881, ff. 198$^v$-206$^r$.

Lilio, Martín de. *Segunda parte del Flor sanctorum ahora nuevamente corregido y de muchos errores alimpiado*, 1558.

Loayza, Pedro de. *Vida de Santa Rosa de Lima [1619].* Lima: Iberia, 1965.

Loomie, Albert J. *Guy Fawkes in Spain: The 'Spanish Treason' in Spanish Documents.* London: Univ. of London, Institute of Historical Research, 1971.

Loomie, Albert J. "'A Seminarie': Joseph Creswell, S.J." *The Spanish Elizabethans. The English Exiles at the Court of Philip II.* New York: Fordham Univ. Press, 1963. 182-229.

Loomie, Albert J. *Spain and the Jacobean Catholics. Vol. II: 1613-1624.* London: The Catholic Record Society, 1978.

Luis de Granada. *Obras completas.* Ed. Álvaro Huerga. Madrid: Fundación Universitaria Española, 1995. 40 vols.

Luke, Helen. "Suffering." *Vox Benedictina* 4.2 (1987): 184-91.

Marguerite, de Navarre. *Dialogue en forme de vision nocturne*. Ed. R. Salminen. Helsinki: Annales Academiae Scientiarum Ferinicae, 1983.

Mooney, Catherine M. "Dutiful Wives and Mothers: The Editorial Recreations of Margaret of Cortona and Angela of Foligno." Berkshire Conference on the History of Women. Vassar College, June 1993.

Muñoz, Luis. *Vida y virtudes de la venerable* virgen doña Luisa de *Carvajal y Mendoza*. 1631; Madrid: Sucesores de Rivadeneyra, 1897.

Olivares, Julián and Elizabeth Boyce. "Doña Luisa de Carvajal y Mendoza." *Tras el espejo la musa escribe. Lírica femenina de los Siglos de Oro*. Madrid: Siglo Veintiuno, 1993. 477-530.

Ortega Costa, Milagros. "Spanish Women in the Reformation." *Women in Reformation and Counter-Reformation Europe: Public and Private Worlds*. Ed. Sherrin Marshall. Bloomington, IN: Indiana Univ. Press, 1989. 89-119.

Peralta, Francisco de. *Copia de una carta que el Padre Francisco de Peralta de la Compañía de Jesús, Rector del Colegio de los Ingleses en Sevilla, escribió al Padre Rodrigo de Cabredo, Provincial de la Nueva España, en que da cuenta de la dichosa muerte que tuvo en Londres la santa señora doña Luisa de Carvajal . . .* Sevilla: Colegio Inglés, 1614.

Pérez de Valdivia, Diego. *Aviso de gente recogida [1585]*. Ed. Álvaro Huerga. Madrid: Fundación Universitaria Española, Univ. Pontífica de Salamanca, 1977.

Plaskow, Judith. *Sex, Sin and Grace. Women's Experience and the Theologies of Reinhold Niebuhr and Paul Tillich*. Durham; New York; London: Univ. Press of America, 1980.

Poutrin, Isabelle. *La voile et la plume. Autobiographie et sainteté féminine dans l'Espagne moderne*. Madrid: Casa de Velázquez, 1995.

Puente, Luis de la. *Vida maravillosa de la venerable virgen doña Marina de Escobar, natural de Valladolid, sacada de lo que ella misma escribió de orden de sus padres espirituales. Escrita por el venerable P. Luis de la Puente de la Compañía de Jesús, su confesor*. Madrid: Francisco Nieto María, 1665.

Rahner, Hugo. *Saint Ignatius Loyola: Letters to Women*. Trans. Kathleen Pond and S. A. H. Weetman. 2nd ed. New York: Herder and Herder, 1960.

Raymond of Capua. *La vida de la bien aventurada santa Caterina de Sena*. Alcalá: Guillén de Brocar, 1511.

Retana, Luis Fernández de. *Doña Juana de Austria*. Ed. Editorial el Perpetuo Socorro. Madrid, 1955.

Rhodes, Elizabeth. "God on Earth: Eucharistic Piety in Post-Tridentine Spanish Female Spirituality." Paper presented at the Sixteenth-century Studies Conference, St. Louis, Oct. 30, 1999.

Rhodes, Elizabeth. "Spain's Misfired Canon: The Case of Fray Luis de Granada's *Libro de la oración*." *Journal of Hispanic Philology* 15 (1990): 3-28.

Rhodes, Elizabeth. "What's in a Name?: On Teresa of Ávila's *Book*." *The Mystical Gesture: Essays on Medieval and Early Modern Spiritual Culture*. Ed. Robert Boenig. New York: Ashgate Press, forthcoming.

Rhodes, Elizabeth. "Women on their Knees: Pornography and in Female Religious Discourse in Early Modern Spain." Paper presented at the Seminar on Women in Early Modern Europe, Center for Cultural and Literary Studies, Harvard Univ., Dec. 7, 1993.

Rhodes, Elizabeth. "Y yo dije 'Sí Señor': Ana Domenge and the Barcelona Inquisition, 1610." In *Women and the Inquisition*. Ed. Mary Giles. Baltimore: Johns Hopkins Univ. Press, 1999. 134-54.

Rodríguez Moñino, Antonio and María Brey Moñino. *Luisa de Carvajal (poetisa y mártir). Apuntes biobibliográficos, seguidos de tres cartas inéditas de la venerable madre*. Madrid: Ayuntamiento de Madrid, 1933.

Schulenburg, Jane Tibbetts. "The Heroics of Virginity. Brides of Christ and Sacrificial Mutilation." *Women in the Middle Ages and the Renaissance. Literary and Historical Perspectives*. Ed. Mary Beth Rose. Syracuse: Syracuse Univ. Press, 1986. 29-72.

Senning, Calvin F. "The Carvajal Affair: Gondomar and James I." *Catholic Historical Review* 56.1 (1970): 42-66.

Serrano y Sanz, Manuel. "Luisa de Carvajal y Mendoza." *Apuntes para una biblioteca de escritoras españolas desde el año 1401 al 1833*. Madrid: Estado español, 1903. 2 vols. I: 233-36.

*A Spanish Heroine in England.* London: The Catholic Truth Society, nd.

Teresa of Ávila. *The Collected Works of St. Teresa of Ávila.* Trans. Kieran Kavanaugh and Otilio Rodríguez. Washington: ICS, 1985. 3 vols.

"Testimonios del Proceso informativo sobre la vida, virtudes y fama de santidad de doña Luisa de Carvajal y Mendoza." Carvajal documents, Convento de la Encarnación, Madrid.

*Tractado de deuotissimas y muy lastimosas contemplaciones de la passion sacratissima del hijo de Dios y compassion de la Virgen su madre. Por esta razon llamado Passio Duorum.* Con las horas de la misma passion devotísimas y muy breves. Valencia: Francisco Diaz Romano, 1538.

Walpole, Michael. "La vida de la Venerable Doña Luisa de Carvajal y Mendoza." Carvajal papers. Convento de la Encarnación, Madrid, nd.

Wiesner-Hanks, Merry E. "Women's Defense of Their Public Role." *Women in the Middle Ages and the Renaissance. Literary and Historical Perspectives.* Ed. Mary Beth Rose. Syracuse: Syracuse Univ. Press, 1986. 1-28.

Wilkinson Zerner, Catherine. "Women's Quarters in Spanish Royal Palaces." *Architecture et Vie Sociale. L'Organisation Intérieure des Grandes Demeures à la Fin du Moyen Age et à la Renaissance.* Ed. Jean Guillaume. Tours: Picard, 1988. 127-34.

Williamsen, Amy R. "Question of Entitlement: Imposed Titles and Intrepretation in Sor Juana and María de Zayas." *Revista de Estudios Hispánicos* 31.1 (1997): 103-12.